Mathematics Teachers' Beliefs about

Anastasios Barkatsas

Mathematics Teachers' Beliefs about Teaching and Learning

An Investigation of Factors that Influence these Beliefs

VDM Verlag Dr. Müller

Impressum

Bibliografische Information der Deutschen Nationalbibliothek: Die Deutsche Nationalbibliothek verzeichnet diese Publikation in der Deutschen Nationalbibliografie; detaillierte bibliografische Daten sind im Internet über http://dnb.d-nb.de abrufbar.

Coverbild: www.purestockx.com

Erscheinungsjahr: 2008
Erscheinungsort: Saarbrücken

Verlag:
VDM Verlag Dr. Müller Aktiengesellschaft & Co. KG, Dudweiler Landstr. 125 a, 66123 Saarbrücken, Deutschland,
Telefon +49 681 9100-698, Telefax +49 681 9100-988,
Email: info@vdm-verlag.de
Zugl.: Perth, Curtin University of Technology, Diss., 2003

Herstellung:
Schaltungsdienst Lange o.H.G., Zehrensdorfer Str. 11, D-12277 Berlin
Books on Demand GmbH, Gutenbergring 53, D-22848 Norderstedt

ISBN: 978-3-639-07838-1

What is laid down ordered, factual, is never enough to embrace the whole truth: life always spills over the rim of every cup

Boris Pasternak

Μηδείς αγεωμέτρητος εισίτω

(Επιγραφή στην είσοδο της Ακαδημίας Πλάτωνος)

Let no one ignorant of Geometry enter this academy

(Entrance to Plato's Academy)

TABLE OF CONTENTS

LIST OF FIGURES

LIST OF TABLES

ACKNOWLEDGMENTS

The research reported here is the result of a multitude of experiences. The study had a great impact on my mathematics education philosophy. This change can be attributed to the influence of several talented people. I have been fortunate in having Professor John Malone as my chief supervisor throughout the study. His knowledge, constructive advice and encouragement, and the fact that he made himself available for advice even on a very short notice, made the course of the study a valuable learning experience.

I would like to thank my family, especially my wife Constantina, who has been an oasis of hope and a bulletin board for many of my thinking aloud sessions during my candidature. Her continuous support and encouragement and her cheerful personality, made this personal journey less monotonous.

To my daughter Liberty and my son Nicholas, who have tolerated my mood changes while preparing the manuscript, I express my deepest thanks for their understanding and compassion. Their encouragement and support was of paramount importance to me especially during zero tolerance periods, and it is much appreciated.

CHAPTER 1

1.1   Introduction to the study

This study represents an exploration of the espoused beliefs and instructional practices of secondary mathematics teachers in Greece. It aimed to investigate the existence of a typology of mathematics teacher's beliefs regarding the nature of mathematics, mathematics teaching, learning and assessment and to explore possible inconsistencies between those beliefs and the teachers' instructional practice. Previous studies (Thompson, 1992; Bishop, 1988; Cooney, 1999; Atweh, Forgasz & Nebres, 2001; Lerman, 1994; Berger, 1999, 2000; Perry, Vistro-Yu, Howard, Wong & Keong, 2002) have suggested that the cultural aspects and contexts of mathematics teachers' beliefs are critical in their implication for student learning. Significant differences in the beliefs among teachers from Australia, Singapore and Indonesia have been reported (Perry, et al., 2002) and a comparison of teachers' beliefs from Singapore, Philippines, Mainland China, Hong Kong and Australia are well under way (Perry, et al., 2002).

The present study aimed to extend the earlier work that has been carried out in various countries through the introduction and analysis of data from hitherto unexplored cultural contexts, namely by investigating Greek secondary mathematics teachers' beliefs about mathematics, about mathematics teaching, learning and assessment, and to contribute to an understanding of the impact that the cultural context could have both as a national and as a transnational phenomenon. If beliefs are considered to be an important factor in good practice teaching, then improving teachers' – and teacher educators' – knowledge of their personal beliefs should, in turn, improve their teaching practices. My journey into the complex topology of the partially chartered terrain of mathematics teachers' beliefs commences below.

1.2   Background to the study

In most modern societies educational institutions are considered key instruments of social purpose. Governments around the world formulate educational policies and finance educational institutions on the assumption that education is necessary for both progress and prosperity. As a major component of an educational system, mathematics education is expected to promote political, economic and social development. However the task of enumerating and empirically validating specific educational functions and uses for any society is a difficult one. Official goals and statements of purpose are often ignored or contradicted in everyday practice, and they cannot be assumed to reflect the daily operation of the system.

Educational systems differ in the extent to which they accommodate broad conceptions about education, its results, and the wide ranges of beliefs and values held within society. For example, the education system of the State of Victoria in Australia is decentralized, permitting more responsiveness to local pressure groups, such as the universities, the Mathematical Association of Victoria and parents' groups. The difficulties inherent in the search for a better education system are not insurmountable. Mathematics education is part of a cycle, perhaps the most valuable link in the chain that supports a mathematically literate society. What is possible and what is achievable in mathematics education is closely bound to the state of school environments as places where mathematical thinking is nurtured and achieved.

This study involves the investigation of inconsistencies between secondary mathematics teachers' beliefs about mathematics, about mathematics teaching, learning and assessment, and the teachers' pedagogical practice.

1.3 The education context in Greece

A synoptic overview of the Greek education system will be presented in this section, with the aim of highlighting those areas of the system that are of relevance to this study.

The Greek education system is centralized, in contrast to that in Australia where the States have responsibility for providing school education. As a consequence, in Australia:

> There are variations in school starting ages, the grade level at which primary-secondary transition takes place, curricula, certification, and tertiary selection procedures (Forgasz, 1995, p.3)

In Greece, the Ministry of National Education and Religious Affairs (MNERA) is the main decision-making body. Policy making, funding, staffing, and the majority of educational establishments, including Universities, are all controlled by the Ministry. The MNERA decides on all issues that concern teaching, personnel, and administration, expenditure and school operations.

Educational development in Greece is characterised by the esteem in which education is held among all sections of the community. It is regarded as a decisive and defining factor, both in shaping the national identity and in advancing the life opportunities of individual members of the community. There is however, a paradoxical quasi-universally held view of the existing system that regards it as incapable of responding to popular demand, or to meeting the expectations of Greece's highly interested population (OECD Examiners' Report, 1996, p. 6). Despite the progress that has been made during the past twenty years on redefining the aspects of the legal and administrative framework within which the system operates, these latter issues have never been resolved, leaving education: "still bound up with an over-legalistic, cenrtalised and politicized patronage-based system which stifles initiative and creativity". (OECD Examiner's Report, 1996, p. 6)

Greek education has the advantage of serving a highly homogeneous society, a cohesive, state-supported religion and strong family solidarity. It is a society strongly committed to equality and social justice. There exists however, great geographical contrasts and variety, with corresponding differences in the distribution of population between urban and rural areas, as well as considerable socio-economic differences between the two. Athens, the capital city of Greece, and Salonica the second largest city, together account for just over 40% of the total Greek population and a similar proportion of economic activity (OECD Examiner's Report, 1996, p. 7).

Another important factor concerning the Greek education system is the political context within which education operates. According to the OECD Examiner's Report (1996), the history of education in Greece over the last twenty years:

> Has been replete with educational reforms that successive governments have legislated
> for, as well as with the confusing array of reforms that were rescinded by subsequent

governments or that remained on the statute book but were not implemented………..A main characteristic of these reform efforts is their episodic and partial nature, attempting to tackle specific aspects of education but without any coherent strategy defining the longer term development of the system as a whole and its place in society. (p. 8)

The Greek education system has a simple structure. Compulsory schooling consists of seven years primary (Grades P-6), followed by a three-year lower secondary level which is called Gymnasium (Grades 7-9). At the post-compulsory upper secondary level there are different types of Lyceum (Grades 10-12). The number of teachers have steadily increased in recent times, resulting in a decrease in teacher/student ratios as compared to two decades ago, and is now on the low side as compared to other Western European countries (OECD Examiners' Report, 1996, p. 14).

As far as teaching is concerned, it continues to be organized in separate disciplines, although the potential of curriculum integration is currently being explored by the Pedagogical Institute of Greece. Today, teachers for all school levels are trained at universities. Secondary mathematics teachers destined for the gymnasium and the lyceum are mathematics graduates, with qualifications including four years of mathematics at university level but with no pedagogical pre-service training. In the past decade, attempts have been made to provide secondary mathematics teachers with pedagogical training before they are appointed to a school.

A new system of pre-service training has now been set in place, designed to remedy the shortcomings of the former system. Newly established Regional Professional Development Centers are located in every prefecture of the country and are thus closer to teachers who seek professional development. In-service training courses last from one to six months, however despite this provision, there is an overriding problem with in-service training: In the Greek system, there is no incentive for in-service training. Promotion and salary levels progression are entirely based on seniority. In this study I have attempted to gauge the impact voluntary in-service has on secondary mathematics teachers' espoused and enacted teachers' beliefs.

1.4 The mathematics education context in Greece

This section provides a brief historical account of changes that have taken place in mathematics education in Greece over the past thirty years. The major influences of mathematics curriculum change will also be presented.

In the late 1970's a number of Greek mathematicians and mathematics educators voiced their concerns regarding the teaching and learning approaches being used at the time, which were based on the then dominant teaching approach to mathematics education. The fundamental premises of these approaches were, according to Karageorgos (2000): (a) an over-emphasis on structure, rigor and formalism, (b) students' alienation from mathematics and science and their applications, (c) the belief that understanding the structures of mathematics was identical to learning mathematics, and (d) the inadequate pre-service pedagogical and school experience, and the inadequate in-service training offered to teachers. By the end of the 70's, a mathematics education movement started taking shape in Greece. This movement promoted innovative ideas and approaches to mathematics teaching: (a) school mathematics was not to be solely based on set theoretical, formalistic proof-based approaches, (b) more emphasis was to be given to applications of mathematics and problem solving, and (c) more emphasis was to be placed on the utilization of interdisciplinary approaches.

Many of those concerns remained at a theoretical level during the 1970's. The debate continued in the early 1980s following the publication of several influential documents. The *Cockcroft Report* (1982) and the National Council of Teachers of Mathematics' (NCTM) *Agenda for Action* (1980) were probably the most influential of the time, and they had an impact on the mathematics education community of Greece. By late 80's a second wave of reforms was being implemented, starting with a total overhaul of the mathematics books of the Gymnasium (Years 7-9). A point of clarification is due at this point however. All the books used by mathematics (and other) teachers in Greek State schools are published by the Pedagogical Institute. They are compulsory and they are distributed to each student free of charge. This process was completed by the end of the academic year 1993-94. As well, new books were prepared during this period by the Pedagogical Institute for the Lyceum levels (Years 10-12).

The discussion to this point has revolved around the preparation of mathematics textbooks. This is the case with most reports that refer to the reform efforts in mathematics education (Karageorgos, 2000). There is a prevailing and indeed a very strongly held belief amongst Greek mathematics educators, mathematicians and mathematics teachers alike, that a necessary and sufficient condition of reforming mathematics education practices consists of replacing existing textbooks by new ones.

The last wave of reforms in Greece is being planned for implementation in the academic years 2002-05. An attempt is being made to introduce an integrated and interdisciplinary curriculum at all levels from P-12. The success or otherwise of this titanic effort for a traditional mathematics education community will be interesting to observe.

Consequently, despite the reform efforts, mathematics classes in Greece are still dominated by teacher chalk-and-talk approaches and remains gender stereotyped (Barkatsas, Forgasz & Leder, 2001, 2002; Katsikas, 2000). One possible interpretation of this is that Greek teachers' perceptions of mathematics are deeply rooted and represent the values of the Greek mathematics education community at large. The system is still largely based on a single textbook published by the Pedagogical Institute. The mathematics curriculum is fragmented and traditional, and it promotes a heavy reliance on testing and final year exams. It focuses on content; it relies heavily on rigor and axiomatic proofs, and it encourages students to invoke deductive and inductive thinking. The influence of pure mathematicians and a rigid mathematics curriculum, based on a rigorous axiomatic approach (Karageorgos, 2000), could account for the observed pattern of beliefs despite the fact that in the past ten years or so girls have been performing at least as well as boys in science and engineering University entrance examinations (Katsikas, 2000). The sole use of teacher-centred traditional chalk-and-talk delivery approaches, and the security associated with them was captured by the view of one of the case studies teachers in this study. In discussing the use of co-operative learning approaches in mathematics teaching and learning the male teacher in the study (Tom) reported at an interview that: "I have never attempted to work with groups in my mathematics classes...Time constraints are very prohibitive. Innovations require time and there is no time available for group work". (Chapter 6, p. 166).

The answer to what constitutes the best practice in learning and teaching mathematics remains open. It seems that another decade of rapid changes in mathematics education has just begun. Teachers' beliefs about mathematics, mathematics teaching and mathematics learning influence their teaching approaches, what is taught, and how it is assessed (Thompson, 1992; Ernest, 1989a, 1989b; Van Zoest, 1994; Howard, Perry & Lindsay, 1997; Pajares, 1992; Hollingworth, 1989). The primary purpose of this study was to gain a better understanding of teaching, via the relationships between teachers' espoused and enacted beliefs about mathematics, mathematics teaching and mathematics learning.

It is my contention, in line with Pajares (1992) and Hollingworth (1989), that mathematics teachers' beliefs represent one of the most important parameters of the success or otherwise of educational reforms. Pajares (1992) argued that knowledge and beliefs are inextricably intertwined and that individuals' beliefs, strongly affect their behaviour and Hollingworth (1989) reported that the way teachers implement new methods or programs in their classrooms relates to whether their beliefs are congruent with the proposed new methods or programs. Teachers' beliefs influence their classroom practices, the beliefs are formed early and beliefs about teaching are well established by the time a prospective teacher starts attending University classes.

In an era of successive mathematics education reforms, it is helpful for the proponents of reforms in mathematics education to understand the impact teachers' beliefs have on their everyday cognitions and classroom practices. In this study I have endeavoured to explore and chart the complexity of the nexus between mathematics teachers' beliefs regarding the teaching and also the learning of mathematics that have attracted a considerable interest in recent non-Greek research studies (McLeod, 1989, 1992; Schoenfeld, 1989; Lester and Garofalo, 1987; Barkatsas and Hunting, 1996; Leder, 1993).

A number of models have been formulated in an attempt to account for the impact beliefs have on mathematics teaching and learning, and they will be considered as part of the literature review in an attempt to weave a coherent picture of the relevant research in the domain of teachers' beliefs.

1.5   Aims of the study

This study represents an exploration of the espoused beliefs and instructional practices of secondary mathematics teachers in Greece. It aimed to investigate the existence of a typology of mathematics teacher's beliefs regarding the nature of mathematics, mathematics teaching, learning and assessment and to explore possible inconsistencies between those beliefs and the teachers' instructional practice. Previous studies have suggested that the cultural aspects and contexts of mathematics teachers' beliefs are critical in their implication for student learning. This study will explore the impact various cultural aspects and a highly centralized curriculum have on Greek secondary mathematics teachers' beliefs about mathematics, and about mathematics teaching, learning and assessment.

The following research questions were addressed to fulfill this purpose:

1.6   Research questions

(1) What are the beliefs of Greek secondary mathematics teachers with regard to mathematics as a discipline, and learning, teaching and assessing mathematics? Specifically, does there exist a typology of teachers' beliefs that correspond to that postulated in the research literature concerning Western teachers?

(2) In what ways do Greek secondary mathematics teachers' biodata, such as professional development background, postgraduate studies background, years of experience, gender and position held, influence their espoused beliefs? In other words, what differences in beliefs exist across professional development undertaken, years of experience, position held, the range of qualifications, and between female and male teachers?

(3) Are there inconsistencies between Greek secondary mathematics teachers' beliefs about mathematics, mathematics teaching, mathematics learning, mathematics assessment and their teaching practice?

1.7   Methodology

To address the above issues the study was conducted in three phases. These are discussed in detail in Chapter 3:

➢ A pilot study was carried out to examine the feasibility of the proposed method of data collection. The sample comprised 345 (207 males, 92 females, 46 no gender specified) mathematics teachers in 37 Greek State High Schools.

➢ A survey was administered to explore the areas of interest and to produce data to examine the research questions statistically. The sample comprised 465 (276 males, 145 females, 44 no gender specified) grade 7-12 mathematics teachers, which included 431 secondary mathematics teachers (244 males, 143 females), 24 secondary mathematics teachers holding a principal's position (22 male, 2 female), and 10 regional mathematics consultants (10 males), in 45 State High Schools throughout Greece.

➢ The quantitative study was followed by a qualitative study focusing on in-depth case studies of two Greek (1M, 1F) veteran secondary mathematics teachers.

1.8   Structure of the book

Chapter 2 consists of the literature review. The literature review forms the theoretical framework for the study.

Chapter 3 describes the procedure chosen to conduct the study. The findings of the pilot study and their implications for the large-scale survey are reported in chapter 4. A large-scale survey explored secondary mathematics teachers' beliefs about mathematics, mathematics teaching, learning and assessment. The purpose of the survey was to provide data in order to statistically analyse the views of the teachers, and to provide a background against which to set the case studies. The findings are reported in Chapter 5. The quantitative study was followed by a qualitative study focusing on two in-depth case studies. Those findings are reported in chapter 6. The research questions are discussed in Chapter 7, along with the study's conclusions, suggestions for future research, and the implications for teacher professional development.

1.9   Summary of chapter

The central concern of this study was to find ways to illuminate the complexity of secondary mathematics teachers' beliefs about mathematics, mathematics teaching, mathematics learning and assessment, and their teaching practice. To explore these complex relationships this study was conducted by utilizing both qualitative and quantitative research methods. The research questions of the study concern mathematics teachers' espoused beliefs about mathematics, mathematics teaching, learning and assessment and factors that contribute to the existence of inconsistencies between the mathematics teachers' espoused beliefs and their teaching practice.

Chapter 2 commences with a discussion of constructivism and its implications for the classroom and the teachers of mathematics. The chapter continues with a literature review of pertinent research.

CHAPTER 2
Literature review

It can certainly be argued that teachers' beliefs play a major role in defining teaching tasks and organizing the knowledge and information relevant to those tasks. But why should this be so? Why wouldn't research-based knowledge or academic theory serve this purpose just as well? The answer suggested here is that the contexts and the environments within which teachers work, and many of the problems they encounter, are ill-defined and deeply entangled, and that beliefs are peculiarly suited for making sense of such contexts. (Nespor, 1987, p. 324)

2.1 Introduction

The purpose of the literature review is to position the present study amongst research studies already conducted, to enable the comparison of the results of such studies with my own and to acknowledge those researchers who assisted me in my endeavour to break new ground in this area of research. The establishment of the dimensions within which the study is placed, and the determination of the context and the various models of teachers' decisions, teachers' beliefs and knowledge, was of paramount importance in the conduct of the literature review. Although the general purpose of the review is to serve primarily the purpose of helping the investigator to: "develop a thorough understanding and insight into previous work and the trends that have emerged" (Borg & Gall, 1983, p.143), these two authors also claim that the review serves a number of other purposes related to pre-research planning, such as: delimiting the research problem, seeking new approaches, avoiding sterile approaches, providing insight into methods and suggesting recommendations for further research.

Borg & Gall's (1983) advice has been attended to in this study in a number of ways. Pre-research planning involved a search for research papers and studies relevant to the research questions (*delimiting the research problem*), a search for an appropriate and broadly acceptable research methodology (*seeking new approaches*), and an examination of teachers' — and mathematics teachers' in particular — beliefs research both in areas that have been sufficiently investigated, and in areas in which research has been sparse and inconclusive (*providing insight into methods and suggesting recommendations for further research*). The research study was carried out by utilizing a combination of qualitative and quantitative methods (*avoiding sterile approaches, providing insight into methods*).

This chapter commences with a discussion of constructivism and beliefs systems, relevant definitions and the distinction between beliefs and knowledge. This is followed by a discussion of beliefs and conceptions of mathematics teachers, including a philosophical analysis of didactical the consequences of prescriptive objectivist and progressive absolutist philosophies of mathematics. In particular the link between beliefs and instructional practice is explored. The chapter concludes with a synstudy of research findings on beliefs and the implications of research findings for the present study.

Since the beginning of the twentieth century, considerable research interest has been invested by social psychologists, in studying the nature of beliefs and their influence on people's actions (Thompson, 1992). Following a recession period during the 1920s, research interest was renewed in the 1930s and the 1960s, but it was not until the 1970s and the emergence of cognitive science that "a place for the study of belief systems in relation to other aspects of human cognition and human affect" was identified (Abelson, 1979, p. 355; cited in Thompson, 1992). Interest in beliefs and belief systems resurfaced in the 1980s. As far as mathematics education is concerned, over the past two decades numerous empirical studies (Berger, 2000) have demonstrated the impact mathematical beliefs have on mathematics teaching and learning processes.

A shift in the direction of research into the study of teachers' beliefs was prompted by a shift in paradigms for research on teaching, according to Thompson (1992). This shift of focus was grounded on the need for an understanding of belief systems and conceptions based on the seminal work of Green (1971) and Rokeach (1960); the need to situate the role of beliefs in the practice of teaching (Nespor, 1987); a focus on teachers' thinking and decision-making processes (Shulman, 1986; Bromme, 1994); and the need for a re-examination of the philosophy and the didactics of mathematics (Ernest, 1994). Pajares (1992) argued that although research on teacher thinking has been thriving, critics have questioned the utility of its findings on teacher education:

> They suggest that another perspective is required from which to better understand teacher behaviors, a perspective focusing on the things and ways that teachers believe. This view is based on the assumption that beliefs are the best indicators of the decisions individuals make throughout their lives. (p. 307)

Pajares (1992) has further documented certain researchers' predictions (Fenstermacher, 1979; Pintrich, 1990; Clark & Peterson; Nespor, 1987; cited in Pajares, 1992) regarding the necessity for disciplined inquiries investigating the role beliefs play on teacher effectiveness and decision-making.

2.2   *Conceptualising beliefs structures*

This study has been framed with constructivist perspectives that endorse both the social and the psychological construction of knowledge (Ernest, 1994, 1989a, 1989b; Bromme, 1994). A review of relevant constructivist issues is presented in what follows.

Constructivism in mathematics education

> *The history of Western epistemology is a history of more or less brilliant failures to resolve the paradox inherent in the traditional conception of knowledge. To make sure that it is "true", the knower would have to compare the known to the unknown reality, which that knowledge is presumed to represent. Such a comparison seems impossible and the sceptics have not tired of reminding us of that. Darwin's theory of evolution opened the path for a different theory of knowledge. Cognition and its results could, as Baldwin and Piaget proposed, be seen as an adaptive procedure. Adaptation, however, is instrumental - and instrumentalist theories of knowledge have had little success in the past because they were unable to supply a reasonable basis for "objectivity". (von Glasersfeld, 1984, p.1)*

It is well known to educators that, in many respects, the traditional classroom is a barrier to innovation. Each individual teacher is isolated in his or her own classroom, and enjoys considerable autonomy in how that classroom is run. Teachers can easily undermine the best-laid plans of ministerial committees, School Boards and curriculum planners and simply refuse to cooperate as they teach hidden from view behind closed classroom doors. Each individual teacher must make a positive decision to adopt a new technique before it can be successfully incorporated into a school's curriculum. A number of reasons can be advanced to explain why teachers are reluctant to make that decision. First, teachers may reject innovations that detract from their authority in the classroom. In the traditional classroom the teacher is in charge and he or she is the processor of knowledge and the dispenser of information.   Second, the efficient use of many new techniques may require alterations in teachers' relationships with each other. If teaching is done in an open classroom, in teams, or in conjunction with specialist teachers, the privacy of the traditional classroom is reduced. Third, the knowledge upon which teaching rests is limited. A great deal is still unknown about how individuals learn and which teaching methods are best for various types of students.

It could be argued that the traditional view of learning considers the mind as an empty vessel and the teacher as the one who fills up all the little vessels. Dengate & Lerman (1995) alternatively refer to the metaphor of tabula rasa or blank state, which "has been utilized for centuries to characterize passive-receptive learning" (Dengate & Lerman 1995, p.27). In the relativistic view, mathematics learning should be considered from at least two frames of reference – from the point of view of the student, and from the point of view of the teacher with whom the student has sustained communication and interaction. Steffe (1985) represented the relationship between mathematics knowledge of the teacher and mathematics knowledge of the child using the diagram in Figure 2.2.1. The diagram indicates that a teacher's and a child's knowledge of mathematics are not identical, either in scope or in kind.   The child's mathematical concepts and ideas develop dynamically over time and formal schooling directly influences some of them. The broken line indicates that the development of mathematics knowledge can be precipitated by appropriate teacher-initiated activities.

The zone of proximal development (zpd, Figure 2.2.1) has been defined by Vygotsky (Wertsch, 1985) as:

The distance between the child's actual developmental level as determined by independent problem solving and the higher level of potential development as determined through problem solving under adult guidance or in collaboration with more capable peers. (p. 6)

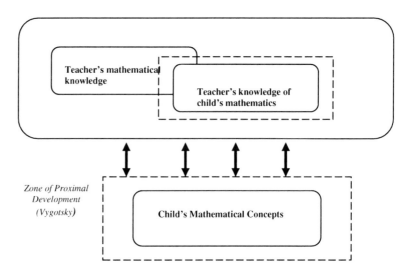

Figure 2.2.1. Children's mathematics (Steffe, 1985).

Instruction plays an important role in development and its focus should be on how the interpsychological functioning can be structured such that it will maximize the growth of intrapsychological functioning. Dengate & Lerman (1995) claimed that a synstudy of Lave and Wenger's (1991) study that "the direction in which cognition is situated is from the social to the individual and not vice-versa" (p.31) and Thompson's (1992) analysis of mathematics "as a kind of activity, a social construction" (p.32), could lead to the conclusion that if the individual is no longer regarded as ultimately autonomous, the position attributed to Vygotsky's school of thought and usually deemed "social constructionism", must fit a model of learning theory that has exogenic-endogenic dualistic nature.

There is an apparent contradiction between the plausible belief that students construct knowledge for themselves by reorganising their internal structures on the one hand, and the seemingly obvious assumption that the goal of teaching is to transmit knowledge to students. According to research literature (Confrey, 1990; von Glasersfeld, 1991a, 1991b, 1990; Steffe 1990, 1991; Hunting, 1983, 1987), a theory that seems to offer an alternative paradigm to the transmission view of knowledge is that of constructivism. Confrey (1990), stated that:

> Constructivism can be described as essentially a theory about the limits of human knowledge, a belief that all knowledge is necessarily a product of our own cognitive acts. We can have no direct or unmediated knowledge of any external or objective reality. We construct our understanding through our experiences, and the character of our experience is influenced profoundly by our cognitive lenses. To a constructivist, this circularity is both acceptable and unavoidable. One's picture of the world is not, however, static; our conceptions can and do change. The essential fact that we are engaged in living implies that things change. By coordinating a variety of constructions from sensory inputs to meditative reflections, we adapt and adjust to these changes and we initiate others. (p. 108)

Guba and Lincoln (1989) put forward a comparative table, in an effort to determine the differences between the 'conventional paradigm', that has been dominant for at least seven hundred years, (also called the positivist, or scientific paradigm) and the 'constructivist paradigm' (also called the naturalistic, hermeneutic, or interpretive paradigm. The constructivist paradigm has also been in existence for some time, according to Guba and Lincoln (1989), but it has not been widely accepted or understood, particularly in English speaking countries. Their comparison table outlining the essentials of the two paradigms follows (Table 2.2.1):

A by-product of constructivist teaching is that the teacher's attempt to understand the individual student's approach to a problem can generate a climate of positive social interaction. Genuine interest on how students think, on the teacher's part, shows to them, that they are considered important in the teaching-learning process, and it can generate the kind of reflection that is necessary for conceptual reorganisation and advancement. These sentiments were of importance for the present study.

Table 2.2.1

The contrasting conventional and constructivist paradigms

CONVENTIONAL BELIEFS	CONSTRUCTIVIST BELIEFS
ONTOLOGY	
A REALIST ONTOLOGY asserts that there exists a single reality that is independent of any observer's interest in it and which operates according to immutable natural laws, many of which take cause-effect form. Truth is defined as that set of statements that is isomorphic to reality	A MONISTIC RELATIVIST ONTOLOGY asserts that there exist multiple, socially constructed realities ungoverned by any natural laws, casual or otherwise. "Truth" is defined as the best informed (amount and quality of information) and most sophisticated (power with which the information is understood and used) construction on which there is consensus (although there may be several constructions extant that simultaneously meet that criterion).
EPISTEMOLOGY	
A DUALIST OBJECTIVE EPISTEMOLOGY asserts that it is possible (indeed, mandatory) for an observer to exteriorize the phenomenon studied, remaining detached and distant from it (a state often called "subject-object dualism"), and excluding and value considerations from influencing it.	A SUBJECTIVIST EPISTEMOLOGY asserts that an inquirer and the inquired-into are interlocked in such a way that the findings of an investigation are the literal creation of the inquiry process. Note that this posture effectively destroys the classical ontology-epistemology distinction.
METHODOLOGY	
AN INTERVENTIONIST METHODOLOGY strips context of its contaminating (confounding) influences (variables) so that the inquiry can coverage on truth and explain nature as it really is and really works, leading to the capability to predict and to control.	A HERMENEUTIC METHODOLOGY involves a continuing dialectic of iteration, analysis, critique, reiteration, reanalysis, and so on, leading to the emergence of a joint (among all the inquirers and respondents, or among etic and emic views) construction of a case.
	(Guba and Lincoln, 1989, p. 84)

The transmission view of teaching works to attribute two general functions to the teacher's words and actions. Firstly, the teacher's words and actions carry meanings in and of themselves that are waiting to be comprehended by students. Secondly, the teacher's word and actions serve to draw the student's attention to mathematical structures in the environment that are embodied in concrete materials, pictures, diagrams or problem statements. The nucleus of the transmission view of teaching and learning is that meaning is inherent in the words and actions of the teacher or in objects in the surrounding environment. This assumption seems to work well in several day situations, and it has been for many years the bottom line of many curriculum documents in mathematics education. According to constructivist theory, mathematical knowledge is not perceived or intuited but it is constructed by reflectively abstracting, (Ginsburg and Opper, 1979), from and reorganising sensory motor and conceptual activity. Mathematical knowledge is an invention of the mind. The teacher who refers to mathematical structures is therefore consciously reflecting on mathematical objects that he or she has previously constructed. Communication often breaks down, since teachers and students each construct their own meanings for words and actions in the context of the ongoing interaction.

Constructivism challenges the assumption that there is one-to-one correspondence between a student's observable behaviours and the underlying conceptual structures. Constructivism (von Glaserfled, 1991a) thus makes the distinction between teaching and training. Teaching aims at generating understanding, whereas training aims at competent performance. Teachers' actions constrain students' construction of new knowledge structures. This idea can be clarified by considering the analogy between the students' construction of mathematical knowledge, and the mathematician's construction of theoretical knowledge. A scientific theory remains unchallenged until conceptual or empirical anomalies become apparent. So, students operating on the frontiers of their own conceptual knowledge have no reason to build new conceptual structures unless their current knowledge results in obstacles, contradictions, or surprises. The difference between the mathematician and the student is that the student interacts with a teacher, who can guide his or her construction of knowledge as the student attempts to complete instructional activities. So the meanings given to the teacher's actions serve as an additional set of observations that can indicate to the students that their current conceptions are inadequate.

Adopting a constructivist view of learning has implications for the mathematics curriculum. According to Driver and Oldham (1986), an important difference between a constructivist curriculum and a more "traditional" one is that 'The curriculum is seen not a body of knowledge or skills but the program of activities from which such knowledge or skills can possibly be acquired or constructed' (p. 112). The constructivist approach also has relevance for this study. Some of the basic tenets of constructivism will be used to facilitate the analysis and interpretation of the research findings especially the case study teachers' classroom practice. This use of the theory is discussed later in this chapter.

Another important aspect of constructivism for the current study concerns the matter of how constructivists view language. Meanings for words and phrases is not fixed somewhere outside the users of language. Each person can only put her own subjective meanings into the words and phrases that have been communicated to them. According to von Glasersfeld (1991a):

> Language frequently creates the illusion that ideas, concepts and even whole chunks of knowledge are transported from a speaker to a listener. This illusion is extraordinarily powerful because it springs from the belief that the meaning of words and phrases is fixed somewhere outside the users of the language. (p.XIV)

Our subjective meanings tend to become intersubjective because we learn to modify and adapt them so that they fit the situations in which we interact with others. Using this method we manage to achieve a great deal of compatibility. Individual meanings however, do not have to be identical in order to be compatible. New concepts and new knowledge cannot be transmitted to another person by speaking, since throughout our lives we discover that the meaning(s) we have associated with a certain word is not compatible with the use others make of that word.

To account for the phenomenon of miscommunication Maturana (1978), proposed the idea of a "consensual domain". A consensual domain is the linguistic behaviour in which two (or more) individuals, with respect to an observer, act in accord as if they have come to agreement regarding their underlying assumptions. Relative agreements are the essence of consensual domains, where subjective experiences of each of the parties overlap. Once we realise the subjectivity of linguistic meaning, we can no longer, according to constructivism, maintain the notion that words convey ideas and that the listener must have conceptual understanding identical with ours. In mathematics classes, a conversation usually turns to predominantly abstract matters and usually it does not take long before conceptual discrepancies can generate perturbations in the course of the interaction.

Miscommunication between the teacher and his/her students was observed in both cases studies teachers' classes in this study, and it was one of the causes of inconsistencies between mathematics teachers' beliefs and their teaching practice (Chapter 6). It was found that in both case studies teachers' classes, a conversation usually turned to abstract matters and it did not take long before conceptual discrepancies would generate perturbations in the course of the teacher-student interaction without the teacher realising it.

In the next section, the difficulties encountered while attempting to formulate a definition of beliefs and belief systems are discussed.

Toward a definition of beliefs and belief systems

There are five principal literatures that have been used in this study for the dual purpose of informing and framing my research and they are analysed in the next sections of the literature review. These are the literatures on:

> *The affective domain and teachers' beliefs and belief systems generally* (McLeod, 1989, 1992; Pajares, 1992; Rokeach, 1960; Berger, 1999, 2000; Nespor, 1987; Hofer and Pintrich, 1997; Perry, 1970)

> *Mathematics teachers' conceptions of mathematics* (Ernest, 1989a, 1989b)

> *Mathematics teachers' conceptions of teaching and learning in mathematics* (Ernest, 1989a, 1989b; Kuhs and Ball 1986; Van Zoest, Jones and Thornton, 1994; Perry, Howard and Tracey, 1999; Fennema, Carpenter, Franke, Levi, Jacobs and Empson, 1996; Cooney, Shealy & Arvold, 1998; Cooney, 1999; Askew, Brown, Rhodes, Johnson and Williams, 1997; Tanner and Jones, 1998),

> *Mathematics teachers' beliefs about the relationship between teaching, learning and instructional practice* (Thompson, 1992; Pajares, 1992; Cooney, 1999; Nespor, 1987; Ernest, 1989a, 1989b; Baird, 2001; Davis, 1998; Raymond, 1997), and

> *Mathematics teachers' beliefs about assessment* (Clarke, 1996; Clarke and Stephens, 1996; Nisbet and Warren, 2000; Cooney, 1999; Shepard, 2000)

Affective issues in mathematical problem solving have attracted considerable attention by mathematics educators and cognitive psychologists in the past decade (Leder, 1993; McLeod, 1989, 1992; Lester & Garofalo 1987;

Schoenfeld, 1985a, 1985b, 1987, 1989, 1992; Dreyfus & Eisenberg, 1986; Mandler, 1989; Silver, 1994). Some investigators (McLeod, 1989; Schoenfeld, 1985a, 1992; Lester & Garofalo, 1987) have postulated that the inclusion of affective aspects of mathematical problem solving is necessary for any useful theory of problem solving in school contexts. One obstacle to progress in this domain is the non-alignment of terminology used by mathematics education researchers. Schoenfeld (1992), in an attempt to assemble a theory of mathematical thinking and problem solving, listed beliefs and affects as one of five aspects of cognition. Leder (1993) used Corsini's definition of affect as a term which is used to:

> Denote a wide range of concepts and phenomena including feelings, emotions, moods, motivation and certain drives and instincts (p. 1-46).

Despite lack of consensus among mathematics education researchers on the use of terminology, the affective domain is generally regarded as referring to constructs that, according to McLeod (1992), go beyond the cognitive domain, and that beliefs, attitudes and emotions can be considered as *subsets* of affect.

There is a need to probe further into the affective domain and to achieve an integration of research on the affective and the cognitive domains, on affect and learning, and on affect and teaching. There is also ongoing debate over which research methodology should be used to measure and evaluate affective aspects of mathematics learning and problem solving. That particular issue is being discussed in depth in Chapter 3.

Beliefs are phenomena that defy direct observation. They may be studied via a thorough and complex process of inference in an attempt to interpret the multitude of their manifestations in human behaviour and practices. Beliefs, attitudes and emotions have attracted considerable interest in recent research studies (McLeod, 1989, 1992; Schoenfeld, 1989, 1992; Lester and Garofalo, 1987; Barkatsas and Hunting, 1996; Leder, 1992, 1993; Berger, 1999, 2000; Buzeika, 1996; Malone, 1995; Malone, Thornton, Langrall, & Jones, 1997; Howard, Perry & Lindsay, 1997; Perry, Howard & Conroy, 1996; Perry, Howard & Tracey, 1999; Nisbet & Warren, 2000; Perry, Vistro-Yu, Howard, Wong & Keong, 2002). As a result of such studies and their diverse foci, various researchers have proposed numerous definitions of beliefs over the past two decades. McLeod's (1992) definition of beliefs has been considered adequate for this study, since it makes clear the distinction between the cognitive and affective dimensions of beliefs:

> Beliefs are largely cognitive in nature, and are developed over a relatively long period of time. Emotions, on the other hand, may involve little cognitive appraisal and may appear and disappear rather quickly, as when the frustration of trying to solve a hard problem is followed by the joy of finding a solution. Therefore we can think of beliefs, attitudes and emotions as representing increasing levels of affective involvement, decreasing levels of cognitive involvement, increasing levels intensity of response, and decreasing levels of response stability. (p. 579)

McLeod (1992) further claimed that beliefs, attitudes and emotions could be considered as subsets of affect. Other researchers (Lester and Garofalo, 1987; (Leder, Pehkonen and Torner, 2002).) have expressed the view that research evidence indicates that beliefs shape attitudes and emotions and that they greatly affect the disposition of students towards mathematics. Pekhonen and Safuanov (1996) too argued that students' prior experiences affect their beliefs at an unconscious level:

> Pupils' mathematical beliefs usually act as a filter that influences almost all their thoughts and actions concerning mathematics. Pupils' prior experiences of mathematics affect their beliefs completely - usually unconsciously. (p. 33)

It could be argued that in a similar way, teachers' prior schooling and cultural experiences too affect their beliefs at an unconscious level, acting as a sieve that filters the majority of their mathematical thoughts and actions, especially at the instructional level.

A certain obstacle to progress in this domain is the non-alignment of the meaning of the concept referred to by researchers. A point of convergence however, may be the agreement of most researchers that attitudes and beliefs are shaped and transformed via appropriately tuned instructional models. Pajares (1992) argued that the confusion arising from the many terms that have been used to describe the same phenomena and the consequent attempts of the researchers to provide definitions for the terms they had introduced, could be generally attributed to the distinction between beliefs and knowledge. In all cases, according to Pajares (1992):

> It was difficult to pinpoint where knowledge ended and belief begun, and the authors
> suggested that most of the constructs were simply different words meaning the same
> thing. (p.309)

The difficulty in defining *educational beliefs* is highlighted by the fact that for research purposes, the term 'beliefs' has been presented in the literature as a concept that is very broad and difficult to operationalise. Pajares (1992) cited a number of constructs which can be considered as subsets of the broadly defined 'educational beliefs' term, the most commonly used being: teacher efficacy, epistemological beliefs, attributions, anxiety, self-concept, self-esteem, self-efficacy and specific subject matter beliefs. What is needed for research purposes is, according to Thompson (1992), a careful consideration of the concept of beliefs from both a philosophical and a psychological perspective. Green (1971) proposed a multidimensional perspective on the structure of beliefs – one that incorporated both philosophical and psychological constructs. He claimed that there are three dimensions of belief structures: the quasi-logical relation between beliefs, the central-peripheral dimension introduced by Rokeach (1968), and the premise that beliefs are held in clusters. An explanation of Green's (1971) proposals and the terms he used, along with a conceptualisation of beliefs from a philosophical perspective are discussed in the forthcoming sections. The psychological perspective is discussed first in order to shed light on the conscious-subconscious dichotomy.

Rokeach (1968, cited in Pajares, 1992) pioneered the introduction of the notion of *belief systems* and his analysis included three assumptions:

> Beliefs differ in intensity and power; beliefs vary along a central-peripheral dimension;
> and, the more central a belief, the more it will resist change...Rokeach defined
> centrality in terms of connectedness: the more a given belief is functionally connected
> or in communication with other beliefs, the more central the belief...He proposed four
> assumptions for connectedness that form a set of priorities for the perceived importance
> of the self. Beliefs on an individual's identity or self are more connected, as are beliefs
> one shares with others. Derived beliefs are learned from others; underived beliefs are
> learned by direct encounter with the belief object. Underived beliefs have more
> functional connections, partly because the: "I saw with my own eyes" phenomenon is
> existential and connected to one's sense of self. (p. 320)

Berger (1999), drawing on Rokeach's (1968) ideas described beliefs as subconscious, conscious or surface, or entrenched. He argued that as far as the research process is concerned central beliefs are less important than subconscious beliefs as long as they are surface beliefs. Subconscious beliefs, according to Berger (1999) render the change process difficult, since changing one's beliefs about something, requires a conscious realisation of what to change. He further claimed that of particular importance to the researcher is the concept of *entrenched beliefs*, which are both central and subconscious and they embody very deep phenomena of beliefs research. Pajares (1992) argued that beliefs are prioritised according to their connections to other cognitive and affective structures. Kitchener's *forms of epistemic cognition* (Pajares, 1992) can be considered as an attempt to define epistemological beliefs. These sets of beliefs are associated with the nature of knowledge itself, and how with a person comes to know and certain beliefs they hold about knowing. Hofer & Pintrich (1997) argued that since the time of Piaget's (1950) theory of intellectual development and Perry's (1970) scheme of intellectual and ethical development, research on epistemological beliefs has addressed six general issues:

- Refining and extending Perry's developmental sequence
- Developing more simplified measurement tools for addressing such development
- Exploring gender-related patterns in knowing
- Examining how epistemological awareness is a part of thinking and reasoning processes
- Identifying dimensions of epistemological beliefs
- Assessing how these beliefs link to other cognitive and motivational processes

(p. 89)

Hofer & Pintrich (1997) arrived at the conclusion that there is very little agreement:

On the construct under study, the dimensions it encompasses, whether epistemological beliefs are domain specific or how such beliefs might connect to disciplinary beliefs".

(p.89)

Hofer & Pintrich (1997) also concluded that it is not clear – from a research point of view – if beliefs about learning, intelligence, and teaching should be considered as central components of the construct of epistemological beliefs. They proposed that as far as the definition of the content of epistemological beliefs is concerned, it should be "limited to individuals' beliefs about the nature of knowledge and the process of knowing" (Hofer & Pintrich, 1997, p.117). They went on to propose that the development of a widely acceptable definition of the construct of epistemological beliefs constitutes one of the most important issues to be resolved by future research efforts.

Most of the researchers' conceptions about beliefs and belief systems have been derived from the psychological and educational research literature. The present study has been influenced, shaped and guided by previous research on the concept of beliefs and belief systems, as well as previous research findings on issues pertaining to teachers' beliefs about the nature of mathematics and mathematics teaching, learning and assessment. Previous findings provide the foundations for the conception of belief-related behaviours and an understanding of the relationship between beliefs and belief-related behaviours. In concluding her detailed historical and psychological discussion of the concept of attitude, Forgasz (1995) elaborated on some commonalities among the models under consideration and was able to discern five common features. Three of those features are of interest to the present study, namely:

- Beliefs are learnt and evolved from interactions with the environment,
- The affective, cognitive and behavioural components are inter-related and there is a tendency to consistency among them
- The components are implicated in overt behaviour but other factors related to the social context are also involved. (adapted from Forgasz, 1995, p. 44)

Although all previously mentioned conceptualisations of beliefs and belief systems provide valuable insights for the understanding of educational beliefs, we are still in need of a broadly acceptable theoretical model (Berger, 2000). A preliminary model proposed by Nespor (1987) was an attempt to develop a theoretically grounded model of belief systems that could provide the necessary scaffolding for systematic and comparative research studies. Nespor (1987) listed six structural features of beliefs 'that serve to distinguish them from other forms of knowledge' (p. 318). At least four out of these six structural features can serve to distinguish 'beliefs' from 'knowledge', according to Nespor (1987):

- Existential presumption
- Alternativity
- Affective and evaluative loading

- Episodic storage

Existential presumptions could play an important role in the formation, duration and strength of teachers' beliefs about certain student characteristics such as ability, maturity and laziness. Nespor (1987) described two diametrically opposite mathematics teachers' beliefs about mathematics learning. She claimed that those beliefs were not simply descriptions but they were labels for entities or deeply rooted beliefs held by the teachers concerned. One of them believed that learning mathematics was primarily a function of drilling and students would not learn if they were lazy. This view was partly shared by one of the case study teachers (Tom) in this study (Chapter 6). The deeply rooted beliefs, held by the other teacher - which was partly shared by the second case study teacher (Ann) in this study (Chapter 6) - was that mathematics learning was primarily a function of maturity.

Nespor (1987), drawing from Abelson (1979), described the term *alternativity* as representations often being part of individuals' belief systems. They could be conceived as:

> Conceptualizations of ideal situations differing significantly from present realities. In this respect, beliefs serve as means of defining goals and tasks, whereas knowledge systems come into play where goals and the paths to their attainment are well defined.
> (p. 319)

Affective and evaluative aspects of belief systems can rely more on evaluative components than knowledge systems do, according to Nespor (1987), a view that was shared by McLeod (1989, 1992). Her conclusion was that the affective and evaluative components of belief systems could act, as regulators to the amount of energy teachers will expend during their classroom activities.

The idea that knowledge is stored in semantic networks, while belief systems are mainly composed of the episodic or experiential material, suggested by Abelson (1979), was stressed by Nespor (1987) in her attempt to incorporate the concept of *episodic storage* into her model. One of Nespor's (1987) conclusions is of particular importance to this study, since both case study teachers stated that their experiences as students and the influence of some of their teachers were pivotal factors in their decision to become mathematics teachers. Nespor (1987) claimed that some crucial experiences or some influential teachers produce a 'richly-detailed episodic memory, which later serves the student as an inspiration and a template for his or her own teaching practice' (p. 320).

Nespor (1987) conceptualized two more features as being useful for the characterization of the ways beliefs are organized as systems:

- Non-consensuality
- Unboundedness

Non-consensuality could be conceived of as a feature of belief systems and derives as a consequence of a disagreement on how they are to be evaluated. Non-consensuality could be conceived as a by-product of the four features of beliefs described earlier, Nespor (1987) argues, and they "consist of propositions, concepts, arguments, or whatever is recognized by those who hold them as being in dispute, or as in principle disputable" (p. 321). It was also argued that beliefs are static and that when they change it is "likely to be a matter of conversion or gestalt shift than the result of argumentation or a marshalling of evidence" (p. 321).

The sixth and final structural feature of a belief system was termed *unboundedness.* This particular feature offers another critical filter through which to view some of the differences that exist between belief and knowledge systems. Nespor (1987) suggested that the unboundedness component of a belief system could be conceived as having: 'stable core applications…but that they can be extended in radical and unpredictable ways to apply to very different types of phenomena' (p.321).

One of the implications of the above-mentioned model for teaching and teacher education is that if beliefs have the structural characteristics suggested by Nespor (1987), then they cannot be proven unreasonable or false, since as was claimed previously, beliefs do not consist of sets of propositions or statements in the same way as conceptual systems do. One can then argue that teachers' orientations to knowledge structures presented to them during pre-service or in-service programs may be influenced by pre-existing belief systems which could be beyond the sphere of influence of the trainers. In a similar manner, the multitude of ways beliefs concerning teachers' understanding of teaching contexts develops over a period of time, appears to be similarly difficult to predict, control or influence (Nespor, 1987). Regarding the issue of successfully transforming teachers' beliefs and practices,

Nespor (1987) nominated the following conclusion as the crux of the problem: 'we do not know very much about how beliefs come into being, how they are supported or weakened, how people are converted to them' (p.326).

Defining the boundaries between 'knowledge' and 'beliefs' has proven to be just another daunting task (Pajares, 1992), researchers investigating the nature of beliefs have had to tackle. It is important for this study to clarify the differences between the two concepts since they have been used interchangeably in numerous research studies as if they were synonymous. According to Nespor (1987) and Pajares (1992) knowledge and beliefs are inextricably intertwined, but the potent affective, evaluative, and episodic nature of beliefs makes them a filter through which new phenomena could be interpreted. Nespor's (1987) position that at least four out of the six structural features of her model. *Existential presumption, Alternativity, Affective and evaluative loading* and *Episodic structure* can serve to distinguish 'beliefs' from 'knowledge', has been discussed in the previous section.

The concepts of ''knowledge' and 'beliefs' have been used interchangeably in numerous research studies as if they were synonymous. Fenstermacher (1994) voiced his disagreement to Kagan's (1990) assertion that she used the two terms interchangeably since there is sufficient evidence that teachers' craft knowledge could be defined in purely subjective terms. Fenstermacher (1994) argued that there is a need to clarify the epistemological distinctions between the two terms. By analyzing what local, craft, situated and tacit knowledge have been conceived to be, he concluded that when referring to teachers' activities, the term knowledge could be considered as:

1. A type of knowing, either formal or practical, that has considerable epistemic import

2. Simply a generic name to describe a broad range of mental states of teachers that arise from their training, experience and reflection and has little if any epistemological import

3. A deliberate selection of a socially valued term, used with the primary intention of legitimating the insights, understandings, beliefs, and so forth that teachers possess (Adapted from Fenstermacher, 1994, p. 34)

In the next section, important aspects of the research literature on beliefs and mental conceptions of mathematics teachers are examined. The importance of this section lies in the fact that beliefs and conceptions of mathematics teachers are the focus of this investigation.

2.3   Beliefs and conceptions of mathematics teachers

This section begins with a short discussion of the distinction between beliefs and knowledge, acknowledging that knowledge and beliefs are inextricably intertwined, followed by issues of primary interest for the present study: mathematics teachers' conceptions of mathematics, mathematics teachers' beliefs about teaching and learning; relationship between beliefs about mathematics, mathematics teaching and learning and instructional practice; mathematics teachers, beliefs about assessment; teachers' beliefs and the classroom environment, and inconsistencies between teachers' espoused beliefs and beliefs in practice.

Mathematics teachers' conceptions of mathematics

It is my contention that four of the most significant aims of mathematics education are the development of a positive attitude toward mathematics in school-aged students, as well as the encouragement of young people to actively participate in solving mathematical problems, in modelling real life situations and to experience the pleasure and fascination of conducting mathematical investigations, thus enabling them to become embedded in potential mathematical microcosms, in much the same way practising mathematicians experience their mathematical endeavours.

Ernest (1989a) developed a detailed model of mathematics teachers' knowledge, beliefs and attitudes – including the impact beliefs have on teaching mathematics – by treating mathematics teachers' cognitive structures, knowledge, and beliefs as *schemas* stored in the mind of mathematics teachers. His model has been influenced by Shulman's (1987) seminal paper on the foundation of knowledge and teaching. The idea of a *schema* has recently helped explain many aspects of human knowledge organisation and recall. Silver (1987) borrowed a description of schema from Thorndyke and Yelcovich (1980), as representing a prototypical abstraction of a complex and frequently encountered concept or phenomenon. As such, a schema is usually derived from past experience with numerous exemplars of the concept involved. Ernest's (1989a) model of mathematics teachers' knowledge, beliefs, and attitudes is depicted in Figure 2.3.1:

COMPONENTS OF THE MODEL

Knowledge
        of mathematics
        of other subject matter
        of teaching mathematics
            Mathematics pedagogy
            Mathematics curriculum
        classroom organization and management for mathematics teaching
        of the context of teaching mathematics
            The school context
            The students taught
        of education
            Educational psychology
            Education
            Mathematics education

Beliefs
        Conception of the nature of mathematics
        Models of teaching and learning mathematics
            Model of teaching mathematics
            Model of learning mathematics
        Principles of education

Attitudes
        Attitudes to mathematics
        Attitude to teaching mathematics

Figure 2.3.1. A model of mathematics teachers' knowledge, beliefs, and attitudes (Adapted from Ernest, 1989a, pp. 15-16)

Ernest (1989a) noted that the term 'beliefs' is not an isolated construct but it consists of the mathematics teachers' beliefs system, values and ideology in much the same way as Kuhs & Ball's (1986) teachers' dispositions, referred to later on (p.34). The impact such conceptions have on the selection of content, styles of teaching and modes of learning, has been the subject of another model proposed by Ernest (1989b). He theorised that teachers' conceptions of the nature of mathematics as a whole (Figure 2.3.2) provide the foundation for teachers' mental models regarding the teaching and learning of mathematics. The following diagram depicts

Ernest's (1989b) model regarding the relationship between beliefs, and their impact on teaching practice.

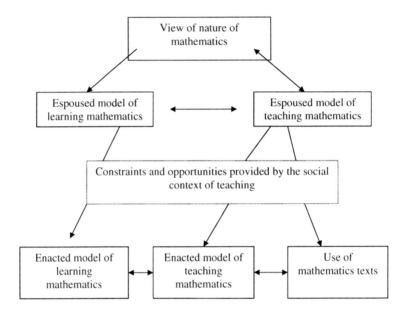

Figure 2.3.2. Relationship between beliefs, and their impact on teaching practice (Ernest, 1989b, p.252)

The relative positions of the elements making up the model in Figure 2.3.2, indicate Ernest's (1989b) awareness of the dominance teachers' beliefs about the nature of mathematics exert on their espoused beliefs about teaching and learning and of his awareness of the fact that the social context may constrain mathematics teachers' enacted approaches concerning the teaching and learning of mathematics.

Ernest (1989a) put forward the view that teachers' beliefs about the nature of mathematics are not necessarily to be thought of as consciously held views. He claimed that they should rather be thought of as 'implicitly held philosophies' (p.

20), and he went on to distinguish three philosophies of mathematics among the many variations possible:

- *The dynamic - problem solving view*: Mathematics is a continually expanding field of inquiry and its results are open to revision. It is also a field of creativity and invention and a cultural product
- *The Platonist view:* Mathematics is a set of monolithic and immutable structures and truths, and a static but unified body of expert knowledge. Mathematics is not created but discovered
- *The instrumentalist view:* Mathematics consists of an accumulation of useful but unrelated facts, rules and skills to be mastered in the pursuit of some unclearly defined end

A combination of the three views or a strong allegiance by teachers regarding one of the views is possible in their daily practice. Mathematics teachers' philosophical worldviews have an impact on their classroom practice, on the ways they perceive teaching, learning and assessment and on the ways they perceive students' potential, abilities, dispositions and capabilities. Accepting a multiplicity of methods and diversified approaches while students solve mathematical problems in class is the result of an active, problem solving view of mathematics. An active problem solving view of mathematics was one of the case study teachers' philosophical stances. This is discussed in detail in Chapter 6. A teacher's insistence on guiding students to a pre-determined correct solution signifies a Platonist or instrumentalist view of mathematics. A Platonist or instrumentalist view of mathematics was the second case study teacher's philosophical stance. This is discussed in detail in Chapter 6.

Mathematics teachers' beliefs about teaching and learning

Systemic reforms are currently being implemented in mathematics education in Greece and it is my contention along with that of Pajares' (1992) and Hollingworth's (1989), that mathematics teachers' beliefs represent one of the most important parameters of the success or otherwise of educational reforms. Pajares (1992) argued that knowledge and beliefs are inextricably intertwined and that individuals' beliefs strongly affect their behaviour, and Hollingworth (1989) reported that the way teachers implement new methods or programs in their classrooms relates to whether their beliefs are congruent with the proposed new methods or programs.

As a result of their personal dispositions with regard to the nature of mathematics teachers develop their own sets of ideas about learning and teaching. Ernest (1989a) developed the following model of possible mathematics teaching approaches:

> ➢ The pure investigational, problem posing and solving model
> ➢ The conceptual understanding enriched with problem-solving model
> ➢ The conceptual understanding model
> ➢ The mastery of skills and facts with conceptual understanding model
> ➢ The mastery of skills and facts model
> ➢ The day to day survival model   (Ernest, 1989a, p. 22)

Kuhs and Ball's (1986) model of teaching mathematics consists of four dominant beliefs:

- *Learner-focused beliefs* emphasising the learner's personal construction of mathematical knowledge
- *Content-focused beliefs* with an emphasis on conceptual understanding
- *Content-focused beliefs* with an emphasis on performance (i.e. mastery of rules and facts)
- *Classroom-focused beliefs* emphasising the use of knowledge to produce effective classroom environments

Van Zoest et al. (1994) conducted a study which compared the beliefs about mathematics and mathematics teaching of pre-service primary mathematics teachers' involved in a mentorship program, to the beliefs of peer pre-service teachers not involved in the mentorship program. The mentorship intervention was grounded on a socio-constructivist approach to mathematics instruction and the treatment group teachers participated in small group teaching activities. Van Zoest, et al. (1994) used a variation of Kuhs and Ball's (1986) model for their study by collapsing two of the four components proposed by Kuhs and Ball's (1986): the classroom-focused view and the two content focused views into one they called *learner-focused with an emphasis on social interaction,* they did this because they theorised that there was an overlap between the classroom-focused view and the two content focused views (see page 34) proposed by Kuhs and Ball's (1986).

Van Zoest et al. (1994), found that the intervention group acted as if, initially, its views had been influenced by the socio-constructivist approach to mathematics instruction, promoted by the mentorship program. Later on in the program however, their actions indicated that they favoured a more traditional pattern of beliefs about mathematics teaching. Van Zoest et al.'s (1994) model of teachers' actions (1994) during the four phases identified by the research program, are described in the comparative overview of mathematics teachers' beliefs models (Appendix B2).

Perry et al. (1999), and his colleagues (Perry et al., 1996; Howard et al., 1997) made their own contribution to teachers' beliefs research by providing a model aimed to describe the espoused beliefs of both primary and secondary mathematics teachers, as a result of a series of studies conducted in Australia. They identified two factors, which they considered sufficient for a full description of the espoused beliefs of mathematics teachers. They defined the two beliefs factors of their model, which they called *transmission view* and *child-centredness view* as follows:

> *Transmission:* the traditional view of mathematics as a static discipline which is taught and learned through the transmission of mathematical skills and knowledge from the teacher to the learner and where "mathematics [is seen] as a rigid system of externally dictated rules governed by standards of accuracy, speed and memory".
>
> *Child-centredness:* students are actively involved with mathematics through "constructing their own meaning as they are confronted with learning experiences which build on and challenge existing knowledge". (Perry, Howard and Tracey, 1999, p. 40)

Perry et al. (1999) stressed that they consider the two factors making up their model as being distinct factors and not as the two ends of a continuum of one belief factor.

Of particular interest to the present study is these authors' transmission factor which is identical to the one identified in this study (Chapter 5) a *traditional - transmission - information processing orientation,* consisting of the following (not mutually exclusive but complementary) views:

❑ The static view (factor 3)

❑ The mechanistic view (factor 4)

Of interest to the present study is also Perry et al.'s (1999) child-centredness factor which shares many characteristics with the *contemporary - constructivist orientation* of this study (Chapter 5), consisting of the following (not mutually exclusive but complementary) views:

❑ The socio-constructivist view (factor 1)

❑ The dynamic problem driven view (factor 2)

❑ The cooperative view (factor 5)

Fennema, Carpenter, Franke, Levi, Jacobs & Empson (1996) conducted a study of mathematics teachers' beliefs and instructional practices as they learned about students' thinking and decided how to utilise that knowledge to enable them to finalise instructional decisions. They categorised teachers' beliefs into four levels:

➢ Level A: Teachers in this category believed that students learn best by being told how to do mathematics.

➢ Level B: Teachers in this category were beginning to question the idea that children needed to be shown how to do mathematics, but they have conflicting beliefs.

➢ Level C: Teachers thought that children would learn mathematics as they solved many problems and discussed their solutions.

➢ Level D: The beliefs in this category were characterized by the acceptance of the idea that children can solve problems without direct instruction and that the mathematics curriculum should be based on children's abilities.

Fennema et al. (1996), observed subtle differences in the beliefs patterns of teachers they had categorised as belonging to Level 4 and decided to separate the two Levels into Level 4A and Level 4B, noting that belief differences between the two levels centered on the degree to which *the teacher believed that children's thinking should be used to make instructional decisions*. Level B teachers, *more than* Level A teachers, reported that they *should use their knowledge of children's thinking consistently*. The researchers reached the conclusion that with regard to the relationship between levels of instruction and beliefs: "there was no consistency in whether a change in beliefs preceded a change in instruction or vice versa" (p. 423). Fennema et al.'s (1996) scheme has been used in the analysis of this study's case studies (Chapter 6), and it is further discussed in the comparative overview of mathematics teachers' beliefs models (Appendix B1).

Cooney and his collaborators (Cooney, Shealy & Arvold, 1998; Cooney, 1999) developed a characterization of secondary mathematics teachers' belief structures, based on their research. Cooney's (1999) scheme has been used in the analysis of this study's case studies (Chapter 6), and it is further discussed in the comparative overview of mathematics teachers' beliefs models (Appendix B1). The researchers acknowledged the contributions Dewey (1933), Schon (1983) and von Glaserfeld (1991) have made on shaping the notion of reflection, and proposed the following partial scheme for the conceptualization/characterization of teachers' knowledge belief structures:

- *Isolationist*: Teachers in this category tend to have belief structures in such a way that beliefs remain separated or clustered away from others. Accommodation is not a theme that characterizes an isolationist.

- *Naïve idealist*: Teachers in this category tend to be received knowers in that, unlike the isolationists, they absorb what others believe to be the case but often without analysis of what he/she believes.

- *Naïve connectionist*: This position emphasizes reflection and attention to the beliefs of others as compared to one's own. The naïve connectionist fails however, to resolve conflict or differences in beliefs.

- *Reflective connectionist*: This position emphasizes reflection and attention to the beliefs of others as compared to one's own. The reflective connectionists however, resolve conflict through reflective thinking.

As a general concluding comment, Cooney (1999) stated that the "inculcation of doubt and the posing of perplexing situations" (p. 173) would seem to be central to the shift from being a naïve idealist (or even an isolationist) to being a reflective connectionist. Inciting doubt and making the previously unproblematic problematic can have significant impact on a person's world and could lead to varied and perhaps unsettling responses.

Askew, Brown, Rhodes, Johnson & Wiliam (1997) conducted a study designed to explore the knowledge, beliefs and practices of effective teachers of numeracy in the United Kingdom. Effectiveness for their project was defined in terms of learning gains. They identified three orientations of teachers' belief systems: (i) the *connectionist* orientation, (ii) the *transmission* orientation and (iii) the *discovery* orientation. These orientations are discussed in the comparative overview of mathematics teachers' beliefs models (Appendix B2).

Of particular interest to the present study is that part of the summary of findings reported by Askew et al. (1997), which is related to highly effective teachers' beliefs, since it will be of use in the analysis of the classroom practices of the case study teachers:

➤ Highly effective teachers were distinguished from other teachers via a particular set of coherent beliefs and understandings, which underpinned their teaching numeracy. Their beliefs related to:
  - The meaning of being numerate
  - The relationship between teaching and students' learning of numeracy
  - The presentation and intervention strategies.

➤ Highly effective teachers believed that being numerate requires:
  - Having a rich network of connections between different mathematical ideas
  - Being able to select and use strategies which are both efficient and effective

➤ Highly effective teachers believed, in relation to teaching that it is the teacher's responsibility to intervene to assist the student to become more efficient in the use of specific strategies

➤ Teachers' beliefs and conceptualizations of the mathematical and pedagogical purposes behind a particular spectrum of classroom practices seemed to be more important than the forms of practice themselves.

Tanner and Jones (1998) conducted a study aimed to identify successful teaching styles by utilizing an action research network of six secondary schools.

They identified two matched pairs in each school, one to act as an intervention group and the other as a control group. Participant observation revealed the existence of four groups, classified according to the teaching styles adopted by its teacher members: *taskers, rigid scaffolders, dynamic scaffolders* and *reflective scaffolders*. The four groups bear many similarities to those identified by Cooney (1999). Tanner and Jones' (1998) are discussed in the comparative overview of mathematics teachers' beliefs models (Appendix B2).

The comparative overview depicted in the Appendices B1 and B2 was developed by me for the present study. The reason for breaking down what was originally one table into two (Appendices B1 and B2) resides in the fact that the information would have been difficult to follow.

Relationship between teachers' beliefs about mathematics and mathematics teaching and learning, and their instructional practice

A number of studies conducted by Australian researchers have investigated various aspects of mathematics teachers' beliefs, for example, how teachers' beliefs (and belief systems) impact on teachers' daily practices (Buzeika, 1996); encouraging reflection on their teaching practices (Malone, 1995); providing alternative models for mathematics teaching (Malone, 1995; Malone, Thornton, Langrall & Jones, 1997); espoused primary and secondary teachers' beliefs about mathematics and the learning and teaching of mathematics (Barkatsas & Malone, 2002; Barkatsas, 2001; Howard, Perry & Lindsay, 1997; Perry, Howard & Conroy, 1996; Perry, Howard, & Tracey, 1999; Nisbet & Warren, 2000).

Other relevant recent research findings, which have been used to inform this study (Thompson, 1992; Pajares, 1992; Cooney, 1999; Nespor, 1987; Ernest, 1989a, 1989b), suggest that teachers' beliefs about the nature of mathematics and about mathematics teaching and learning have an impact on teaching practice. Many researchers have stressed the importance of teachers' beliefs on the success or otherwise of contemporary mathematics curricular reforms (Thompson, 1992; Pajares, 1992; Askew et al., 1997; Van Zoest et al., 1994). Thompson (1992) argued that the likelihood that the implementation of proposed or mandated changes in teachers' classrooms might be influenced by their deeply rooted espoused beliefs. Pre-service high school mathematics teachers experienced difficulties in the implementation of their espoused beliefs in practice, according to Parmelee (1992, cited in Van Zoest, 1994, p. 42).

Nisbet & Warren's (2000) review of the relevant research investigating potential interrelationships between mathematics teachers' espoused beliefs and their classroom practice offers some insights on the current state of affairs:

- The relationship between teachers' beliefs and classroom practice is dynamic with each influencing the other
- Teachers' practices are shaped by their beliefs about the nature of mathematics, teaching and learning
- Changes in teachers' beliefs about teaching and learning are derived largely from classroom practice
- Changes in teachers' beliefs about teaching and learning are influenced by the production of valued outcomes (i.e. student learning) resulting from classroom experimentation (Adapted from Nisbet & Warren, 2000, p. 35)

Regarding the causes of disparities between teachers' espoused (stated) and enacted beliefs (classroom actions) three possible explanations have been offered by Ernest (1989a), specifically the:

- Depth of the teacher's espoused beliefs and the extent to which they are integrated with his/her other knowledge and beliefs, especially pedagogical knowledge
- Level of the teacher's consciousness of his/her beliefs and the extent to which the teacher reflects on his or her teaching practice
- The powerful influence of the social context and its effect on teachers' actions and behaviours

Baird (2001) went a step further by developing a taxonomy of influences on teaching practice by pursuing the nexus between a teacher's intention and the resulting action. Baird's (2001) taxonomy follows has four levels:

- Teacher *Values/Beliefs*
- Teacher *Intentions/Purposes*
- *Approaches/Behaviours* exhibited by teacher
- *Methods/Procedures* selected by teacher to foster student learning (p. 274)

Each level influences the level below it. The superordinate level is "Teacher *Values and Beliefs*". Conscious or tacit values and beliefs held by the teacher influence teaching intentions and purposes. These intentions and purposes in turn, influence observable teaching approaches and behaviours that again, influence the teachers' selection of methods and procedures for student learning.

In an attempt to emphasise the role of different types of teacher's *listening* in mathematics classrooms, Davis (1998) developed a framework which may be used as an analytical multi-encompassing device to guide the analysis of complex classroom interactions occurring in the context of this study's case studies. He developed a categorisation called 'listening for differences in mathematics classrooms', which has been used in this study to facilitate interpretation of classrooms' videotaped sessions, and to draw conclusions regarding teachers' instructional practices (Chapter 6 and 7). Davis (1998) proposed the following categories of teachers' listening in mathematics classrooms:

➢ *EVALUATIVE LISTENING*

The primary reason for listening in such mathematics classrooms tends to be limiting and limited. The communicant (a questioner or otherwise) is not really interested in what the other person is saying and the communication is constrained by the fact that the teacher is listening *for* something in particular (her own pre-determined answer) rather than listening *to* the speaker. Rather, the person's actions (including his or her questions) are generally pre-determined and allow little room for deviation. As a result students may feel that their contributions are not valued. This situation is illustrated in the classroom interactions of one of the participants in this study, which is discussed in detail in Chapter 6. *In such classes listening occurs at a trivial level.* It seems that teachers utilising this type of approach may conceive it as a complement to their questioning. Thus, the teacher whose own listening is merely evaluative would strive for unambiguous explanations and well-structured lessons (Davis, 1998). The teacher has a correct answer in mind or a pedagogical question since no one is attending to the answer in a way that will make a difference to the course of subsequent events. In interactions of that form it is possible that teachers who use this type of interaction as the major teaching approach in their classrooms are not picking up potentially powerful learning opportunities.

> *INTERPRETIVE LISTENING*

This category is characterised by a somewhat different manner of listening. More attention is being paid to students' articulations and subjective sense - making are more important. In this case the teacher is listening *to* what the student is saying but he/she is still listening *for* particular responses. The sorts of questions asked by the teacher, although permitting for a greater range of response, they are constrained and they do not foster much divergence. This mode of listening is grounded on awareness that an active interpretation – a sort of reaching out rather than taking in – is involved. Unlike evaluative listening, such an attending mode of listening is deliberate, and the listener is aware of the fallibility of his or her sense making. The enacted conception of mathematics knowledge is still little different from the preceding account of the evaluative listening mode. Mathematics still seems to be about constructing associations between signifiers. As for the authority in the classroom it remains with the teacher. Students' explanations are being modelled on the teacher's explanations. This case has been elucidated Ann's (one of the case study teachers) classroom interactions, which is discussed in detail in Chapter 6. The teacher in this case is not merely trying to assess the knowledge students have acquired, but to access the subjective sense being made.

> *HERMENEUTIC LISTENING*

This mode of teaching seems to be concerned more with delivering a flexible response to ever-changing circumstances than of unyielding progress toward imposed goals. The rigid structure, the preset goals, the formulated explanations, the entrenched roles are being dissolved in some extent as the unanticipated, the surprising, and the intuitive find places for expression. In classrooms following this particular approach, a conflation of roles is occurring. The teacher becomes a participant in the exploration of a shared project. The authority is becoming collective and there is a sense of community-established standards.

Thus *hermeneutic listening* reflects the participatory and negotiated nature of this manner of interaction with learners. Hermeneutic listening requires the willingness to interrogate the taken for granted and the prejudices that frame our perceptions and actions. It is a consequence of this theoretical disposition that in our joint actions we are capable of forming more complex unities (Davies, 1998). What seems to have been abandoned in everyday teaching activities is:

> The belief that teaching is a matter of *causing* learners to acquire, master, or construct particular understandings through some pre-established (and often learner independent) instructional sequence. Learning is a social process, and the teacher's role is one of participating, of interpreting, of transforming, of interrogating-in short, of listening. (Adapted from Davis, 1998, p.371)

Another area of research that is related to this study's last research question: *"Are there inconsistencies between Greek secondary mathematics teachers' beliefs about mathematics, mathematics teaching, mathematics learning, mathematics assessment and their teaching practice?"* explores the inconsistencies between mathematics teachers' espoused beliefs and instructional practice and the reasons for their existence. Raymond (1997) proposed a model (Figure 2.3.3) of relationships between primary teachers' mathematics beliefs and their teaching practice. The researcher proposed a model of relationships between mathematics beliefs and teaching practice, which was used in this study. The model is presented in Figure 2.3.3 and provides a useful starting point and a way of structuring discussion.

The main elements of Raymond's (1997) model are: (a) teachers' mathematics beliefs and (b) mathematics teaching practice. The model suggests complex relationships between mathematics teachers' beliefs and their practice and contributes to a better understanding of some factors that are considered to be important, when teachers' attempted to explain the existence of inconsistencies between them. Raymond (1997) reported that the main causes of inconsistencies were due not so much on teachers' beliefs but on practices other than beliefs. The cumulative effect of these other influences, for example, past school experiences, teacher education program, personality traits of the teacher, social teaching norms and so on, were the main cause of inconsistencies between beliefs and practice. The manifestation of teachers' beliefs in mathematics classrooms would be likely to be influenced by: (a) the teacher's prior experiences of learning mathematics, classroom teaching, peer interactions, awareness of research results in mathematics education, using mathematics in other life experiences, teacher education programs; and (b) by various socio-historical, socio-economic, socio-political and socio-cultural factors.

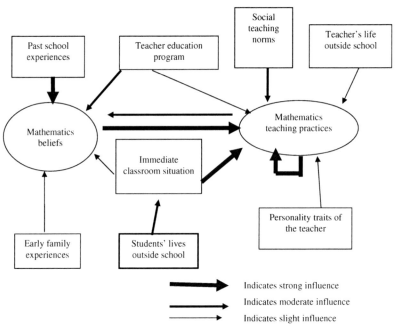

Mathematics beliefs: about the nature of mathematics and mathematics pedagogy
Mathematics teaching practices: Mathematical tasks, discourse, environment, and evaluation
Immediate classroom situation: students' (abilities, attitudes, and behaviour) time constraints, the mathematics topic at hand
Social teaching norms: School philosophy, administrators, standardised tests, curriculum, textbook, other teachers, resources
Teachers' life: Day-to-day- occurrences, other sources of stress

Students' lives: Home environment, parents' beliefs (about children, school, and mathematics)
Teacher education program: Mathematics content courses, field experiences, student teaching
Past school experiences: Successes in mathematics as a student, past teachers
Early family experiences: Parents' view of mathematics, parents' educational background, interaction with parents (particularly regarding mathematics)
Personality traits: confidence, creativity, humour, openness to change

Figure 2.3.3. A model of relationships between mathematics beliefs and practice
(Raymond, 1997)

Mathematics teachers' beliefs about assessment

There has been a growing interest in mathematical assessment during the last two decades and a wealth of research reports has led to the development of authentic assessment strategies and tasks (NCTM, 1989; Webb, 1993; Clarke, 1996; Clarke & Stephens, 1996). Clarke (1996) proposed that assessment should been assigned a proactive role in the process of determining what kind of learning and instruction will be planned. He proposed that assessment should be 'constructive' in the sense that its principal aim is to inform 'a constructive consequent action' (Clarke, 1996, p. 336). A number of assessment strategies could be used to exemplify the new (constructivist) approach: Student portfolios, group work, open-ended tasks, student self-assessment, extended investigations and projects.

Clarke & Stephens (1996) claimed that as far as the Victorian Certificate of Education (VCE) is concerned, 'the Challenging Problem and the Investigative Project components best characterise the shift in curriculum and assessment embodied in the VCE Mathematics'. Nisbet & Warren (2000) have noted that 'there is a paucity of research on what teachers believe about the purpose of assessment and how they use the data they collect during the assessment process'. They also extended the Clarke, Clarke & Lovitt (1990) scheme on the major uses of assessment-which focuses on three areas-teachers, students and parents-with the third area extended to become 'for accountability purposes' (Nisbet & Warren, 2000, p. 37). Accountability constitutes one of the factors resulting from the Factor Analysis (Chapter 5) conducted in the present study.

Nisbet & Warren (2000) noted that despite the fact that much has been written about the purposes of assessment 'there is a paucity of research' (p.36) on how mathematics teachers use assessment information and on what they actually believe about assessment. The same can be said about research efforts regarding the relationship between espoused beliefs about assessment and the actual teaching practice. Assessment approaches may be considered as extensions of mathematics teachers' beliefs about mathematics, and mathematics teaching and learning. Cooney (1999) cited a study by Senk, Beckmann and Thompson (1997), in which they found that:

About 68% of teachers' tests focus on lower level outcomes and that only about 5% of
the items require any depth of thinking. Further, they found that virtually no teachers
used open-ended items on tests. (p. 167)

Both of the case study teachers' tests in the present study, focused on lower
level outcomes too. Cooney (1999) remarked that according to his studies: "teachers
felt uncomfortable in answering and unlikely to use open-ended items with their
students" (p. 167). A similar conclusion has been drawn from the current study, as a
result of one of the case study teachers' interview responses and classroom
observations (Chapter 6).

With regard to the introduction of contemporary assessment practices into
mathematics classrooms, the role of teachers is considered pivotal. Shepard (2000)
noticed that mathematics teachers' prevailing ideas about assessment could be far
from what new trends on assessment aim to tackle. It could be argued that, if
mathematics educators aim to bring about change in outdated assessment practices
in mathematics classrooms, then "teachers' knowledge and beliefs should be a
primary site for research" (Shepard, 2000, p. 71).

2.4   Chapter summary

I have argued that the manifestation of teachers' beliefs in mathematics
classrooms would most likely be influenced by a number of factors, including the
teacher's prior experiences of learning mathematics, classroom teaching, peer
interactions, awareness of research results in mathematics education, using
mathematics in other life experiences, teacher education programs, and various
socio-historical, socio-economic, socio-political and socio-cultural inputs.
Relationships between secondary mathematics teachers' beliefs and their
instructional practice are important to explore because many secondary mathematics
teachers communicate an authoritarian and thereby limited view of mathematics
(Thompson, 1992), which influences their instructional practices, even when they
profess contemporary views about mathematics learning and teaching. Teachers'
instructional practices are influenced by their own schooling experiences long before
they participate in formal mathematics and mathematics education training. Further,
these beliefs "seldom change dramatically without significant intervention"

(Cooney, et al., 1998). Changing secondary mathematics teachers' beliefs is a daunting task that requires carefully planned intervention strategies. It is therefore important to develop a workable theoretical framework of teachers' beliefs, in conjunction with an understanding of how these beliefs are developed and held, and how they influence instructional practice.

The lack of a theoretical framework of mathematical beliefs research has been pointed out by Berger (2000), who proposed a new multi-perspective model of beliefs research as a result of studies in fields of inquiry as diverse as computer science, mathematics and computer culture. According to Berger (2000), his belief system model extends 'the classical psychological perspective by aspects current sociology, ethnography, and cognitive science, especially of neuroscience and cognitive linguistics' (p. 12). The model is based on the conceptualization that teachers' multiple realities may be conceived as socio-cultural frames consisting of 'world views or belief systems' such as the world view of mathematics, the world view of computers, and the world view of didactics. Belief could then be conceived as personal conceptualizations of those multiple realities, which represent possible cognitive representations of frame-specific personal attitudes, implicit theories and knowledge forms. As a result, the individual may produce specific schemes of perception and evaluation. Themes, fields, habits, belief systems/worldview, practice and diction could all be conceived as elements of a specific frame such as the frame of the world of mathematics.

The conclusion reached by Berger (2000) was that belief systems are metaphorically organized and therefore a qualitative methodological framework incorporating a linguistic interview analysis could provide an appropriate vehicle for the investigation of belief systems. In the present study a qualitative methodology framework incorporating a linguistic interview analysis has been used as part of the analysis, aiming to provide an appropriate vehicle for the investigation of belief systems.

This study is significant in providing evidence on the existence of a typology of secondary mathematics teachers' beliefs, and the impact these beliefs have on mathematics instructional environments. It is also significant in examining whether various models of teachers' beliefs postulated by previous studies would be confirmed by inferential statistical methods, in examining the influence particular bio-data exert on these beliefs, and in exploring reasons for the existence of inconsistencies between beliefs and instructional practice.

Teachers' role as facilitators of students' thinking, make their participation in the implementation of instructional reforms instrumental. The implications for teacher preparation and ongoing professional development programs emerge from the recognition that:

> Teachers' beliefs are compatible with the ideas that underlie a professional development program, these beliefs support the change…the change process appears to be cyclical and gradual with both beliefs and classroom experimentation being considered as important components" (Nisbet & Warren (2000, p. 35).

In the next chapter the methodology used in this study will be outlined along with some critical issues regarding the use of quantitative and qualitative methodologies in mathematics education research.

CHAPTER 3
Methodology

3.1   Introduction

This chapter describes the methods used to answer the research questions. Following a discussion of the purpose of the study and a statement of the research questions, the reasons for adopting a combination of quantitative and qualitative research approaches are discussed. The details of the techniques used in the Pilot study (Chapter 4), in the quantitative part of the study (Chapter 5) and in the qualitative part of the study (Chapter 6) are provided along with the information concerning the instruments and the methods of data analysis.

3.2   Purpose of the study and research questions

The central concern of this study was to contribute to an understanding of secondary mathematics teachers' beliefs about mathematics, mathematics teaching, mathematics learning and assessment, and their teaching practice. To explore these complex affective factors, this study was conducted by utilizing both qualitative and quantitative research methods. The research questions are as follows:

(1) What are the beliefs of Greek secondary mathematics teachers with regard to mathematics as a discipline, and learning, teaching and assessing mathematics? Specifically, does there exist a typology of teachers' beliefs that correspond to that postulated in the research literature concerning Western teachers?

(2) In what ways do Greek secondary mathematics teachers' biodata, such as professional development background, postgraduate studies background, years of experience, gender and position held, influence their espoused beliefs? In other words, what differences in beliefs exist across professional development undertaken, years of experience, position held, the range of qualifications, and between female and male teachers?

(3) Are there inconsistencies between Greek secondary mathematics teachers'
beliefs about mathematics, mathematics teaching, mathematics learning,
mathematics assessment and their teaching practice?

3.3   Qualitative and/or quantitative: Deciding on an appropriate research methodology

The issue of what constitutes an acceptable approach for the research process
will be addressed in this section. According to Shulman (1988) 'when we speak of
research we speak of a family of methods which share the characteristics of
disciplined inquiry'. Cronbach and Suppes (1969) attempted to define disciplined
inquiry, in the following way:

> The disciplined inquiry is conducted and reported in such a way that the argument can
> be painstakingly examined. The report does not depend for its appeal on the eloquence
> of the writer or on any surface plausibility. (p.15)

The researchers also suggested that the report of a disciplined inquiry should
have a texture that:

> Displays the raw materials entering the argument and the logical processes by which
> they were compressed and rearranged to make the conclusion credible. (pp. 15-16)

The report of a disciplined inquiry must conform to the following
requirements: (a) it should provide sufficient information on the nature of the raw
materials and the context or contexts in which they were collected, (b) the processes
of manipulating, analysing and synthesizing the data via statistical or other methods
of extrapolating, the interpretations, conclusions and recommendations, should all be
readily available and make sense to the informed reader, and (c) the logic, reliability
and validity used to arrive at a credible result can be easily tested by the informed
reader.

Lincoln and Guba (1985) proposed a definition of research that conforms to
these three requirements. Their contention was that their definition circumvented the
basic/applied research dilemma, and that it was congenial to those with a naturalistic
orientation to research, while not abandoning the rationalistic position:

> Research is a type of disciplined inquiry undertaken to resolve some problem in order to
> achieve understanding or to facilitate action. (p.6)

The researcher alone determines the adoption of a particular research methodology and the associated research methods and techniques. The methodology is the system that guides the researcher's investigation. It could be conceived as a representation of the researcher's 'world view'.

The word *methodology* is a synthesis of *the* Greek words *μετά-meta* (after, with), *οδός-odos* (path, trail, the way) and *λόγος-logos* (discourse, reason, cause). The first two parts make up the word *method (meta+odos)*. Methodology can therefore be conceived as the ideological *(ιδέα-idea+λόγος-reason)* and/or philosophical stance underlying the reasoning that informs particular discourses or methods of doing research. Before elaborating on the issue of methodological categories, research methods will be discussed. Research methods are ways of conducting a research inquiry, informed by particular methodologies. The terms methodology and method are sometimes used interchangeably in research studies, causing confusion.

3.4   *Categorising methodologies*

Ways of categorizing methodologies can be made by reference to the purposes of the research being undertaken. Research in mathematics education has, according to Schoenfeld (2000) two main purposes. Pure research aims to understand the nature of mathematical thinking, teaching and learning, and applied research aims to use such understandings to improve mathematics instruction. Schoenfeld claimed that these two purposes are deeply intertwined, both sharing equal importance. The reason for this is that there is no way that progress can be made on the applied front without having acquired a deep understanding of the interconnections of learning, teaching and thinking. Over the last twenty years there has been a continuing and heated debate on the merits of qualitative and quantitative research methods (Miles & Huberman, 1994; Kvale, 1996). Various researchers have also examined the question of combining the two methodological approaches (Miles & Huberman, 1994).

Two opposing paradigms have emerged: (a) The positivist or quantitative paradigm (random sampling, statistical significance testing, empirical methods, scientific methods), and (b) the post-positivist, interpretive, naturalistic or qualitative paradigm (non-random sampling, non-empirical methods, ethnographic interviews, participant observation).

The debate over qualitative versus quantitative methods has resulted in researchers considering the two methodologies not as mutually exclusive, but rather as complementing each other. Evidence of the recognition of the complementarity of the two dominant paradigms in mathematics education research in the past twenty years is manifest in the numerous studies that have been conducted in mathematics education employing a combination of qualitative and quantitative research methods (Van Zoest, et al., 1994; Schoenfeld, 1985, 1989, 2000; Forgasz, 1995; Leder, 1992; Thompson, 1992; McLeod, 1992). McLeod (1992), argued that:

> The debate over qualitative versus quantitative appears to be almost over, and the time for intelligence use of multiple research methods that fit the research problems is here. The use of clinical interviews and detailed observations should provide the field with a deeper understanding of the role of affective issues in mathematics learning and teaching. (p. 591)

It is interesting to note that, though the multi-method approach to research is now generally encouraged, Kilpatrick (2000) expressed the view that mathematics education researchers of the future will return to a scientific view of mathematics education, in their search for reliable methods. In his words:

> I think there is good reason to expect that over the next decade or so researchers in mathematics education will begin to rethink their research approaches. They will recognize the value of developing a conception of research in which reliable evidence is gathered, justifications are offered, knowledge claims are tested, and the resulting knowledge is made public and can be independently verified. In other words, I foresee a return to the view that research in mathematics education ought to be scientific-not in the narrow sense of the physical sciences but in the sense of an interpretive science of human thought and behavior. (Kilpatrick, 2000, p.90)

In the field of mathematics teachers' beliefs and conceptions too, most contemporary research has been conducted, according to Thompson (1992), by employing a combination of qualitative and qualitative research methods and research designs, depending on the purpose of the study. Thompson (1992) concluded that:

The diversity of purposes, methods, designs, and analytical frameworks used by researchers has led to great variability in how teachers' conceptions have been described. (p.131)

Classroom research is about meaning and its construction. Researchers, teachers and students alike construct meaning during classroom interactions. To account for classroom human interactions and teachers' beliefs, the researcher has to balance the strengths and weaknesses of the qualitative and quantitative approaches with the sole purpose of presenting a report of an investigation that at the same time reflects the complexity of teachers' beliefs, and is also generalisable, credible, reliable and valid. For this reason a multiple perspectives methodology has been adopted for this investigation.

The issue of compatibility of combining quantitative and qualitative research methods is the basis of another heated debate in education research. Forgasz (1995) referred to a number of researchers (Firestone, 1987; Linn, 1992; Wiersma, 1986) who argued that the two method types are incompatible because they are grounded on paradigms that make different ontological, epistemological and methodological assumptions. Other researchers have acknowledged a blurring of the boundaries, and yet others propounded the view that mutual acceptance of complementary paradigms has been recognized at the practical level by researchers. Generally, researchers agree that validity and reliability should be always considered and the methods adopted should follow high standards. Schoenfeld (2000) proposed a set of criteria for judging theories, models and results in mathematics education:

- *Descriptive power*, which means the capacity to capture "what counts" in ways that seem faithful to the phenomenon being described
- *Explanatory power*, which means the provision of explanations of how and why things work
- *Scope* i.e. the of phenomena "covered" by the theory
- *Predictive power* of a theory means the degree by which some results may be predicted in advance of their taking place
- *Rigor and specificity*, which means the specification of certain objects and the relationships among them
- *Falsifiability* meaning making non-tautological claims or predictions whose accuracy can be tested empirically
- *Replicability* means that any research program should have well defined procedures and constructs and relates to the following two sets of issues: (i)

will the same thing happen if the test is repeated under identical circumstances? (ii) will other researchers "see" the same things in the data?

- *Multiple sources of evidence (triangulation)* i.e. to seek as many sources of information as possible and to provide compelling evidence about the phenomena being investigated, and to make sure that they portray a consistent "message" to the reader of the research report.

Strenuous efforts to conform to these criteria were made in the present study.

The issues of generalisability, reliability and validity in quantitative and qualitative methods

In quantitative research in the social sciences the Hawthorn effect looms large. Positivist researchers make every effort to avoid influencing the behaviour of their subjects through their physical presence. In searching for a state of affairs that is not affected by their presence, they attempt to create a barrier between themselves and the human phenomenon they are investigating, perhaps through the use of paper and pencil instruments and non-participant observation. In qualitative research the researcher and the subject are engaged and virtually bound together. The qualitative researcher is likely to use interviews and participant observations, and in this regard, there are a number of issues which concern the data collection methods, the possibility of researcher bias, data coding and processing, the adequacy of sampling in qualitative research, the generalisability of the findings and the credibility and quality of conclusions drawn.

The concepts of generalisability and the reliability and validity of research findings are important to the scientific community. According to Kvale (1996) three forms of generalisability can be attributed to Stake's (1994) analysis – statistical, analytic and naturalistic. Kvale (1996, p. 234) added a fourth: that of researcher and reader generalisation. His analysis, however, focused on the practical issue of targets of generalisation (Schofield, 1990; cited in Kvale, 1996). According to Schofield there are three targets of generalisation:

- *What is,* that is attempting to establish the typical, the common and the ordinary

- *What may be,* that is attempting to predict future trends for a particular situation, by generalising from the findings
- *What could be,* rather than mapping what is, or predicting future trends, research may attempt to be transformative in nature by identifying exemplary situations

The findings of qualitative research, examined by traditional methods, could create serious doubt, according to Miles and Huberman (1994). They argued that:

> Increasingly we see "multisite, mutlimethod" studies that may combine qualitative and quantitative inquiry, carried out by a research team working with comparable data collection and analysis methods. (p.2)

This sentiment echoes Clarke's (2001) complementary accounts methodology, the characteristics of which are reportedly different from other approaches to classroom research in terms of:

> ➢ The nature of the data collection procedures, leading to the construction of "integrated data sets" combining videotape and interview data,
>
> ➢ The inclusion of the reflective voice of participant students and teachers in the data set,
>
> ➢ An analytical approach that utilises a research team with complementary but diverse areas of expertise to carry out a multi-faceted analysis of a common body of classroom data. (p.14)

Clarke (2001) argued that multiple analyses of qualitative or quantitative data should serve the purpose of achieving a synthesis of the findings. He went on to state that:

> The value of triangulation in such [mathematics education] research is employed because of the intrinsic value of multiple perspectives and not with the aim of determining 'what really happened'. (p. 14)

Explication of the procedures of qualitative analysis, the use of multiple perspectives and verifying the sturdiness of the conclusions drawn, can provide more confidence in the findings of qualitative research.

Qualitative researchers have developed *criteria* to parallel the quantitative research criteria of:

- *Internal validity*: how can the researcher establish confidence in the truth of the findings of the research, for both the respondents and the context of the research process?),

- *External validity:* how can the researcher determine the degree to which the findings of the research have applicability in other contexts or with other respondents?),

- *Reliability:* the level of internal consistency or stability of the measuring device over time, and

- *Objectivity*: how can the researcher establish the degree to which the findings of an inquiry stem from the characteristics of the respondents and the context, and not from the motivations, biases and perspectives of the researcher? These parallel qualitative research criteria are termed:

  - ➢ *Credibility* (the counterpart of internal validity),
  - ➢ *Transferability* (the counterpart of external validity),
  - ➢ *Dependability* (the counterpart of reliability), and
  - ➢ *Confirmability* (the counterpart of objectivity).

In order to establish that the qualitative criteria are met, the qualitative researcher can utilise the following techniques respectively:

- For *credibility*: prolonged engagement, persistent observation, peer debriefing, negative case analysis, progressive subjectivity, and member checks (Lincoln and Guba, 1985; Schaller and Tobin, 1998), and triangulation (cross-checking) of data,

- For *dependability and confirmability*: an external audit in two parts; one that examines the process results in a dependability judgement and another that is concerned with the product results in a confirmability judgement (Lincoln and Guba 1985, 1986),

- For *transferability*: thick descriptive data developed on the notion of a narrative about the context to allow for the degree of fit to be made by other investigators.

These techniques have been utilised in this study in order to establish the validity, reliability, objectivity and the credibility of the research.

In an attempt to substantiate the findings of qualitative research, Lincoln and Guba (1986) devised five criteria to parallel quantitative research criteria. The criteria refer to the *authenticity* of qualitative research. They include

- *Fairness*: the inquirer aims to present a balanced view that encompasses all constructions and the values that undergird them,

- *Ontological authenticity*: the aim of qualitative research ought to be to raise consciousness so that each person in the situation studied can achieve a more sophisticated construction of what is being studied,

- *Educative authenticity*: each person in the situation studied should have the opportunity to enrich its educational background about others of different persuasions, values and constructions and hence to appreciate how diversified opinions, judgements and actions are evoked,

- *Catalytic authenticity*: qualitative inquiry must facilitate and stimulate action, and

- *Tactical authenticity*: the question about whether the evaluation is empowering or impoverishing, and to whom, may be answered by this criterion. A positive step toward empowerment can be taken by providing all persons with something at stake in the inquiry, with the opportunity to control it as well.

The abovementioned authenticity criteria have been closely adhered to in the qualitative part of this study.

Linking qualitative and qualitative data

Linking qualitative and quantitative data in educational research and its subset mathematics education research is not the issue, according to Salomon (1991, cited in Miles & Huberman, 1994), but rather whether "we are taking an 'analytic' stance to understanding few controlled variables or a systemic approach to understanding the interaction of variables in complex environments" (p.41). Miles & Huberman (1994) have suggested that qualitative and quantitative data should be linked in educational research for the following reasons:

- To enable confirmation or corroboration of each other via triangulation

- To elaborate or develop analysis, providing richer detail

- To initiate new lines of thinking through attention to surprise or paradoxes, 'turning ideas around,' providing fresh insight
- To help sequentially (results of the first method inform the second's sampling, instrumentation, etc.)
- To expand the scope and breadth of a study by using different methods in different components
- Quantitative studies "persuade" the reader through de-emphasising individual judgement and stressing the use of established techniques, leading to a more precise and generalisable results, while qualitative research persuades through rich depiction and strategic comparison across cases, thereby overcoming the 'abstraction inherent in quantitative studies

Combining properly conducted qualitative and quantitative studies provides a powerful mix, where the qualitative methods can provide the "glue that cements the interpretation of multi-method results" (Jick, 1979; cited in Miles and Huberman, 1994, p. 42).

Since one of the aims of this study was to explore possible inconsistencies between secondary mathematics teachers' espoused beliefs about mathematics, mathematics teaching, mathematics learning and mathematics assessment along with their teaching practice, research methods which would provide a powerful mix of the best available data analysis methods were sought and as a result, a combination of qualitative and quantitative methods were employed in this study.

3.5 Procedure for the present study

The study was conducted in three parts:

- ➢ A pilot study was carried out to examine the feasibility of the proposed method of data collection. It involved the development and statistical analysis of the questionnaire survey.
- ➢ A survey was administered to explore the areas of interest and to produce data to examine the research questions statistically. The survey was sent to to a random selection of six hundred grade 7-12 mathematics teachers. The return rate was 78%, (n=465) and the resulting sample comprised 465 (276

males, 145 females, 44 no gender specified) participants, which included 431 secondary mathematics teachers (244 males, 143 females), 24 secondary mathematics teachers holding a principal's position (22 male, 2 female), and 10 regional mathematics consultants (10 males), in 45 State High Schools throughout Greece. The returned surveys reflected a reasonably well-balanced distribution of grade level experience (Chapter 5, Section 5.2, Table 5.2.1).

➢ The survey was followed by a study focusing on two in-depth case studies (1M, 1F), following strict directives pertaining to classroom access set by the Ministry of Education of Greece. The Ministerial directives required the consent of both the principal and the mathematics teacher. Through extensive interviews, observation and video taping of mathematics lessons of the two case study participants, a detailed picture of the complex relationships between enacted beliefs and teaching practice has emerged. Close examination of some of their lessons, using detailed analytical criteria developed by me, allowed insight into the vast terrain of everyday teaching practice, and displayed the complexity and the pervasive nature of emotions, values and beliefs, and everyday practice. It also showed that certain beliefs and values are intertwined in the work of veteran (20+ years of experience) secondary mathematics teachers.

Overview

This section is divided into three parts:

(i)   **Pilot study**

(ii)   **Main study part 1: Questionnaire survey**

(iii)   **Main study part 2: Case studies**

Pilot study

The pilot study focused on the development and administration of the questionnaire and on the statistical analysis of the questionnaire survey data. Its aim was to gather material to assist in the development of the questionnaire survey and to trial its factorability. The results of the pilot study are presented in Chapter 4. Its procedures are reported in the following sections.

Questionnaire survey

A questionnaire was sent to to six hundred grade 7-12 mathematics teachers, their principals (only if they were mathematics teachers), and their regional mathematics consultants. The resulting sample comprised 465 (276 males, 145 females, 44 no gender specified), in Greek schools (Appendix C1). Questions explored teachers' conceptions regarding the nature of mathematics, mathematics teaching, learning and assessment. Data from these responses were analysed using SPSS$_{win}$ and Excel. The results are examined in Chapter 5 and provide a summary of reported orientations that are characteristic of secondary mathematics teachers' espoused beliefs, along with the details of the background against which to present the detailed analysis of case study teachers that appear in Chapter 6.

Case studies

The quantitative study was followed by a qualitative study in an attempt to identify differences between teachers' espoused beliefs and beliefs in practice. Close examination of the work of two teachers of Years 10-12 (Senior High school) makes up this component of the study. This section illustrates the complexity of teachers' everyday cognitions and their enacted beliefs. Detailed criteria were developed for both the interview and the classroom observation components of this section of the study. Transcripts of audiotapes and videotapes were used to ensure that the analysis was based as closely as possible on the reality of the classrooms observed.

(i)   Pilot study

The aim of the pilot study was to trial the 80-item questionnaire (Appendix C1) on secondary mathematics teachers working during 1999-2000 in State High schools in Greece in order to establish a typology of their espoused beliefs.

Psychometrically "poor" items (that is, variables loading on more than one factor) were eliminated and the *resulting questionnaire for the main study consisted of a total of 53 items* (Appendix C2)

Development of the pilot study questionnaire

In developing the questionnaire items, I drew on previous research findings about teacher beliefs issues in mathematics education (Ernest, 1989; Van Zoest, et al., 1994; Howard, Perry & Lindsay, 1997; Clark & Stephens, 1996), obtained feedback from 5 volunteer mathematics educators (ME), 3 mathematics consultants (MC), 10 mathematics curriculum developers (MCD) and 10 secondary mathematics teachers (SMT). Various items were omitted or further modified on the basis of reactions obtained from these groups. An 80-item researcher designed questionnaire was the instrument for this investigation. The validity and reliability of the questionnaire items were examined by statistical analyses (Chapter 4, sections 4.2 and 4.3).

The questionnaire was divided into four sections. Sections I, II and III (56 items – beliefs about mathematics, beliefs about mathematics teaching and beliefs about mathematics learning – Appendix C1) and section IV (24 items – beliefs about mathematics assessment – Appendix C1).

The pilot study questionnaire drew on previously validated research questionnaires and the following items were directly taken from the following questionnaires:

- Items 1, 2, 4, 12, 24 (Van Zoest, et al, 1994)
- Items 5, 6, 7, 8, 9, 10, 15, 16, 17, 18, 19, 21, 22, 47, 48, 49, 50 (Howard, Perry & Lindsay, 1997)
- Items 57-71 (Clark & Stephens, 1996)

The analysis of the questionnaire was carried out in two parts:

➤ A Likert-type scoring format was used for Sections I, II and III

➤ In Section IV, teachers were asked to indicate the degree of importance they attached to each of the aspects described on each item.

A more detailed analysis of Sections I, II, III and IV of the pilot study questionnaire is presented in what follows:

Sections I, II, and III: Beliefs about mathematics, mathematics teaching and mathematics learning

This investigation of the espoused beliefs of secondary mathematics teachers, working during 1999-2000 in State High schools in Greece, included the collection of information on the following subject demographics: gender, age, and professional development background, length of teaching experience, position held, postgraduate studies background, and beliefs about mathematics, mathematics learning and mathematics teaching.

In Sections I, II and III of the questionnaire (Appendix C1), a Likert-type scoring format was used – teachers were asked to indicate the extent to which they agreed (or disagreed) with each statement presented. A five-point scoring system was used – strongly disagree (SD) to strongly agree (SA). A score of 1 was assigned to the SA response and a score of 5 to SD. The survey contained three subsets of items: Beliefs about Mathematics (BM: 10 items), Beliefs about Mathematics Learning (BML: 12 items) and Beliefs about Mathematics Teaching (BMT: 34 items). A space was also provided for teachers to add comments on any aspect (of each part) of the instrument and its items.

Section IV: Beliefs about mathematics assessment

In Section IV of the questionnaire (Appendix C1), teachers were asked to indicate the degree of importance they attached to each of the aspects described on each item of the questionnaire. A four-point scale was used [highly important (HI), of some importance (SI), beneficial but not essential (BNE), of little importance (LI)]. A score of 1 was assigned to the HI response and a score of 4 to LI. A space was also provided for teachers to comment on any aspect of the instrument and its items.

Clarke and Stephens (1996) used 15 items in the questionnaire part of their study and the participants were asked to indicate the degree of importance they attached to the aspect described by each item. The 15 items were designed to reflect different ways in which problem solving and investigations could be valued and used by teachers. One of the aims of the study was to compare the assessment views of teachers teaching VCE mathematics at the time, with those of teachers from Greece with no VCE (or equivalent) mathematics teaching experience.

In the present study, the 15 items used by Clarke and Stephens (1996) formed part of a larger questionnaire on secondary teachers' beliefs about assessment. Two of the items used by Clarke and Stephens have been slightly reworded for the purposes of this study.

Administration of pilot study questionnaire

The questionnaire survey was conducted in October 1999. An 80-item researcher designed questionnaire was the instruments for this investigation. Six hundred survey forms were sent to a random selection of grade 7-12 mathematics teachers. Twenty questionnaires were sent out to each selected school with the request to reproduce the questionnaire if it was necessary. The questionnaire was also sent out to the relevant regional mathematics consultant. A stamped, addressed envelope was attached to each questionnaire to facilitate return, and a 'return by' date was provided. The resulting sample comprised 345 (207 males, 92 females, 46 gender not specified) mathematics teachers from 37 Greek State High Schools.

Analysis of pilot study questionnaire

Descriptive statistics (tests of normality, frequencies) as well Chi-squared tests, t-tests, ANOVA, MANCOVA, PCA and Factor Analyses were used to analyse the data.

(ii)   Main study part 1: Questionnaire survey

Development of questionnaire

The development of the questionnaire was carried out in four parts (Appendix C2), following the procedure used in the pilot study. A Likert-type scoring format was used for the items making up Sections I, II and III *(Beliefs about mathematics, mathematics teaching and mathematics learning)* of the questionnaire whereas in Section IV (**Beliefs about mathematics** *assessment*) of the questionnaire, teachers were asked to indicate the degree of importance they attached to each of the aspects described on each item. The items in each part of the questionnaire are presented below:

Sections I, II and III: Beliefs about mathematics, mathematics teaching and mathematics learning

A 34-item researcher designed questionnaire (Sections I, II and III, Appendix C2) was the instrument for this investigation. This investigation took place during 1999-2000 in State High schools in Greece, and covered the following subject demographics: gender, age, professional development background, length of teaching experience, position held, postgraduate studies background, and beliefs about mathematics, mathematics learning and mathematics teaching.

A Likert-type scoring format, identical to the pilot study's questionnaire was used, and teachers were asked to indicate the extent to which they agreed (or disagreed) with each statement presented. A five point scoring system was used – strongly disagree (SD) to strongly agree (SA). A score of 1 was assigned to the SA response and a score of 5 to SD. The survey contained three subsets of items: Beliefs about Mathematics (BM: 6 items), Beliefs about Mathematics Learning (BML: 7 items) and Beliefs about Mathematics Teaching (BMT: 21 items). A space was also provided for teachers to comment on any aspect (of each part) of the instrument and its items.

Section IV: Beliefs about mathematics assessment

The data for this investigation were collected using a 19-item researcher designed questionnaire (Appendix C2, Section IV). The investigation was carried out during 1999-2000 in State High schools in Greece, and collected exactly the same information about subject demographics and used exactly the same methods as those used in the pilot the following subject demographics: gender, age, professional development background, length of teaching experience, position held, postgraduate studies background, and beliefs about mathematics, mathematics learning and mathematics teaching. The format used was identical to the pilot study's questionnaire, and teachers were asked to indicate the degree of importance they attached to each of the aspects described on each item of the questionnaire. A four-point scale was used [highly important (HI), of some importance (SI), beneficial but not essential (BNE), of little importance (LI)]. A score of 1 was assigned to the (HI) response and a score of 4 to (LI). A space was also provided for teachers to comment on any aspect of the instrument and its items. Both parts of the main study questionnaire are contained in Appendix C2.

Administration of the main study questionnaire

The questionnaire survey was conducted in the period between December 1999 and March 2000. As mentioned earlier, a 53-item researcher designed questionnaire was the instruments for this investigation. Six hundred survey forms were mailed to a random selection of grade 7-12 mathematics teachers. A stamped, addressed envelope was attached to each questionnaire to facilitate return, and a 'return by' date was provided. The resulting sample comprised 465 (276 males, 145 females, 44 gender not specified) mathematics teachers from 39 Greek State High Schools.

Analysis of the main study questionnaire

Descriptive statistics (tests of normality, frequencies), t-tests, PCA and Factor Analyses were conducted along with ANOVA, Trend Analysis with Scheffe pair-wise comparisons, Cluster Analysis and Multiple Discriminant Analysis. The statistical techniques used, including the reasons/criteria for the choice of the most appropriate techniques for this study, are discussed in Chapter 5.

(iii)   Main study part 2: Case studies

The case studies focused on the work of two veteran secondary mathematics teachers in Greece named Ann and Tom. The analyses drew on their own words as well as on detailed analyses of their lessons, stimulated video recall, my field notes, and pre- and post-instructional interviews with the teachers. The case studies serve the purpose of illuminating the findings from the quantitative data and hence their selection is embedded in the scales delineated in the statistical data.

Selection of teachers

The principals of 10 schools in the Metropolitan area of the Greek capital Athens were contacted and requested to participate in the project. During meetings with the principals, I provided an outline of the study and the principals were invited to nominate a staff member for participation in this study. Strict directives pertaining to classroom access set by the Ministry of Education required the consent of the nominated teacher.

At the culmination of the process four (2M, 2F) of the six (3M, 3F) nominated teachers agreed to participate in the qualitative component of the study. One of the female participants decided to withdraw from the study soon after the first videotaped session, and one of the male participants did not wish to participate in the post-instructional interview, rendering that case study incomplete. Credit should be given to the principals and the individual teachers who were prepared to participate in a project that may have been seen by many as an intrusion or disturbance, within their classrooms.

Time frame

A pre-instructional interview took place before classroom observations. Two weeks of taping were spent with each teacher, with a gap of two weeks between each taping. During this period, the teachers watched videotapes of their lessons and post-instructional interviews took place. One further weekly gap took place between my first visit and the video taping to facilitate students' familiarization with the presence of the equipment and of my presence in their classrooms.

Data collection

The data collected consisted of:

(I)   Structured interviews recorded on audiotape (Appendix C5)

- Before classroom video taping
- After the completion of classroom observations

 (II)   Lesson observations

An interview and a video analysis scale (Appendices C3 and C4) was designed to assess the extent to which secondary mathematics teachers adopted one of the following five orientations to instruction, which represent a slightly varied form of those used by Raymond (1997): *Traditional, Primarily Traditional, Even mix of Traditional and Alternative, Primarily Contemporary, Contemporary.* An attempt was also made to tap the task specific strategies used by the teachers via a researcher-designed checklist (Appendix C6).

Presentation and selection of data

An attempt was made to capture the multitude of mathematics classroom microcosms, by approaching the very essence of classroom life in diverse ways. The format of presentation was decided to be in two columns. The text of the lesson is in the left hand column, and the analysis, drawing on my criteria (indicated by symbols in brackets) for teaching practice to describe the teacher's beliefs and associated behaviours, is given on the right hand column. The text is broken at various points to allow the case study teacher's voice to be heard, as he/she made comments while watching the taped lessons a week after his/her lessons were videotaped.

Although many classes of each teacher were observed and video taped, I decided that only a single lesson of mathematics would be used as the focus for full analysis and interpretation. I could have chosen to discuss more briefly a greater number of lessons taught by Ann and Tom, but to do so it would have necessitated the fragmentation of the process of teaching and it would not have allowed me to focus on an exploration of the many aspects of classroom life. It could also have led me to forego my intention to acknowledge the complexity of mathematics teachers' work. The lessons took place after a week spent observing and appearing to record information in order to accustom students to the equipment. When the actual taping took place, students appeared to take no notice of me or of the equipment. Professionals transcribed the dialogue as completely and accurately as the equipment would permit, and the final transcript was double-checked by me. The transcription process was completed when a professional translator, an Englishman who has lived and worked in Athens as a translator for thirty years, translated all Greek transcripts to English. These were in turn double-checked by me using the back-translation technique and by paying special attention to the accuracy of mathematical nomenclature.

Verification procedures

When the analysis of the videotaped sessions (using the criteria categories) was completed, each teacher was given a copy and was asked to comment. None of the case studies teachers expressed any disagreement or concern. Two further checks of the transcripts of the videotaped sessions were administered. Randomly selected sections were analysed by another experienced coder (a mathematics education university lecturer) for inter-coder reliability and I then re-examined the whole analysis "blind" to ensure an intra-coder reliability check.

3.6 Summary and concluding comments

The task of this chapter was to describe the research methodology on which this study was grounded, and the research methods by which it was carried out. The three research questions which emerged from the literature review surveyed in Chapter 2, were presented in section 3.2.

It was decided to adopt Raymond's (1997) model of relationships between mathematics beliefs and teaching practice (Figure 2.3.3, Chapter 2) as the framework for the discussion on inconsistencies. The models proposed by Ernest (1989a, 1989b), Fennema, et al. (1996), and Cooney (1999) were adopted as the framework for the discussion on teachers' beliefs about mathematics and mathematics teaching and learning.

The questionnaire survey (Appendix C2) results are analysed in Chapter 5 and provide a summary of reported orientations that are characteristic of Greek secondary mathematics teachers' espoused beliefs. At the same they set the background against which to detail the analysis of individual mathematics teachers' espoused beliefs and instructional practices which are described in Chapter 6.

The final conclusions drawn from the study are presented in Chapter 7.

In the following chapter the findings of the pilot study are presented. The aim of the pilot study was to gather material to assist in the development of the questionnaire survey and to trial its factorability.

CHAPTER 4
Results of the Pilot study

4.1 Introduction

This study represents an exploration of secondary mathematics teachers' beliefs regarding mathematics, mathematics teaching, learning and assessment. Pajares (1992) argued that knowledge and beliefs are inextricably intertwined and that individuals' beliefs strongly affect their behaviour, while Hollingworth (1989) reported that the way teachers implement new methods or programs in their classrooms relates to whether their beliefs are congruent with the proposed new methods or programs. As noted in Chapter 2, teachers' beliefs influence their classroom practices. The beliefs are formed early, and beliefs about teaching are well established by the time a prospective teacher starts attending University classes. It is therefore instrumental to understand the impact teachers' beliefs have on their everyday cognitions and classroom practices.

The aim of the pilot study was to gather material to assist in the development of the questionnaire survey and to trial its factorability. The procedures of the pilot study were presented in section 3.5.2.

4.2 Beliefs about mathematics, mathematics teaching and mathematics learning

The instrument

A 56-item researcher designed questionnaire (Sections I, II and III, Appendix C1), interview protocol and video analysis teacher action criteria (Appendices C3 and C4), were the instruments for this investigation.

In the questionnaire, a Likert-type scoring format was used - teachers were asked to indicate the extent to which they agreed (or disagreed) with each statement presented. A five point scoring system was used – strongly disagree (SD) to strongly agree (SA). A score of 1 was assigned to the SA response and a score of 5 to SD. The survey contained three subsets of items: *Beliefs about Mathematics (BM: 10 items), Beliefs about Mathematics Learning (BML: 12 items) and Beliefs about Mathematics Teaching (BMT: 34 items). A space was also provided for teachers to comment on any aspect (of each part) of the instrument and its items.*

Examples of the questions that participants had to answer during the interviews included the following: Can you describe the learning environment in your class? Which factors do you consider to have a significant influence on your beliefs about mathematics teaching and learning? Which factors may explain the existence of inconsistencies between espoused beliefs and beliefs in practice?

The sample

The sample comprised 345 (207 males, 92 females, 46 no gender specified) mathematics teachers in 37 Greek State High Schools. Data from these responses were analysed using SPSS$_{win}$ (ver. 8.0).

Data analysis

It could reasonably be expected that teachers' beliefs about mathematics, mathematics learning and mathematics teaching would be linked in various ways. Inferential statistical techniques (Multiple Analysis of Covariance – MANCOVA and t-tests) as well as Principal Component Analysis (PCA) was used in order to analyse the 56 questionnaire items for a typology of teachers' espoused beliefs, using an Analysis of Variance (ANOVA) and the scree plot technique. The significance level was set at 0.05.

Results and discussion

Principal Component Analysis

A Principal Component Analysis (PCA) was used in order to interrogate the 56 questionnaire items for a typology of teachers' espoused beliefs. The scree plot (Figure 4.2.1) graphically displays the eigenvalues (eigenvalues represent variance – a component with an eigenvalue less than 1 is not deemed as important, from a variance perspective, as an observed variable). for each factor and would suggest that there are three predominant factors, accounting for 20% of the variance.

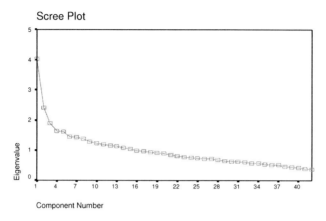

Figure 4.2.1. Scree plot (Beliefs about mathematics, and mathematics teaching and learning)

According to Coakes & Steed (1999) if the Kaiser-Meyer-Olkin Measure of Sampling Adequacy is greater than 0.6 and the Bartlett's Test of Sphericity is significant – both verified in Table 4.2.1 – then factorability of the correlation matrix is assumed.

Table 4.2.1

KMO Measure of Sampling Adequacy and Bartlett's Test of Sphericity (Beliefs about mathematics, and mathematics teaching and learning)

Kaiser-Meyer-Olkin Measure of Sampling Adequacy.		.685
Bartlett's Test of Sphericity	Approx. Chi-Square	978.177
	df	861
	Sig.	.003

A final confirmatory factor analysis (Table 4.2.2) was run following the elimination of psychometrically "poor" items (double loadings, negative loadings and reliability and normality tests.

Table 4.2.2

Factors related to views regarding mathematics, mathematics teaching and

mathematics learning

ITEM NUMBER AND ITEM DESCRIPTION	Factor loadings		
Component 1			
(S53) Students should be given the opportunity to feel confident and to attempt to maximise their potential in mathematics	.673		
(S54) The education system should be preparing critically thinking citizens who are able to utilise their mathematical skills	.614		
(S42) It is important for students to be provided with opportunities to reflect on and evaluate their own mathematical understanding	.592		
(S22) Mathematics learning is enhanced by challenging activities within a supportive environment	.559		
(S46) It is important that mathematics content be presented to students in the correct logical sequence	.556		
(S26) A vital task for the teacher is motivating students to resolve their own mathematical problems	.523		
(S24) Ignoring the mathematical ideas generated by the students can seriously limit their learning	.506		
(S32) Teachers should be able to present mathematical ideas in a variety of ways	.504		
(S56) Teachers should respect the mathematical knowledge of their students which is consisting of a nexus of experiences, beliefs, attitudes, representations, concepts, strategies, connections, values, judgments and emotions	.432		
(S51) The comprehension of mathematical concepts by students should correspond to their cognitive development and it should be a decisive factor in the content sequence to be taught	.422		
(S9) Mathematics is a beautiful, creative and useful human endeavour that is both a way of knowing and a way of thinking	.377		
(S34) Teachers always need to hear students' mathematical explanations before correcting their errors	.346		
(S19) Students are capable of much higher levels of mathematical thought than has been suggested traditionally	.316		
(S49) Teachers should negotiate social norms with the students in order to develop a cooperative learning environment in which students can construct their knowledge	.313		
Component 2			
(S4) Mathematics is a static and immutable knowledge with objective truth		.620	
(S48) The role of the mathematics teacher is to transmit mathematical knowledge and to verify that learners have		.586	

received that knowledge		
(S41) It is the teacher' responsibility to provide students with clear and concise solution methods for mathematical problems	.474	
(S11) The most effective way to learn mathematics is by listening carefully to the teacher explaining a mathematics lesson	.471	
(S47) Teachers or the textbook-not the student-are the authorities for what is right or wrong	.448	
(S43) It is important that mathematics content be presented to students in the correct sequence	.431	
(S20) The memorisation of mathematical facts is important in mathematics learning	.350	
(S40) Telling students the answer is an efficient way of facilitating their mathematics learning	.316	
(S8) Mathematics is no more sequential than any other subject	.306	
Component 3		
(S13) Students can learn more mathematics together than by themselves		.546
(S16) Students are rational decision makers capable of determining for themselves what is right and what is wrong		.522
(S15) Mathematics knowledge is the result of the learner interpreting and organising the information gained from experiences		.504
(S14) Students always benefit by discussing their solutions to mathematical problems with each other		.446
(S3) Justifying the mathematical statements that a person makes is an extremely important part of mathematics		.372
(S38) An effective way to teach mathematics is to provide students with interesting problems to investigate in small groups		.369
(S55) All students are able to be creative and do original work in mathematics		.358

The three factors represent three apparently differing beliefs about mathematics, mathematics teaching and mathematics learning. The three factors loaded on each of the following items respectively:

- *Item 53:* Students should be given the opportunity to feel confident and to attempt to maximise their potential in mathematics
- *Item 4:* Mathematics is a static and immutable knowledge with objective truth
- *Item 13:* Students can learn more mathematics together than by themselves

Fourteen items loaded on Factor 1, 9 items loaded on Factor 2 and 7 items loaded on Factor 3 (Table 4.2.2). In interpreting the factors, teachers whose espoused beliefs are those expressed by Factor 1 can be assumed to espouse a *constructivist (or alternative) orientation* to teaching and learning mathematics. They may be considered to believe that they should create problematic situations for learners, that mathematics learning is enhanced by activities which build upon students' experiences, that students are rational decision makers and that mathematics knowledge is the result of the learner interpreting and organising the information gained from experiences and that mathematics learning is enhanced by challenging activities within a supportive environment.

Teachers whose espoused beliefs are those expressed by Factor 2 may be assumed to espouse a traditional (and for many centuries dominant) *transmission orientation* to teaching and learning mathematics, believing that their role is to transmit knowledge. Teachers in this category may be considered to believe that mathematics problems given to students should be quickly solvable in a few steps and quickly, mathematics is computation, and memorization, and that mathematics is a static and immutable knowledge with objective truth.

Teachers whose espoused beliefs are those expressed by Factor 3, on the other hand, may be assumed to espouse a *collaborative learning (socio-constructivist) orientation* to teaching and learning mathematics, believing that mathematics knowledge is the result of the learner interpreting and organising the information gained from experiences and that students always benefit by discussing their solutions to mathematical problems with each other and that an effective way to teach mathematics is to provide students with interesting problems to investigate in small groups.

The similarities between factors 1 and 3 could represent some uncertainty or apprehension on the part of the teachers to fully adopt contemporary mathematics education philosophies and methods. It could also be due to the number of years these teachers have been exposed to traditional mathematics education techniques.

A reliability analysis was also conducted on the items comprising each factor. For each factor, item-total correlations (no value < 0.3) confirmed the internal consistency of the items. Cronbach Alpha values for the three factors were as follows:

- Factor 1: $\alpha = .79$
- Factor 2: $\alpha = .60$
- Factor 3: $\alpha = .60$

Statistically significant differences due to gender, experience and position

A MANCOVA test (Table 4.2.3) was conducted in order to investigate the possibility of statistically significant differences between the 3 Factors (dependent variables), gender as the independent variable and experience, and position and postgraduate studies as covariates.

Bartlett's test of sphericity has been used to facilitate a decision being made on whether step-down analysis is appropriate. According to Coakes and Stead, (1999) if Bartlett's test is significant at an alpha level of .05, then the dependent variables are related and thus MANCOVA should be conducted. For this part of the study, BTS<.05 (Table 4.2.1) so the validity of the results in Table 4.2.3 is established.

Table 4.2.3

Tests of Between-Subjects Effects (Beliefs about mathematics, and mathematics teaching and learning)

Source	Dependent Variable	Type III Sum Of Squares	df	Mean Square	F	Sig.
EXPER SENIOR HIGH	REGR factor score 2	4.007	1	4.007	8.435	.020
POSITION	REGR factor score 3	5.896	1	5.896	10.859	.011
GENDER	REGR factor score 3	3.591	1	3.591	6.613	.033

Statistically significant differences were obtained between *experience at senior high school level* (185M, 80F) and espoused beliefs expressed by *Factor 1 and Factor 2.* Statistically significant differences were also obtained between *position* (Teacher=256, Principal=10, Asst. Principal=13, Contract teacher=7, Consultant=10) and espoused beliefs expressed by *Factor 3;* and *gender* (207 males, 92 females, 46 no gender specified) and espoused beliefs expressed by *Factor 3.*

Mean scores for the questionnaire items corresponding to Factor 2 for responses by teachers with experience at senior high level (Years 10-12) are illustrated in Figure 4.2.2. The similarities in the directions of the responses are evident:

- For all items, the direction of the responses in all teacher experience categories was the same.
- For 5 of the items (20, 43, 11, 41 & 48) the responses for all teacher experience categories were in the "agree" (mean scores < 3) direction.
- For 4 of the items (8, 40, 47 & 4) the responses for all teacher experience categories were in the "disagree" (mean scores > 3) direction.

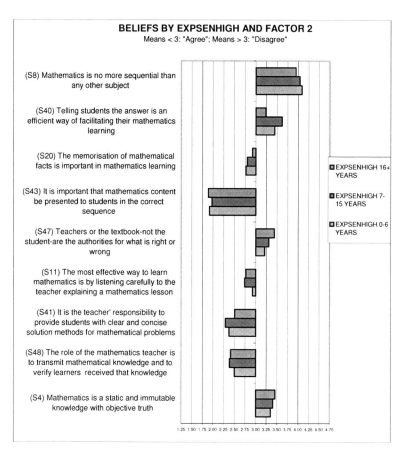

Figure 4.2.2. Teachers' responses by experience at senior high school mean scores for the questionnaire items corresponding to Factor 2.

Teachers' responses by position (Teacher=256, Principal=10, Asst. Principal=13, Contract teacher=7, Consultant=10) mean scores for the questionnaire items corresponding to Factor 3 are illustrated in Figure 4.2.3 The similarities and differences in the directions of the responses are evident:

- For 4 of the items (38, 3, 14 & 15) the responses for all position categories were in the "agree" (mean scores < 3) direction.

There were 3 items (13, 16 & 55) for which there were differences in the direction of the teachers' responses by position. Teachers and consultants' responses were in the same direction for all 3 items.

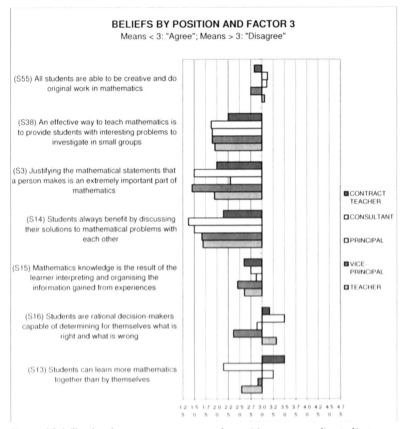

Figure 4.2.3. Teachers' responses mean scores by position corresponding to Factor 3.

Teachers' responses by gender (207 males, 92 females, 46 no gender specified) mean scores for the questionnaire items corresponding to Factor 3, are illustrated in Figure 4.2.4. The similarities and differences in the directions of the responses are evident:

- For all items, the directions of the responses for both male and female teachers were the same
- For 5 of the items (3, 13, 14, 15 & 38) the responses for both male and female teachers categories were in the "agree" (mean scores < 3) direction
- For 2 items (16 & 55) the responses for both male and female teachers were in the "disagree" (mean scores > 3) direction.

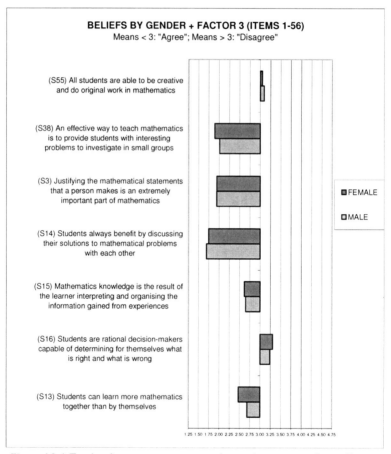

Figure 4.2.4. Teachers' responses mean scores by gender corresponding to Factor 3.

4.3   Beliefs about assessment

The instrument

The data for this investigation were collected using a 24-item researcher designed questionnaire (Chapter 3, section 3.5). Teachers were asked to indicate the degree of importance they attached to each of the aspects described on each item of the questionnaire. A four-point scale was used [highly important (HI), of some importance (SI), beneficial but not essential (BNE), of little importance (LI)]. A score of 1 was assigned to the HI response and a score of 4 to LI. A space was also provided for teachers to comment on any aspect of the instrument and its items. A limitation of this study is that all results must be considered in the context that responses to the questionnaire items depend on the interpretations assigned to them by each respondent.

The sample

The sample comprised 345 (207M, 92F, 46 no gender specified) randomly selected mathematics teachers in 37 Greek State High schools. Data from these responses were analysed using SPSS$_{win}$ and Excel. The quantitative study was followed by a qualitative study in an attempt to identify differences between teachers' espoused beliefs and beliefs in practice.

Results and discussion

Principal Component Analysis

It could reasonably be expected that teachers' beliefs about mathematics, mathematics learning and mathematics teaching would be linked in various ways. Inferential statistical techniques (MANCOVA and t-tests) as well as Principal Component Analysis (PCA) was used in order to interrogate the 24 questionnaire items for a typology of teachers' espoused beliefs about mathematics assessment, using an Analysis of Variance (ANOVA) and the scree plot technique. The significance level was set at .05.

The scree plot (Figure 4.3.1) graphically displays the eigenvalues for each factor and would suggest that there are three predominant factors, accounting for 33.3% of the variance.

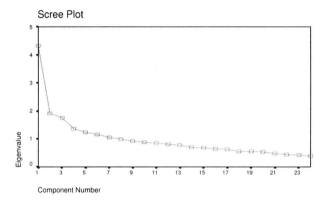

Figure 4.3.1. Scree plot (Beliefs about assessment)

According to Coakes & Steed (1999) if the Kaiser-Meyer-Olkin Measure (KMO) of Sampling Adequacy is greater than 0.6 and the Bartlett's Test of Sphericity (BTS) is significant — both verified in Table 4.3.1 — then factorability of the correlation matrix is assumed.

Table 4.3.1

KMO Measure of Sampling Adequacy and Bartlett's Test of Sphericity (Beliefs about assessment)

Kaiser-Meyer-Olkin Measure of Sampling Adequacy.		.774
Bartlett's Test of Sphericity	Approx. Chi-Square	1213.622
	df	276
	Sig.	.000

For this study KMO =.774 and BTS < .0001, so factorability of the correlation matrix is assumed. The Gronbach's coefficient for factor 1 was 0.80, for factor 2 was 0.60 and for factor 3 was 0.60. Varimax results for factor analysis are shown in Table 4.3.2.

Table 4.3.2

Factors related to views regarding mathematics assessment

ITEM NUMBER AND ITEM DESCRIPTION	Factor loadings		
Component 1			
(S68) TOOMAI: Students undertaking extended mathematical activities	.661		
(S70) TOOMAI: Students posing their own problems	.657		
(S69) TOOMAI: Students undertaking open-ended mathematical activities	.611		
(S73) TOOMAI: The encouragement of student participation via properly designed activities	.575		
(S63) TOOMAI: Developing students' report writing skills	.556		
(S65) TOOMAI: Presenting problems spanning a range of content areas in mathematics	.442		
(71) TOOMAI: The regular completion of student mathematical journals	.425		
Component 2			
(S59) TOOMAI: Teaching problem solving skills		.696	
(S58) TOOMAI: The use of different mathematical skills in combination		.673	
(S57) TOOMAI: Students developing investigating skills		.658	
(S60) TOOMAI: Presenting problems which require a range of problem solving techniques		.589	
(S62) TOOMAI: The application of mathematics to real world contexts		.475	
Component 3			
(S80) TOOMAI: To succeed in university entrance exams			.786
(S75) TOOMAI: To assess students' work and to verify if they should be promoted to the next grade			.731
(S79) TOOMAI: To provide students and parents with feedback on progress being made			.468

TOOMAI means: The Objective Of Mathematics Assessment Is

The three factors represent three apparently differing beliefs about mathematics assessment. The three factors loaded on each of the following items respectively:

- *Item 68:*   TOOMEI: Students undertaking an extended mathematical activity
- *Item 59:*   TOOMEI: Teaching problem solving skills
- *Item 80:*   TOOMEI: To succeed in university entrance exams

Seven items loaded on Factor 1, 5 items on Factor 2 and 3 items on Factor 3 (Table 4.3.2). Teachers whose espoused beliefs are those expressed by Factor 1 may be assumed to espouse a *socio-constructivist orientation* to mathematics assessment. This implies that they are likely to believe that the objective of mathematics education is that: students should be undertaking open-ended mathematical activities, students posing their own problems and students undertaking extended mathematical activities.

Teachers whose espoused beliefs are those expressed by Factor 2 may be assumed to espouse a *problem solving orientation* to mathematics assessment. Teachers in this category are likely to believe that the objective of mathematics education is that: students should develop investigating skills, teachers should be presenting problems which require a range of problem solving techniques and that mathematics should be applied to real world contexts.

Teachers whose espoused beliefs are those expressed by Factor 3 may be assumed to espouse an *accountability orientation* to mathematics assessment. Teachers in this category are likely to subscribe to the view that assessment in mathematics is used for accountability purposes. The inclusion of 'TOOMEI: To succeed in University entrance exams' in this factor may imply that if teachers are assessing for an 'outside audience' it is easier for them to justify the purposes of the assessment used (Nisbet & Warren, 2000).

The similarities between factors 1 and 2 could represent some uncertainty or apprehension on the part of the teachers to fully adopt contemporary mathematics education philosophies and methods. It could also be due to the number of years these teachers have been exposed to traditional mathematics education techniques.

Statistically significant differences due to gender experience and position

A MANCOVA test (Table 4.3.3) was conducted in order to investigate the possibility of statistically significant differences between the 3 Factors (dependent variables), gender as the independent variable and experience, and position and postgraduate studies as covariates.

Table 4.3.3

Tests of Between-Subjects Effects (Beliefs about assessment)

Source	Dependent Variable	Type III Sum	df	Mean Square	F	Sig.
EXPSENHIGH	REGR factor score 1	4.530	1	4.530	17.894	.003
POSITION	REGR factor score 1	5.295	1	5.295	20.917	.002

Statistically significant differences were obtained between *experience at senior high school level* (185M, 80F), *position* (Teacher=256, Principal=10, Asst. Principal=13, Contract teacher=7, Consultant=10). The statistical significance of gender differences was assessed by independent groups t-tests. No significant differences were found.

4.4 Summary

In preparation for the main study psychometrically unsatisfactory items were deleted from the original questionnaire to produce the main study's questionnaire. Criteria used to eliminate items are described in Appendix D1. The reasons for the elimination of items are described in Appendix D2. Both parts of questionnaire used in the main study (Chapter 5) appear in Appendix C2. The following statistical analyses were carried out to examine the psychometric properties of the new instrument:

Using SPSS:

(1) For 80 items, descriptives with mean, standard deviation, skewness, kurtosis

(2) Reliability analysis (Alpha analysis) for each factor

(3) Exploratory factor analysis (for 80 items): forced to 3+3 factors; replace missing data with means (insufficient number of cases due to large loss through listwise deletion); varimax rotation; loading only above .3 accepted

(4) Printouts for 2-3 above analysed

As mentioned above, a full report of the criteria used to eliminate items from the Pilot study's questionnaire and the reasons for elimination of items from the questionnaire of the Pilot study, may be found in Appendices D1 and D2.

In the next chapter the methods used, and the results of the large-scale questionnaire survey are presented. The details of the techniques used in parts 1 and 2 of Chapter 5 are described. In part 1 the results of the statistical analysis of mathematics teachers' beliefs about mathematics, mathematics teaching and mathematics learning are presented. In part 2 the results of the statistical analysis of mathematics teachers' beliefs about mathematics assessment are also presented along with details of the instruments and the methods of data analysis.

CHAPTER 5

Data Analysis

Part 1: Beliefs about mathematics, mathematics instruction and learning

5.1 Introduction

In this chapter the methods used to answer the research questions are presented. The reasons for adopting both large scale and case study methods have already been discussed in chapter 3. The details of the techniques used in parts 1 and 2 of the main study are described and in part 1 the results of the statistical analysis of mathematics teachers' beliefs about mathematics, mathematics teaching and mathematics learning are presented. In part 2 of this chapter the results of the statistical analysis of mathematics teachers' beliefs about mathematics assessment are also presented along with details of the instruments and the methods of data analysis.

5.2 Data analysis

The instrument

A 34 items researcher-designed questionnaire, interview protocol and video analysis teacher action criteria list were the instruments for this investigation (Chapter 3, Section 3.5). On the survey, a Likert-type scoring format was used – teachers were asked to indicate the extent to which they agreed (or disagreed) with each statement presented. A five point scoring system was used – strongly disagree (SD) to strongly agree (SA). A score of 1 was assigned to the SA response and a score of 5 to SD. The questionnaire contained three subsets of items: *Beliefs about Mathematics (BM: 6 items), Beliefs about Mathematics Learning (BML: 7 items) and Beliefs about Mathematics Teaching (BMT: 21 items).*

Participants

The sample consisted of 465 secondary mathematics teachers, principals and regional mathematics consultants (Chapter 3, Section 3.5). The returned surveys reflected a reasonably well-balanced distribution of grade level experience (Table 5.2.1).

Table 5.2.1
Percentage distribution of teachers by experience

	Years of experience		
	0-5	6-15	16+
Experience at high school (Years 7-9)	53.7	25.8	20.5
Experience at senior high school (Years 10-12)	46.2	30.4	23.4

Two teachers, named Ann and Tom for this study, were the subjects of the case studies (Chapter 3, Section 3.5).

Data analysis

Data from the questionnaire responses (see Appendix C2) regarding beliefs about mathematics, mathematics teaching and mathematics learning were analysed using SPSS$_{win}$. Inferential statistical techniques as well as Principal Component Analysis (PCA) was used in order to interrogate the 34 questionnaire items for a typology of teachers' espoused beliefs, using an Analysis of Variance (ANOVA) and the scree plot technique. The significance level was set at .05.

Principal Component Analysis

It could reasonably be expected that teachers' beliefs about mathematics, mathematics learning and mathematics teaching would be linked in various ways. A Principal Component Analysis (PCA) was used in order to interrogate the 34 questionnaire items for a typology of teachers' espoused beliefs. Given the exploratory nature of the study and guided by the Analysis of Variance (ANOVA), the scree plot and the interpretability of the factors, a five factor orthogonal solution (Table 2) was accepted after the extraction of principal components and a Varimax rotation. The solution accounted for 39% of the variance, and 22 of the 34 items were used to delineate the factors.

According to Coakes & Steed (1999), if the Kaiser-Meyer-Olkin (KMO) Measure of Sampling Adequacy is greater than 0.6 and the Bartlett's Test of

Sphericity (BTS) is significant (Table 5.2.2) then factorability of the correlation matrix is assumed. A matrix that is factorable should include several sizable correlations. For this reason (Tabachnick & Fidell, 1996) it is helpful to examine matrices for partial correlations where pairwise correlations are adjusted for effects of all other variables. Tabachnick & Fidell (1996) further stated that:

> Significance tests of correlations in the correlation matrix provide an indication of the reliability of the relationships between pairs of variable. If the correlation matrix is factorable, numerous pairs are significant........... (*and*) there are mostly small values among the variables with effects of the other variables removed. ...... Finally, Kaiser's measure of sampling adequacy is a ratio of the sum of squared correlations to the sum of squared correlations plus sum of squared partial correlations. The value approaches 1 if partial correlations are small. Values over .6 and above are required for good FA (Factor Analysis). (p.642)

For this part of the study, the KMO=.679 and BTS<.01, so factorability of the correlation matrix is assumed.

Table 5.2.2

Kaiser-Meyer-Olkin (KMO) Measure of Sampling Adequacy and Bartlett's Test of Sphericity

Kaiser-Meyer-Olkin Measure of Sampling Adequacy.		.679
Bartlett's Test of Sphericity	Approx. Chi-Square	656.478
	df	561
	Sig.	.003

The analysis yielded 13 factors with eigenvalues greater than 1. Given the exploratory nature of the study and guided by the interpretability of the factors, as well as the scree plot (Figure 5.2.1), a five-factor orthogonal solution was accepted after the extraction of principal components and a Varimax rotation.

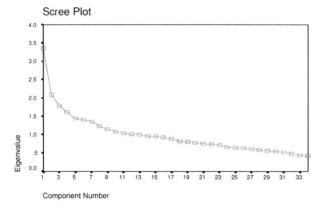

Figure 5.2.1. Scree plot (Beliefs about mathematics, mathematics teaching
and mathematics learning)

A final confirmatory factor analysis (Table 5.2.3) was carried out, following the elimination of psychometrically "poor" items. Variables loading on more than one factor were eliminated, Cronbach's alpha coefficient of internal consistency were used to ensure that the items comprising the resulting factors produced a reliable scale, and normality test were carried out to assess normality among single variables by examining their skewness and kurtosis. If a variable has substantial skewness or kurtosis, the variable needs to be transformed (Tabachnick & Fidell, 1996). In this study, no variable had any substantial skewness or kurtosis, so no transformation of variables was necessary. The extraction method used was Principal Component Analysis and the rotation method was a Varimax with Kaiser Normalization. The rotation converged in 7 iterations.

Table 5.2.3

Factors related to views about mathematics, mathematics teaching and

mathematics learning

Item	Item description	Loading
	Factor 1:	
	A socio-constructivist orientation to mathematics, mathematics teaching and mathematics learning	
P42+M24	It is important for students to be provided with opportunities to reflect on and evaluate their own mathematical understanding	.594
P24+M14	Ignoring the mathematical ideas generated by the students can seriously limit their learning	.594
P54+M32	The education system should be preparing critically thinking citizens who are able to utilise their mathematical skills	.583
P30+M17	Mathematics teachers should be fascinated with how students think and intrigued by alternative ideas	.482
P27+M16	Teachers should encourage their students to strive for elegant solutions when they solve problems	.385
P3+M1	Justifying the mathematical statements that a person makes is an extremely important part of mathematics	.306
	Factor 2:	
	A dynamic problem-driven orientation to mathematics, mathematics teaching and mathematics learning	
P22+M13	Mathematics learning is enhanced by challenging activities within a supportive environment	.650
P51+M30	The comprehension of mathematical concepts by students should correspond to their cognitive development and it should be a decisive factor in the content sequence to be taught	.608
P56+M34	Teachers should respect the mathematical knowledge of their students, which is consisting of a nexus of experiences, beliefs, attitudes, representations, concepts, strategies, connections, values, judgements and emotions	.558
P9+M6	Mathematics is a beautiful, creative and useful human endeavour that is both a way of knowing and a way of thinking	.463
P34+M19	Teachers always need to hear students' mathematical explanations before correcting their errors	.447
P7+M4	Mathematics is the dynamic searching for models and problems and their results are open to review	.358
	Factor 3:	
	A static-transmission orientation to mathematics, mathematics teaching and mathematics learning	
P11+M7	The most effective way to learn mathematics is by listening carefully to the teacher explaining a mathematics lesson	.718
P4+M2	Mathematics is a static and immutable knowledge with objective truth	.675
P48+M28	The role of the mathematics teacher is to transmit mathematical knowledge and to verify that learners have received that knowledge	.637

Factor 4:

A mechanistic-transmission orientation to mathematics, mathematics teaching and mathematics learning

P20+M12   The memorisation of mathematical facts is important in   .623
           mathematics learning
P47+M27   Teachers or the textbook-not the student-are the authorities   .602
           for what is right or wrong
P15+M10   Mathematics knowledge is the result of the learner   .532
           interpreting and organising the information gained
           from experiences

Factor 5:

A collaborative orientation to mathematics, mathematics teaching and mathematics learning

P38+M20   An effective way to teach mathematics is to provide   .551
           students with interesting problems to investigate
           in small groups
P16+M11   Students are rational decision makers capable of determining   .536
           for themselves what is right and what is wrong
P55+33   All students are able to be creative and do original work   .469
           in mathematics
P13+M8   Students can learn more mathematics together than   .447
           by themselves

Note: P means Pilot study items and M means Main study items

The five factors represent five apparently differing but not mutually exclusive beliefs about mathematics, mathematics teaching and mathematics learning. The five factors loaded on each of the following items respectively:

- *Item P42+M24:* It is important for students to be provided with opportunities to reflect on and evaluate their own mathematical understanding

- *Item P22+M13:* Mathematics learning is enhanced by challenging activities within a supportive environment

- *Item P11+M17:* The most effective way to learn mathematics is by listening carefully to the teacher explaining a mathematics lesson

- *Item P20+M12:* The memorisation of mathematical facts is important in mathematics learning

- *Item P38+M20:* An effective way to teach mathematics is to provide students with interesting problems to investigate in small groups

Six items loaded on Factor 1, six items on Factor 2, three items on factor 3, three items on factor 4 and four items loaded on Factor 5 (Table 5.2.3). The naming of factors was guided by the nature of the items (see main study questionnaire, Appendix C3) associated with each factor. The factors are as follows:

Teachers whose beliefs are expressed by Factor 1 (15.3% of total sample) can be assumed to espouse *a socio-constructivist or contemporary orientation* to mathematics, mathematics learning and mathematics teaching. They believe that they should create problematic situations for learners, that mathematics learning is enhanced by activities which build upon students' experiences, that students are rational decision makers, that mathematics knowledge is the result of the learner interpreting and organising the information gained from experiences, that mathematics learning is enhanced by challenging activities within a supportive environment and that the education system should be preparing critically thinking citizens who are able to utilise their mathematical skills.

Teachers whose beliefs are expressed by Factor 2 (23.2% of total sample) can be assumed to espouse *a dynamic problem-driven orientation* to mathematics, mathematics learning and mathematics teaching. They believe that challenging activities within a supportive environment enhances mathematics learning, that mathematics is a beautiful, creative and useful human endeavour that is both a way of knowing and a way of thinking, that mathematics teachers always need to hear students' mathematical explanations before correcting their errors, and that mathematics is the dynamic searching for models and problems and their results are open to review.

Teachers whose beliefs are expressed by Factor 3 (30.8% of total sample) can be assumed to espouse *a static – transmission orientation* to mathematics, mathematics learning and mathematics teaching. Teachers in this category believe that mathematics is computation, that the most effective way to learn mathematics is by listening carefully to the teacher explaining a mathematics lesson, that mathematics is a static and immutable knowledge with objective truth, and that the role of the mathematics teacher is to transmit mathematical knowledge and to verify that learners have received that knowledge.

Teachers whose beliefs are expressed by Factor 4 (26.2% of total sample) can be assumed to espouse *a mechanistic transmission orientation* to mathematics, mathematics learning and mathematics teaching. They believe that the memorisation of mathematical facts is important in mathematics learning, that teachers and the textbooks are the authorities for what is right or wrong.

Teachers whose beliefs are expressed by Factor 5 (4.5% of total sample) can be assumed to espouse *a cooperative orientation* to mathematics learning and mathematics teaching. They believe that an effective way to teach mathematics is to provide students with interesting problems to investigate in small groups, that students are rational decision makers capable of determining for themselves what is right and what is wrong, and that all students are able to be creative and do original work in mathematics.

The results of the factor analysis can be summarized as follows. There seem to be *two orientations* that are characteristic of secondary mathematics teachers' beliefs with regard to the nature of mathematics and the learning and teaching of mathematics:

- A *contemporary – constructivist orientation*, consisting of the following (not mutually exclusive but complementary) views:
    - ❏ The socio-constructivist view (factor 1)
    - ❏ The dynamic problem driven view (factor 2)
    - ❏ The cooperative view (factor 5)
- And a *traditional – transmission – information processing orientation*, consisting of the following (not mutually exclusive but complementary) views:
    - ❏ The static view (factor 3)
    - ❏ The mechanistic view (factor 4)

The outcome was that mathematics teachers' beliefs about mathematics could not be separated from their beliefs about teaching and learning mathematics. The results will be further discussed in Chapter 7.

Average mean responses

To gain some insight into how the sample responded overall to each of the factors, the average mean responses were also calculated for the items that contributed to each factor. Table 5.2.4 summarizes the average mean frequency for each factor together with the range of mean frequencies for the items in each factor.

Table 5.2.4
Average mean frequencies of responses to each factor

Factor		Average Mean response	Range of item mean frequencies
1.	Contemporary-social constructivist	1.72	1.48 – 1.93
2.	Dynamic problem solving	2.07	2.00 – 2.17
3.	Traditional-Static	2.96	2.43 – 3.51
4.	Traditional-Mechanistic	3.63	3.35 – 3.79
5.	Contemporary-Collaborative	2.41	1.97 – 2.61

Note: Responses are based on a 5-point Likert scale: 1 is Strongly Agree and 5 is Strongly Disagree, for the items in factors 1-5. The items in factors 6-8 are based on a 4-point scale: 1 is Highly Important and 4 is of Little Importance.

These results indicate that overall, neither the static nor the mechanistic view of mathematics, mathematics teaching and mathematics learning rated highly among mathematics teachers. The static view however, was stronger than the mechanistic view. It should also be pointed out that all dimensions of the contemporary view, that is, the socio-constructivist, the problem solving and the cooperative dimensions rated more highly than both dimensions of the traditional view – the static and the mechanistic dimensions. In the light of the discussion following the results of the factor analysis, i.e. the fact that the largest two groups were those associated with factor 3 and factor 4, a tenable explanation is that a distinction may exist between the strength of views of Greek mathematics teachers in the sample and the spread/popularity of these views.

Cluster Analysis and Multiple Discriminant Analysis

Cluster analysis can be used to determine homogeneous and clearly discriminated classes of teachers. The results of cluster analysis have been used in this study to confirm the results of the PCA and Factor Analysis and to enhance the depth of the analysis by developing more interpretable classes of the participating teachers. The selection of a cluster solution is facilitated by the interpretation of the agglomeration schedule, which provides information about the homogeneity of the clusters being combined at each stage (Drew & Bishop, 1999). The distance between the successive stages reported in the schedule, becomes progressively larger from stage to stage and there often exists a point at which the distance between the reported coefficients shows sudden and large increases. This enables a decision to be made about the number of clusters that will be used in the analysis. Figure 5.2.2 depicts a graph of the coefficients in the final stages of the agglomeration schedule for the present study.

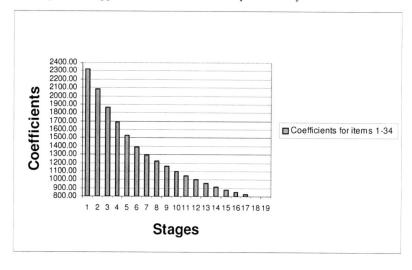

Figure 5.2.2. Agglomeration graph for items related to beliefs about mathematics, and mathematics teaching and learning

According to Diekhoff (1992, cited in Coakes & Steed, 1999) 'because the distances listed in the agglomeration schedule become progressively larger from stage to stage, there will be often a point at which the distance shows a sudden, exceptionally large increase'. It is evident (Figure 5.2.2) that there is a large jump in the coefficient value from 1528.12 to 1685.53 in the stages between the fifth last and the fourth last. This strongly supports the selection of a five clusters solution.

Multiple Discriminant Analysis (MDA) can be used, according to Coakes & Steed (1999), to determine how reliable cluster membership is and to enable the researcher both in describing the nature of the differences between clusters and in testing these differences for significance. MDA allows the researcher to predict which variables discriminate between the groups entered in the analysis. The use of MDA to predict cluster membership for our research is explained in what follows. The grouping variable for this analysis was the cluster membership variable from the five cluster solution. The independent variables used for the MDA were the five factors obtained from the factor analysis.

There are a number of assumptions underlying the use of MDA and the following statistical analyses were carried out in order to rule out any violations of assumptions regarding linearity, univariate and multivariate normality, homogeneity of variance-covariance matrices and multicollinearity, in accordance with current statistical practices (Coakes & Steed, 1999; Tabachnick & Fidell, 1996).

To test for multicollinearity, the within group correlation matrix (Table 5.2.5) is examined. Multicollinearity or singularity, according to Tabachnick & Fidell (1996), may occur when correlations among dependent variables are high since one dependent variable is a near-linear combination of other dependent variables and 'the dependent variable provides information that is redundant to the information available in one or more of the other dependent variables' (p. 383). The within-group correlation matrix (Table 5.2.5) for this study indicates that the correlations between the variables are low ranging from -.06 between factors 1 and 5 to .0239 between factors 3 and 5. Low correlations indicate that multicollinearity does not constitute a problem.

Table 5.2.5
Pooled Within-Groups Matrices

		REGR factor score 1	REGR factor score 2	REGR factor score 3	REGR factor score 4	REGR factor score 5
Correlation	REGR factor score 1	1.000	.066	-.004	-.138	-.064
	REGR factor score 2	.066	1.000	-.027	.197	-.214
	REGR factor score 3	-.004	-.027	1.000	-.153	.239
	REGR factor score 4	-.138	.197	-.153	1.000	-.082
	REGR factor score 5	-.064	-.214	.239	-.082	1.000

The one-way comparisons are reported (Table 5.2.6), using the Wilks' Lambda statistic. Significant differences exist for all the predictor variables. It was concluded that the five groups differ significantly on all the predictor variables (p .0001).

Table 5.2.6
Tests of Equality of Group Means

	Wilks' Lambda	F	df1	df2	Sig.
REGR factor score 1	.735	41.477	4	460	.000
REGR factor score 2	.553	92.952	4	460	.000
REGR factor score 3	.762	35.866	4	460	.000
REGR factor score 4	.495	117.509	4	460	.000
REGR factor score 5	.749	38.631	4	460	.000

An examination of the canonical discriminant functions output (Table 5.2.7) indicates that four discriminant functions have been extracted. The eigenvalues (eigenvalues represent variance), percentage of variance explained and significance of these discriminant functions are also reported. The first row of the table indicates the significance of all functions (with zero functions removed). The chi-squared value of 1086.436 is highly significant ($p<.0001$), indicating that the two functions together discriminate between the sectors very well. The second row indicates the significance after the first function has been removed. This measures the significance of functions two to four. The same procedure is used for rows 3 and 4 of the table. All functions are significant at an alpha .0001 ($p<.0001$).

Table 5.2.7
Wilks' Lambda

Test of Function(s)	Wilks' Lambda	Chi-square	df	Sig.
1 through 4	.094	1086.436	20	.000
2 through 4	.254	629.264	12	.000
3 through 4	.487	330.189	6	.000
4	.771	119.155	2	.000

In Table 5.2.8 it can be seen that the first function has an eigenvalue of 1.707, which accounts for 48.7% of the total explained variance. The second function is smaller with an eigenvalue of .919 and accounts for 26.2% of the variance. Similarly the third function has an eigenvalue of .584 and accounts for 16.6% of the explained variance and the fourth function has an eigenvalue of .296 and accounts for only 8.5% of the explained variance. The canonical correlation is the ratio of the between – groups variation and varies, like normal correlation, from 0.00 to 1.00. Function 1 has a high canonical correlation (r=.794) and explains almost half of the variation.

Table 5.2.8
Canonical discriminant functions

Function	Eigenvalue	% of Variance	Cumulative %	Canonical Correlation
1	1.707	48.7	48.7	.794
2	.919	26.2	74.9	.692
3	.584	16.6	91.5	.607
4	.296	8.5	100.0	.478

Note: First 4 canonical discriminant functions were used in the analysis.

A further part of the Multiple Discriminant Analysis (MDA) relates to the standardized canonical discriminant function coefficients. This matrix (Table 5.2.9) is used to calculate predicted group membership using the products of raw scores and the function coefficients, in a manner similar to the β weights in multiple regression (Coakes & Steed, 1999).

Table 5.2.9
Standardized Canonical Discriminant Function Coefficients

	Function			
	1	2	3	4
REGR factor score 1	.292	.306	-.207	.896
REGR factor score 2	-.713	.467	.560	.081
REGR factor score 3	.350	-.261	.740	.217
REGR factor score 4	.831	.531	.196	-.236
REGR factor score 5	-.294	.743	-.347	-.115

The structure matrix (Table 5.2.10) shows, according to Coakes & Steed (1999) the correlation of each variable with each function. These are similar to factor loadings in factor analysis and are ordered in descending magnitude for function 1 then function 2 and so on. Function 1 is comprised of the variable factor 4. Function 2 is comprised of the variables factor 4 and 5. Function 3 is comprised of the variables factor 2 and 3. Function 4 is comprised of the variable factor 1. These sets of variables are seen to be the variables, which maximally predict differences between the five factors.

Table 5.2.10
Structure Matrix

	Function			
	1	2	3	4
REGR factor score 4	.621*	.560	.250	-.368
REGR factor score 5	-.145	.517*	-.293	-.118
REGR factor score 2	-.476	.440	.640*	.113
REGR factor score 3	.169	-.178	.613*	.220
REGR factor score 1	.147	.217	-.178	.941*

Pooled within-groups correlations between discriminating variables and standardized canonical
discriminant functions. Variables ordered by absolute size of correlation within function.
* Largest absolute correlation between each variable and any discriminant function

Table 5.2.11 represents the Canonical discriminant functions evaluated at
group means (group centroids). These means are joint means based on the linear
combinations of predictor variables and they are standardised. They are used to
interpret the differences between the groups. It can be seen (Table 5.2.11) that
factor 3 has a high score on function 2 and a low score on function 1, and also a
relatively low score on functions 3 and 4.

Table 5.2.11
Canonical discriminant functions evaluated at group means (group centroids)

	Function			
	1	2	3	4
1	-.943	-1.244	-1.336	.259
2	1.407	.581	2.341E-02	.719
3	-.391	.993	-.263	-.530
4	.557	-1.035	.780	-.340
5	-4.623	.472	1.656	1.013

Figure 5.2.3 is a territorial map, which provides a graphical representation
of the group centroids and the participants' scores. An examination of the group
centroids (Table 5.2.11) and the graph (Figure 5.2.3) provides an indication of
the differences between the 5 groups (Factors) and the corresponding
mathematics teachers' beliefs categories. It can be seen (Figure 5.2.3) that group
5 differs from the other 4 groups on the first function, that group 1 differs from
group 2 on the first function. It can also be seen that group 1 differs from groups
3 and 2 on the second function, but this difference is less clearly defined. A full
discussion of the results will be provided in chapter 6.

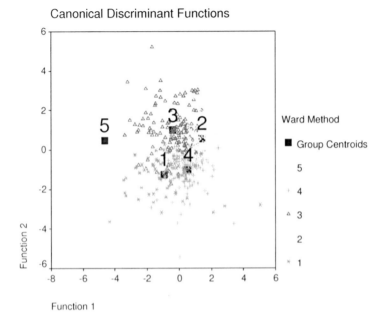

Figure 5.2.3. Canonical discriminant functions map of the participants' scores

Cluster Analysis produces typologies of items or groups by using the similarities or proximities between people as the basis for producing clusters. One measure of the outcome of the analysis is the extent to which it is able to correctly assign predicted group membership (Coakes & Steed, 1999). Table 5.2.12 represents a classification of the group membership, indicating that 84.5% of original grouped cases were correctly classified. The percentage of cases correctly classified in each predicted group is given along the diagonal of the table. Chance prediction would be approximately 20% per group since there are five groups, but this would vary slightly since there are unequal cell sizes across groups. According to the values in Table 5.2.12, it can be claimed that the functions do discriminate among the groups better than chance (·20%).

Table 5.2.12
Classification Results

			Predicted Group Membership					Total
			1	2	3	4	5	
Original	Count	1	62	1	1	7	0	71
		2	1	95	5	7	0	108
		3	6	15	109	11	2	143
		4	2	10	4	106	0	122
		5	0	0	0	0	21	21
	%	1	**87.3**	1.4	1.4	9.9	.0	100.0
		2	.9	**88.0**	4.6	6.5	.0	100.0
		3	4.2	10.5	**76.2**	7.7	1.4	100.0
		4	1.6	8.2	3.3	**86.9**	.0	100.0
		5	.0	.0	.0	.0	**100.0**	100.0

Note: 84.5% of original grouped cases correctly classified.

There was a 100% prediction for *group 5*, which represents mathematics teachers who espouse *a cooperative orientation* to mathematics learning and mathematics teaching. This means that although a small group (21 cases), teachers who espouse a collaborative view to teaching and learning mathematics hold very strong views, which are quite different from the other four groups.

The prediction was quite satisfactory for groups 1, 2 and 4 but less satisfactory for group 3. There was a 12.7% (1.4%+1.4%+9.9%) misclassification for *group 1* (factor 1) cases. The 11.3% (1.4%+9.9%) drift in predictions towards traditional teaching and learning methods, might have been expected if the protracted exposure of secondary mathematics teachers in Greece to traditional methods of teaching, the traditional nature of the mathematics books and the traditional curricula that have been in use during the past decades were taken into consideration. This percentage could represent some uncertainty or apprehension on the part of the teachers to fully adopt contemporary mathematics education philosophies and methods. It could also be due to the number of years these teachers have been exposed to traditional mathematics education techniques.

There was a 12% (0.9%+4.6%+6.5%) misclassification for *group 2* (factor 2) cases, indicating that mathematics teachers who espouse *a dynamic problem-driven orientation* to mathematics, mathematics learning and mathematics teaching, show a drift in predictions towards traditional teaching and learning methods. The 11.1% (4.6%+6.5%) drift in predictions towards traditional teaching and learning methods, may be expected if we take under consideration the protracted exposure of secondary mathematics teachers in Greece to traditional methods of teaching, the traditional nature of the mathematics books and the traditional curricula that have been in use during the past decades. This percentage could represent some uncertainty or apprehension on the part of the teachers to fully adopt contemporary mathematics education philosophies and methods. It could also be due to the number of years these teachers have been exposed to traditional mathematics education techniques.

There was a 23.8% (4.2%+10.5%+7.7%+1.4%) misclassification for *group 3* (factor 3) cases, indicating that mathematics teachers who espouse *a static – transmission orientation* to mathematics, mathematics learning and mathematics teaching, show a drift (10.5%) in predictions towards a dynamic problem solving orientation. The 7.7% drift in predictions towards traditional teaching and learning methods, may be expected since it represents another category of traditional beliefs.

There was a 13.1% (1.6%+8.2%+3.3%) misclassification for *group 4* (factor 4) cases, indicating that mathematics teachers who espouse *a mechanistic – transmission orientation* to mathematics, mathematics learning and mathematics teaching, show a drift (8.2%) in predictions towards a dynamic problem solving orientation. The 3.3% drift in predictions towards traditional teaching and learning methods, may be expected since it represents another category of traditional beliefs.

Teacher characteristics and their influence on teachers' beliefs

Data were collected on five teacher characteristics, namely, gender, professional development, years of teaching experience at Junior High school, years of teaching experience at Senior High school, position held and postgraduate qualifications possessed. One-way analyses of variance, linear contrasts and Scheffe pair-wise comparisons were performed in order to examine if the five beliefs factors (Table 5.2.3) relating to mathematics, mathematics teaching and mathematics learning, varied according to these five characteristics.

Professional Development

The Professional Development background was not a significant variable for any of the factors, suggesting that the in-service training they had undertaken did not significantly influence secondary mathematics teachers' beliefs about mathematics, mathematics teaching and learning.

Gender

The independent samples t-test (Table 5.2.13) shows that gender was significant for one of the five factors – Factor 1, *A contemporary socio-constructivist orientation to mathematics, mathematics teaching and mathematics learning* (t_{421}=-3.3, p=.001).

Table 5.2.13
Independent Samples Test (Gender)

		t-test for Equality of Means		
		t	df	Sig. (2-tailed)
REGR factor score 1	Equal variances assumed	-3.325	419	.001
	Equal variances not assumed	-3.261	277.268	.001

The mean factor score for female teachers (0.23) was significantly higher than for the male teachers (-0.10) as can be seen from Figure 5.2.4. It appears that female teachers in this study placed more emphasis on a socio-constructivist view of mathematics, mathematics teaching and mathematics learning than did the male teachers.

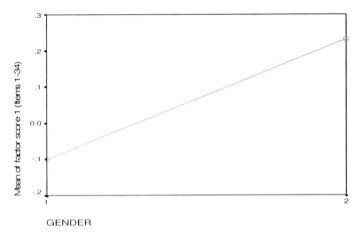

Figure 5.2.4. Means Plot (Gender)

Years of experience at junior high school

The ANOVA summary table (Table 5.2.14) shows that years of experience at Junior High school was significant for one of the five factors – Factor 1: *A contemporary socio-constructivist orientation to mathematics, mathematics teaching and mathematics learning* ($F_{(2, 421)}$=3.514, p=.031). It could be argued that teachers with experience at junior high school (Years 7-9), placed more emphasis on a socio-constructivist view of mathematics, mathematics teaching and mathematics learning than did teachers with experience at other levels (Figure 5.2.5). A tenable explanation is that junior high school teaching offers more opportunity for a child-centred approach, since teachers do not have to face the pressures of preparing their students for University entrance exams, something that both case study teachers – who were both veteran senior high school teachers – felt compelled to do. By examining the Linear term which is also significant across the years of experience at junior high school (Table 5.2.14), it can be concluded that the contemporary socio-constructivist orientation to mathematics, mathematics teaching and mathematics learning increases consistently (Figure 5.2.5) between the inexperienced teachers category (0-6 years of experience) and the experienced teachers category (6-15 years of experience). To further examine these differences across the three levels of experience (0-6 years, 7-15 years and 16+ years), Scheffe pair-wise comparisons were performed. The results of this analysis showed no clear trend and no discernible pattern.

Table 5.2.14
ANOVA (Experience at junior high school)

				df	F	Sig.
REGR factor score 1	Between Groups	(Combined)		2	3.514	.031
		Linear Term	Unweighted	1	3.833	.051
			Weighted	1	5.460	.020
			Deviation	1	1.568	.211

In addition, the Levene test for homogeneity of variances for Factor 1 (Table 5.2.15) is not significant (p>.05), indicating that the assumption has not been violated. Linear trends should be interpreted with caution when the test for homogeneity of variances is significant. Assessing the F-value at a more conservative alpha level of .001 could be the solution. In this case the test is not significant (Table 5.2.15) and therefore there is no need to adjust the alpha level of significance.

Table 5.2.15
Test of Homogeneity of Variances (Experience at junior high school)

	Levene Statistic	df1	df2	Sig.
REGR factor score 1	1.549	2	362	.214

From the means plot (Figure 5.2.5) it can also be seen that the contemporary socio-constructivist view of mathematics, mathematics teaching and learning (factor 1) was more prevalent among experienced teachers (7-15 years experience) and veteran teachers (16+ years of experience) than among inexperienced teachers (0-6 years of experience).

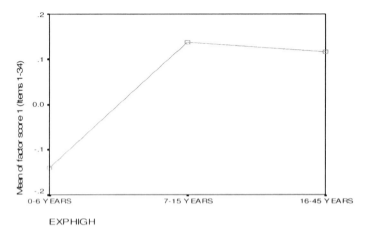

Figure 5.2.5. Means Plot (Experience at junior high school)

Years of experience at senior high school

Years of experience at senior high school was not a significant variable for any of the factors, suggesting that teachers' beliefs about mathematics, mathematics teaching and mathematics learning were not significantly influenced by their experience at senior high school level (Years 10-12). The Linear term however, is significant for Factor 2 (A dynamic problem-driven orientation to mathematics, mathematics teaching and mathematics learning) across the years of experience at senior high school (Table 5.2.16). It can be concluded that the dynamic problem-driven orientation to mathematics, mathematics teaching and mathematics learning increases consistently (Figure 5.2.6) across teachers' experience categories.

Table 5.2.16
ANOVA (Experience at senior high school)

				df	F	Sig.
REGR factor score 2 (Items 1-56)	Between Groups	Combined		2	2.713	.068
		Linear Term	Unweighted	1	4.755	.030
			Weighted	1	3.954	.048
			Deviation	1	1.472	.226

To examine these differences further across the three levels of experience (0-6 years, 7-15 years and 16+ years) Scheffe pair-wise comparisons were performed. The results of this analysis showed no clear trend and no discernible pattern. In addition, the Levene test for homogeneity of variances for Factor 2 is not significant (p>.05), indicating that the assumption has not been violated (Table 5.2.17).

Table 5.2.17
Test of Homogeneity of Variances (Experience at senior high school)

	Levene Statistic	df1	df2	Sig.
REGR factor score 2	2.700	2	300	.069

From the means plot (Figure 5.2.6) it can also be seen that the *dynamic problem-driven orientation to mathematics, mathematics teaching and mathematics* (factor 2) was more prevalent among veteran teachers (16+ years of experience) than among inexperienced teachers (0-6 years of experience) and experienced teachers (7-15 years experience).

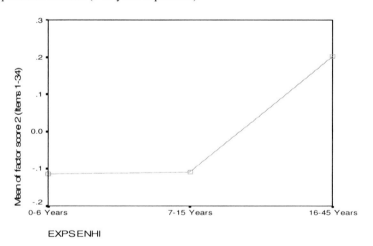

Figure 5.2.6. Means Plot (Experience at senior high school)

Position held

The ANOVA summary table (Table 5.2.18) shows that a participant's *position* was significant for two of the five factors – Factor 1: *A contemporary* socio-constructivist orientation to mathematics, mathematics teaching and mathematics learning ($F_{(2, 412)}$=3.171, p=.043), and Factor 3: A static-transmission orientation to mathematics, mathematics teaching and mathematics learning ($F_{(2, 412)}$=4.919, p=.008 (Table 5.2.18). The three position categories in the survey were: (a) teacher (244 males, 143 females, 44 no gender specified), (b) principal (22 males, 2 females) and (c) regional mathematics consultant (10 males). By examining the Linear term which is also significant across the years of experience at Junior High school (Table 5.2.18), it can be concluded that the contemporary socio-constructivist orientation to mathematics, mathematics teaching and mathematics learning decreases consistently (Figure 5.2.7) between the principal and consultant categories of position held. To further examine these differences across the three different positions (teacher, principal and consultant) Scheffe pair-wise comparisons were performed. The results of this analysis showed no clear trend and no discernible pattern.

Table 5.2.18
ANOVA (Position held)

				df	F	Sig.
REGR factor score 1	Between Groups	Combined		2	3.171	.043
		Linear Term	Weighted	1	4.948	.027
			Deviation	1	1.393	.239
	Within Groups			410		
	Total			412		
REGR factor score 3	Between Groups	Combined		2	4.919	.008
		Linear Term	Weighted	1	.225	.636
			Deviation	1	9.614	.002
	Within Groups			410		
	Total			412		

In addition, the Levene test for homogeneity of variances for Factors 1 and 3 (Table 5.2.19) is not significant (p <.05), indicating that the assumption has not been violated.

Table 5.2.19
Test of Homogeneity of Variances (Position held)

	Levene Statistic	df1	df2	Sig.
REGR factor score 1	1.750	2	410	.175
REGR factor score 3	.874	2	410	.418

From the means plot (Figure 5.2.7) it can also be seen that the contemporary socio-constructivist view of mathematics, mathematics teaching and learning was more prevalent among teachers and principals than among consultants.

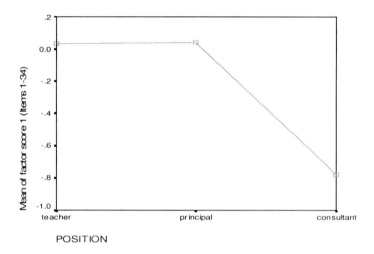

Figure 5.2.7. Means Plot (Position held-Factor 1)

From the means plot (Figure 5.2.8) it can be seen that the static-transmission orientation to mathematics, mathematics teaching and mathematics learning was more prevalent among consultants than among teachers and principals.

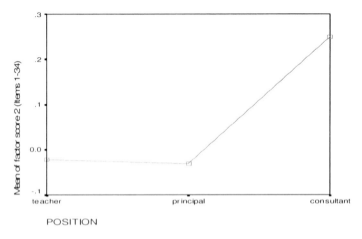

Figure 5.2.8. Means Plot (Position held-Factor 2)

Postgraduate studies background

The ANOVA summary table (Table 5.2.20) shows that the postgraduate studies background was significant for one of the five factors – Factor 4: *A mechanistic-transmission orientation to mathematics, mathematics teaching and mathematics learning* ($F_{(2, 454)}$=3.152, p=.044).

Table 5.2.20
ANOVA (Postgraduate studies background)

				df	F	Sig.
REGR factor score 4	Between Groups	Combined		2	3.152	.044
		Linear Term	Weighted	1	.479	.489
			Deviation	1	5.825	.016
	Within Groups			452		
	Total			454		

In addition, the Levene test for homogeneity of variances for Factor 4 (Table 5.2.21) is not significant (p＞.05), indicating that the assumption of homogeneity has not been violated.

Table 5.2.21
Test of Homogeneity of Variances (Postgraduate studies background)

	Levene Statistic	df1	df2	Sig.
REGR factor score 4	.836	2	452	.434

To examine these differences across the three different qualifications levels (4 year maths degree, Masters, Ph.D.) Scheffe pair-wise comparisons were performed (Table 5.2.22).

Table 5.2.22
Scheffe Multiple Comparisons (Postgraduate studies background)

			Sig.
Dependent Variable	POSTGRAD	POSTGRAD	
REGR factor score 4	Ph.D.	Master	.046

The results of the Scheffe analysis (Figure 5.2.9) showed that there was a significant difference ($p < 0.05$) between the views of the teachers with a Masters qualification and those with a Ph.D. degree on the mechanistic-transmission view of mathematics, mathematics teaching and mathematics learning.

It can also be argued (Figure 5.2.9) that the mechanistic – transmission view of mathematics, mathematics teaching and mathematics learning was more prevalent among teachers with a Masters degree.

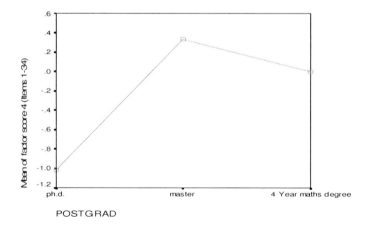

Figure 5.2.9. Means Plot (Postgraduate studies background)

It could be argued that teachers with Master degrees, and to lesser extent teachers with no postgraduate qualifications, placed more emphasis on a mechanistic-transmission orientation to mathematics, mathematics teaching and mathematics learning than did teachers with a Ph.D.

Part 2: Mathematics teacher's beliefs about assessment

5.3   Data Analysis

The instrument

The data for this investigation were collected using a 19 items researcher - designed questionnaire. Teachers were asked (Chapter 3, Section 3.5) to indicate the degree of importance they attached to each of the aspects described on each item of the questionnaire. A four — point scale was used [highly important (HI), of some importance (SI), beneficial but not essential (BNE), of little importance (LI)]. A score of 1 was assigned to the HI response and a score of 4 to LI. A space was also provided for teachers to comment on any aspect of the instrument and its items. A limitation of this study is that all results must be considered in the context of the dependency of responses to the questionnaire items on the interpretations assigned to them by each respondent.

Participants

The sample consisted of 465 secondary mathematics teachers, principals and regional mathematics consultants (Chapter 5, Section 5.2, p. 86).

Data analysis

Data from the questionnaire responses (Appendix C2) regarding beliefs about mathematics assessment were analysed using $SPSS_{win}$. Inferential statistical techniques as well as Principal Component Analysis (PCA) was used in order to interrogate the 19 questionnaire items for a typology of teachers' espoused beliefs, using an Analysis of Variance (ANOVA) and the scree plot technique. The significance level was set at .05.

Principal Component Analysis

A Principal Component Analysis (PCA) was used in order to interrogate the 19 questionnaire items for a typology of teachers' espoused beliefs, using an Analysis of Variance (ANOVA) and the scree plot technique. The significance level was set at .05. According to Coakes & Steed (1999), if the Kaiser-Meyer-Olkin (KMO) Measure of Sampling Adequacy is greater than 0.6 and the Bartlett's Test of Sphericity (BTS) is significant (Table 5.2.2) then factorability of the correlation matrix is assumed. The Kaiser-Meyer-Olkin Measure (KMO) of Sampling Adequacy is greater than .6 (KMO=.774) and the Bartlett's Test of Sphericity (BTS) is significant (<.001) (Table 5.4.1) therefore factorability of the correlation matrix is assumed.

Table 5.4.1
KMO Measure of Sampling Adequacy and Bartlett's Test of Sphericity

Kaiser-Meyer-Olkin Measure of Sampling Adequacy.		.780
Bartlett's Test of Sphericity	Approx. Chi-Square	987.169
	df	171
	Sig.	.000

The analysis yielded 5 factors with eigenvalues greater than 1 (eigenvalues represent variance – a component with an eigenvalue less than 1 is not deemed as important, from a variance perspective, as an observed variable).

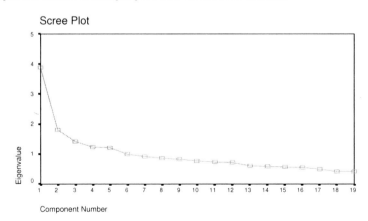

Figure 5.4.1. Scree plot (Beliefs about assessment)

Given the exploratory nature of the study and guided by the interpretability of the factors, as well as the scree plot (Figure 5.4.1), a three-factor orthogonal solution was accepted after the extraction of principal components and a Varimax rotation. The solution accounted for 37.5% of the variance, and 16 of the 19 items were used to delineate the factors.

Table 5.4.2
Factors related to views about assessment

Item	Item description	Loading
Factor 1:		
A socio-constructivist orientation to mathematics assessment		
P68+M44	TOOMAI: Students undertaking an extended mathematical activity	.643
P70+M46	TOOMAI: Students posing their own problems	.642
P69+M45	TOOMAI: Students undertaking open-ended mathematical activities	.607
P63+M40	TOOMAI: Developing students' report writing skills	.592
P73+M49	TOOMAI: The encouragement of student participation via properly designed activities	.560
P65+M41	TOOMAI: Presenting problems spanning a range of content areas in mathematics	.391
P71+M47	TOOMAI: The regular completion of student mathematical journals	.334
Factor 2:		
A problem solving orientation to mathematics assessment		
P58+M36	TOOMAI: The use of different mathematical skills in combination	.725
P59+M37	TOOMAI: Teaching problem solving skills	.661
P57+M35	TOOMAI: Students developing investigating skills	.645
P60+M38	TOOMAI: Presenting problems, which require a range of problem solving techniques	.597
P62+M39	TOOMAI: The application of mathematics to real world contexts	.457
Factor 3:		
An accountability orientation to mathematics assessment		
P80+M53	TOOMAI: To succeed in university entrance exams	.753
P75+M51	TOOMAI: To assess students' work and to verify if they should be promoted to the next grade	.653
P79+M52	TOOMAI: To provide students and parents with feedback on progress being made	.535
P66+M42	TOOMAI: Using problems specific to the topic being taught	.448

Notes (1) P means Pilot study items and M means Main study items
(2) TOOMAI means The Objective Of Mathematics Assessment Is

A final confirmatory factor analysis (Table 5.4.2) was carried out following the elimination of psychometrically "poor" items (double loadings and reliability and normality tests), using Principal Component Analysis as the extraction method and Varimax with Kaiser Normalization as the rotation method. The rotation converged in 5 iterations.

The three factors represent three apparently differing beliefs about mathematics assessment. The three factors loaded on each of the following items respectively:

- *Item 68:*   The objective of mathematics assessment is (TOOMAI): Students undertaking an extended mathematical activity
- *Item 58:*   TOOMAI: The use of different mathematical skills in combination
- *Item 80:*   TOOMAI: To succeed in university entrance exams

Seven items loaded on Factor 1, five items on Factor 2 and four items on Factor 3 (Figure 5.4.2).

Teachers whose beliefs are those expressed by Factor 1 (49.1% of total sample) may be assumed to espouse a *socio-constructivist orientation* to mathematics assessment. They may be considered to believe that they should create problematic situations for learners, that mathematics learning is enhanced by activities which build upon students' experiences, that students are rational decision makers and that mathematics knowledge is the result of the learner interpreting and organising the information gained from experiences and that mathematics learning is enhanced by challenging activities within a supportive environment.

Teachers whose beliefs are those expressed by Factor 2 (17.6% of total sample) may be assumed to espouse a *problem solving orientation* to mathematics assessment. Teachers in this category may be considered to believe that the objective of mathematics education is that: students should develop investigating skills, teachers should be presenting problems which require a range of problem solving techniques and that mathematics should be applied to real world contexts.

Teachers whose beliefs are those expressed by Factor 3 (33.3% of total sample) may be assumed to espouse an *accountability orientation* to mathematics assessment. Teachers in this category may be considered to subscribe to the view that assessment in mathematics is used for accountability purposes. The inclusion of 'TOOMAI: To succeed in University entrance exams' in this factor may imply that if teachers are assessing for an 'outside audience' (Nisbet & Warren, 2000) it is easier for them to justify the purposes of the assessment used.

The absence of items relating to timed-tests, recall items and end of semester exams from the final assessment questionnaire, is the result of the Pilot Study's statistical analysis. Items Q61 and Q66 (Appendix D2), which addressed those areas, were eliminated from the items pool used in the main study. Item Q61: "*The objective of mathematics assessment is to prepare students for the recently introduced objective type tests*" specifically addressed the use of those tests, since they form an integral part of the objective type tests referred to in the item.

Average mean responses

To gain some insight into how the sample responded overall to each of the factors, the average mean responses were calculated for the items comprising each factor. Table 5.4.3 summarizes the average mean frequency for each factor together with the range of mean frequencies for the items in each factor.

Table 5.4.3
Average mean frequencies of responses to each factor

Factor	Average Mean response	Range of item mean frequencies
1. Contemporary-social constructivist	2.24	1.59 2.83
2. Dynamic problem solving	1.99	1.63 2.22
3. Traditional-Accountability	2.06	1.93 2.11

Note: Responses are based on a 4-point scale: 1 is Highly Important and 4 is of Little Importance.

The results indicate that overall, teachers in the sample emphasised the use of contemporary methods of assessment. Next, they used assessment for accountability purposes and lastly they use problem solving methods of assessment. The wide range of responses to the contemporary orientation indicates that it represents a wide spectrum of approaches not sufficiently coherent.

Cluster Analysis and Multiple Discriminant Analysis

Cluster analysis was used to determine homogeneous and clearly discriminated classes of teachers. The results of cluster analysis were used in this study to confirm the results of the PCA and Factor Analysis and to enhance the depth of the analysis by developing more interpretable classes of the participating teachers. The selection of a cluster solution was facilitated by the interpretation of the agglomeration schedule, which provides information about the homogeneity of the clusters being combined at each stage (Coakes & Steed, 1999). The distance between the successive stages reported in the schedule becomes progressively larger from stage to stage, and there often exists a point at which the distance between the reported coefficients shows sudden and large increases. This enabled a decision to be formed about the number of clusters that were to be used in the analysis. Figure 5.4.2 represents a graph of the coefficients in the final stages of the agglomeration schedule for the present study.

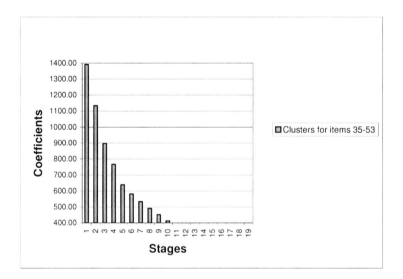

Figure 5.4.2. Agglomeration graph for items related to beliefs about mathematics assessment

From Figure 5.4.2 it is evident that in there is a large jump in the coefficient value from 897.18 to 1134.31 in the stages between the third last and the second last. This strongly supports the selection of a three cluster solution.

It has already been mentioned in Section 5.2 that Multiple Discriminant Analysis (MDA) can be used according to Coakes & Steed (1999), to determine how reliable cluster membership is and to enable a researcher both to describe the nature of the differences between clusters and test these differences for significance. MDA allows the researcher to predict which variables discriminate between the groups entered in the analysis. The use of MDA to predict cluster membership for this study is explained in what follows. The grouping variable for this analysis was the cluster membership variable from the three cluster solution. The independent variables used for the MDA were the three factors obtained from the factor analysis. It has already been mentioned (Section 5.2), that there are a number of assumptions underlying the use of MDA and the following statistical analyses were carried out in order to rule out any violations of assumptions regarding linearity, univariate and multivariate normality, homogeneity of variance-covariance matrices and multicollinearity, in accordance with current statistical practices (Coakes & Steed, 1999; Tabachnick & Fidell, 1996).

To test for multicollinearity, the within-group correlation matrix (Table 5.4.4) was examined. The matrix indicates that the correlations between the variables are low ranging from -.074 between factors 2 and 3, and .075 between factors 1 and 3. Low correlations indicate that multicollinearity is not problematical.

Table 5.4.4
Pooled Within-Groups Matrices

		REGR factor 1	REGR factor 2	REGR factor 3
Correlation	REGR factor 1	1.000	-.048	.075
	REGR factor 2	-.048	1.000	-.074
	REGR factor 3	.075	-.074	1.000

The one-way comparisons are reported in Table 5.4.5. Wilks' Lambda statistic was used here. Significant differences exist for all the predictor variables. It is concluded that the three groups differ significantly on all the predictor variables (p= .0001).

Table 5.4.5
Tests of Equality of Group Means

	Wilks' Lambda	F	df1	df2	Sig.
REGR factor 1	.447	257.737	2	417	.000
REGR factor 2	.497	211.343	2	417	.000
REGR factor 3	.990	2.155	2	417	.117

An examination of the canonical discriminant functions output (Table 5.4.6) indicates that four discriminant functions have been extracted. The eigenvalues, percentage of variance explained and significance of these discriminant functions are also reported. The first row of the table indicates the significance of all functions (with zero functions removed). The chi-squared value of 635.601 is highly significant (p<.0001), indicating that the two functions together discriminate between the sectors very well. The second row indicates the significance after the first function has been removed. This measures the significance of function two. All functions are significant at an alpha .0001 (p<.0001).

Table 5.4.6
Wilks' Lambda

Test of Function(s)	Wilks' Lambda	Chi-square	df	Sig.
1 through 2	.217	635.601	6	.000
2	.497	291.016	2	.000

In Table 5.4.7 it can be seen that the first function has an eigenvalue of 1.289, which accounts for 56.0% of the total explained variance. The second function is smaller with an eigenvalue of 1.013 and accounts for 44.0% of the variance. The canonical correlation is the ratio of the between – groups variation and varies, like normal correlation, from 0.00 to 1.00. Function 1 has a high canonical correlation (r=.750) and explains more than half of the variation.

Table 5.4.7
Canonical correlation

	Function	Eigenvalue	% of Variance	Cumulative %	Canonical Correlation
	1	1.289	56.0	56.0	.750
	2	1.013	44.0	100.0	.709

Note: First 2 canonical discriminant functions were used in the analysis.

A further part of the Multiple Discriminant Analysis (MDA) relates to the standardized canonical discriminant function coefficients. This matrix (Table 5.4.8) is used to calculate predicted group membership using the products of raw scores and the function coefficients, in a manner similar to the Beta (β) weights in multiple regression (Coakes & Steed, 1999).

Table 5.4.8
Canonical discriminant function coefficients

	Function	
	1	2
REGR factor 1	.960	-.288
REGR factor 2	.333	.944
REGR factor 3	-.084	.183

The structure matrix (Table 5.4.9) shows, the correlation of each variable with each function. These are similar to factor loadings in factor analysis and are ordered in descending magnitude for function 1 then function 2 and so on. These sets of variables are seen to be the variables which maximally predict differences between the three factors.

Table 5.4.9
Structure Matrix

	Function	
	1	2
REGR factor 1	.937	-.320
REGR factor 2	.293	.944
REGR factor 3	-.037	.092

Table 5.4.10 represents the Canonical discriminant functions evaluated at group means (group centroids). These means are joint means based on the linear combinations of predictor variables and they are standardised. They are used to

interpret the differences between the groups. It can be seen for example (Table 5.4.10) that factor 2 has a high score on function 2 and a low score on function 1.

Table 5.4.10
Functions at Group Centroids

		Function	
	3 clusters	1	2
	1	-1.075	-.370
	2	.246	2.157
	3	1.452	-.596

Unstandardized canonical discriminant functions evaluated at group means

Figure 5.4.3 is a territorial map, which provides a graphical representation of the group centroids and the participants' scores. An examination of the group centroids (Table 5.4.10) and the graph (Figure 5.4.3) provides an indication of the differences between the 3 groups (Factors) and the corresponding mathematics teachers' beliefs categories. It can be seen (Figure 5.4.3) that group 1 differs from group 3 on the first function, and that groups 1 and 3 differ from group 2 on the second function but this difference is less clearly defined. A full discussion of the results will be provided in chapter 7.

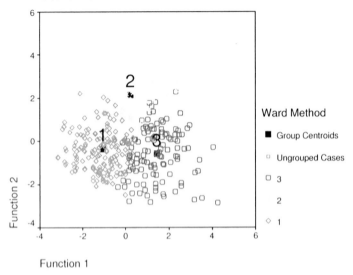

Figure 5.4.3. Canonical discriminant functions map of the participants' scores

As mentioned in section 5.2 cluster analysis produces typologies of items or groups by using the similarities or proximities between people as the basis for producing clusters. One measure of the outcome of the analysis is the extent to which it is able to correctly assign predicted group membership (Coakes & Steed, 1999). Table 5.4.11 represents a classification of the group membership, indicating that 91.2% of original grouped cases were correctly classified. The percentage of cases correctly classified in each predicted group is given along the diagonal of the table. Chance prediction would be approximately 33.3% per group since there are thee groups, but this would vary slightly since there are unequal cell sizes across groups. According to the values in Table 5.4.11, it can be claimed that the functions do discriminate among the groups better than by chance (·33.3%).

Table 5.4.11
Classification Results

			Predicted Group Membership			Total
			1	2	3	
Original	Count	1	189	13	4	206
		2	4	68	2	74
		3	6	8	126	140
	%	1	**91.7**	6.3	1.9	100.0
		2	5.4	**91.9**	2.7	100.0
		3	4.3	5.7	**90.0**	100.0

Note: 91.2% of original grouped cases correctly classified.

The prediction for all groups (91.7%, 91.9% and 90.0%) was satisfactory meaning that the extent to which MDA was able to correctly assign predicted membership was quite high.

The prediction for group 1 (factor 1), which represents mathematics teachers who espouse *a socio-constructivist orientation to mathematics assessment*, was 91.7%. There was 9.2% (6.3%+1.9%) misclassification for group 1 cases. The 6.3% drift in predictions towards problem solving assessment methods was to be expected, since both factors 1 and 2 represent contemporary assessment approaches.

The prediction for group 2 (factor 2), which represents mathematics teachers who espouse *a problem solving orientation to mathematics assessment*, was 91.9%. There was 7.9% (5.2%+2.7%) misclassification for group 2 cases. The 5.2% drift in predictions towards socio-constructivist methods of assessment was to be expected also, since both factors 1 and 2 represent contemporary assessment approaches.

The prediction for group 3 (factor 3), which represents mathematics teachers who espouse *an accountability orientation to mathematics assessment*, was 90.0%. There was 10.0% (5.7%+4.3%) misclassification for group 3 cases. There was a 10.0% drift in predictions towards problem solving assessment and socio-constructivist assessment approaches. This percentage could represent some uncertainty or apprehension on the part of the teachers to fully adopt a traditional orientation towards mathematics assessment.

Teacher characteristics and their influence on teachers' beliefs

Data were collected on five teacher characteristics, namely, gender, professional development, years of teaching experience at Lower High school level, years of teaching experience at Senior High school level, position held and postgraduate qualifications possessed. One-way analyses of variance, linear contrasts and Scheffe pair-wise comparisons were performed in order to test if the three beliefs factors (Table 5.4.2) relating to mathematics assessment, varied according to these five characteristics.

Professional Development

Professional Development was not a significant variable for any of the factors, suggesting that the in-service training they had undertaken did not significantly influence secondary mathematics teachers' beliefs about mathematics assessment.

Gender

Gender was not a significant variable for any of the factors, suggesting that teachers' beliefs about mathematics assessment were not significantly influenced by their gender.

Years of experience at junior high school

The ANOVA summary table (Table 5.4.12) shows that that *Years of experience at junior high school* was significant for one of the three factors – Factor 2: *A problem solving orientation to mathematics assessment* ($F_{(2, 121)}$=4.064, p=.018). It could be argued that teachers with experience at junior high school (Years 7-9) placed more emphasis on a problem solving orientation to mathematics assessment than did teachers with experience at other levels. By examining the Linear term which was also significant across the years of experience at junior high school (Table 5.4.12), it can be concluded that the problem solving orientation to mathematics assessment increases consistently (Figure 5.4.4) across all teachers' experience categories. To further examine these differences across the three levels of experience (0-6 years, 7-15 years and 16+ years) Scheffe pair-wise comparisons were performed. The results of this analysis showed no clear trend and no discernible pattern.

Table 5.4.12
ANOVA (Experience at junior high school)

				df	F	Sig.
REGR factor 2	Between Groups	(Combined)		2	4.064	.018
		Linear Term	Unweighted	1	5.151	.024
			Weighted	1	7.248	.007
			Deviation	1	.880	.349
	Within Groups			319		
	Total			321		

In addition, the Levene test for homogeneity of variances for Factor 1 (Table 5.4.13) is not significant (p>.05), indicating that the assumption has not been violated.

Table 5.4.13
Test of Homogeneity of Variances (Experience at junior high school)

	Levene Statistic	df1	df2	Sig.
REGR factor 2	2.223	2	319	.110

From the means plot (Figure 5.4.4) it can be seen that the problem solving view of assessment in mathematics was more prevalent among experienced teachers (7-15 years experience) and veteran teachers (16+ years of experience) than among the inexperienced teachers (0-6 years of experience).

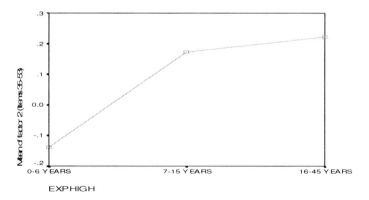

Figure 5.4.4. Means Plot (Experience at junior high school)

Years of experience at senior high school

Years of experience at senior high school was not a significant variable for any of the factors, suggesting that teachers' beliefs about mathematics assessment were not significantly influenced by their experience at senior high school (Years 10-12).

Position held

The ANOVA summary table (Table 5.4.14) shows that *Position* was significant for one of the three factors – Factor 1: *A socio-constructivist orientation to mathematics assessment* ($F_{(2, 367)}$=5.042, p=.007). The three position categories in the survey were: (a) teacher (244 males, 143 females, 44 no gender specified), (b) principal (22 males, 2 females) and (c) regional mathematics consultant (10 males). It could be argued that position held (teacher, principal, consultant) influenced teachers who espoused a socio-constructivist view to mathematics assessment. By examining the Linear term which is also significant across position categories (Table 5.4.14), and taking under consideration the means plot (Figure 5.4.5), it can be concluded that the socio-constructivist orientation to mathematics assessment decreases between the teacher and principal categories and increases between the principal and consultant categories (Figure 5.4.5).

Table 5.4.14
ANOVA (Position held)

				df	F	Sig.
REGR factor 1	Between Groups	Combined		2	5.042	.007
		Linear Term	Weighted	1	5.530	.019
			Deviation	1	4.555	.033
	Within Groups			365		
	Total			367		

From Figure 5.4.5 it can be seen that the socio-constructivist view of mathematics assessment was more prevalent among teachers than among consultants, principals and vice-principals.

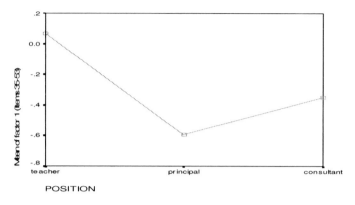

Figure 5.4.5. Means Plot (Position held)

To examine the differences across the three teachers' positions in this study (teacher, principal and mathematics consultant) Scheffe pair-wise comparisons were performed (Table 5.4.15).

Table 2.4.15
Multiple Comparisons-Scheffe (Postgraduate studies)

			Sig.
Dependent Variable	(I) POSITION	(J) POSITION	
REGR factor 1	teacher	principal	.013

The results of this analysis showed that teachers' and principals' views differ significantly with regard to a socio-constructivist orientation to mathematics assessment (Table 5.4.15). In addition, the Levene test for homogeneity of variances for Factor 1 (Table 5.4.16) is not significant (p>.05), indicating that the assumption has not been violated.

Table 5.4.16
Test of Homogeneity of Variances (Position held)

	Levene Statistic	df1	df2	Sig.
REGR factor 1	.772	2	365	.463

Postgraduate studies

The ANOVA summary table (Table 5.4.17) shows that the variable *Postgraduate studies* was significant for one of the three factors – Factor 1: *A socio-constructivist orientation to mathematics assessment* ($F_{(2, 414)}=3.164$ p=.043). By examining the Linear term which is also significant across the years of experience at Junior High school (Table 5.4.17), it can be concluded that the socio-constructivist orientation to mathematics assessment increases consistently (Figure 5.4.6) across teachers' postgraduate qualifications. Of interest is the finding that teachers with Ph.D. degrees have the lowest means for Factor 1 as compared to teachers holding a Masters degree and a first degree in mathematics. To examine the differences across the three levels of qualifications (Ph.D., Masters and 4 year mathematics degree) further, Scheffe pair-wise comparisons were performed. The results of this analysis showed no clear trend and no discernible pattern.

Table 5.4.17
ANOVA (Postgraduate studies)

				df	F	Sig.
REGR factor 1	Between Groups	(Combined)		2	3.164	.043
		Linear Term	Weighted	1	4.225	.040
			Deviation	1	2.102	.148
	Within Groups			412		
	Total			414		

In addition, the Levene test for homogeneity of variances for Factor 1 (Table 5.4.18) is not significant (p>.05), indicating that the assumption has not been violated.

Table 5.4.18
Test of Homogeneity of Variances (Postgraduate studies)

	Levene Statistic	df1	df2	Sig.
REGR factor 1	.564	2	412	.569

From the means plot (Figure 5.4.6) it can be seen that the socio-constructivist view of mathematics assessment was more prevalent among teachers with Masters and 4 year mathematics degrees than among teachers with Ph.D. degrees in mathematics education.

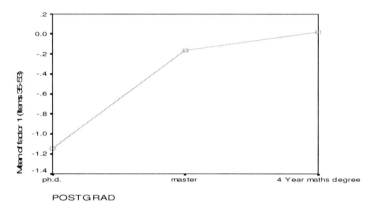

Figure 5.4.6. Means Plot (Postgraduate studies)

A tenable explanation for this finding is that a number of the Ph.D. degrees had been of a theoretical nature in pure mathematics, the history of mathematics or other topics, which bear no direct relevance to mathematics education.

5.5 Chapter summary

Teachers hold beliefs towards the nature of mathematics, as well as towards the learning and teaching of mathematics. It can be conjectured that teachers' beliefs influence their teaching in many ways. There is evidence from this study that there are teachers who espouse sets of beliefs that might be described as 'transmission' beliefs, teachers who espouse sets of beliefs that could be described as 'socio-constructivist' and teachers who espouse a generally non-traditional (alternative) orientation to teaching and learning mathematics. As well as the evidence from interviews with teachers, there is support for the view that teachers' reflection on their classroom experiences can shape and influence their beliefs. Particular emphasis needs to be placed on investigating the effect of classroom experiences on the evaluation and reorganisation of teacher beliefs and the effect of this reorganisation on what occurs in the mathematics classroom.

It is my contention that in attempting to transform current transmission-orientated teaching practices, an understanding of the complex topology of the region where teachers' espoused and enacted sets of beliefs intersect is of paramount importance. Taking under consideration the recent interest being expressed by the mathematics education community on the importance of values in teaching and on their interrelationship to belief systems, It is likely that such an understanding will constitute the 'fulcrum' of both future reforms and the delivery of in-service and pre-service programs.

It could be argued that the data reported in this study illustrate that teachers seem sensitive to, and aware of, socio-constructivist theories about the learning and teaching of mathematics, and that they adjust their beliefs about mathematics and themselves as teachers of mathematics to reflect prevailing societal norms. The findings on teachers' beliefs and expectations reported in this study invite further investigation as to whether the transition from traditional to alternative views about mathematics and mathematics teaching and learning, constitutes a smooth continuous process or there exists a deep chasm between the dominant paradigms.

CHAPTER 6
Case studies: The work of Ann and Tom

6.1 Introduction

This chapter focuses on the work of two Greek teachers fictitiously named in this study as Ann and Tom. It does draw on their own words as well as on detailed analyses of their lessons, my field notes, and pre- and post-instructional interviews with the three teachers. The purpose of this chapter is to provide answers for both the first and third research questions of the study (Chapter 3, pages 48-49), by exploring the interrelationships between espoused beliefs held by mathematics teachers and their beliefs in practice and through a description of factors that influence and shape those beliefs. It was anticipated that by attempting to interpret the nature of two veteran mathematics teachers' beliefs and the factors which influence them, it would be possible to develop a framework that would lead to the establishment of professional development programs which will inform teachers of the impact that beliefs have on everyday practice both for novice and experienced instructors of mathematics.

The material in this chapter is drawn from extensive audio taped interviews, some centered on the teacher concerned watching the videotaped lessons with me, and others describing my comments on each teacher's videotaped lessons, based on a detailed pre-instructional interview on the two teachers' case histories as well as their beliefs about mathematics, mathematics teaching, mathematics learning and assessment. Where appropriate, comparison is made with the data in Chapter 5. The method of data collection and analysis has been discussed in Chapter 3. In the following sections the work of each case study teacher will be described in detail.

6.2 The work of Ann

Introducing Ann

Ann is in her late forties and has been teaching in the Greek State school system for twenty-two years, the last nine in her current coeducational senior high school. She is a veteran teacher having taught at schools with students from low socio-economic backgrounds as well as in middle class suburbs. Her current school is in a middle class suburb. Ann holds a four-year Bachelor of Science degree, with a major in pure mathematics, and a Master of Mathematics Education degree. Ann was selected from a pool of six mathematics teachers (3M, 3F) nominated by their principals (Chapter 3, p. 64). At the culmination of the process only four (2M, 2F) teachers agreed to participate in the qualitative component of the study. One of the female participants decided to withdraw from the study soon after the first videotaped session, and one of the male participants did not wish to participate in the post-instructional interview, rendering that case study incomplete.

Ann spent her own childhood at a State High school and she described herself as having been a very good student of mathematics who initially wanted to study Architecture but did not gain enough points for the School of Engineering, which was her first preference, so she opted for The School of Science, which was her second preference. She described her own mathematics teachers as a bad influence on her decision not to choose mathematics teaching as her first preference. In her words:

> *I did not want to become a mathematics teacher, I think that at that time of my life I hated the mathematics profession, since I used to think that schooling was oppressive and anachronistic and my teachers were authoritative, inflexible and unapproachable.*

(Teachers' responses to interview questions appear in italics throughout the chapter, whereas the full interview may be found in Appendix F1). Ann has taught Years 10-12 for many years and the year the study took place she was teaching Year 10 and 11 classes. The video taped sessions took place in her Year 10 classes. She claimed that she loves teaching mathematics and that she was wrong about her initial feelings towards the profession:

> *My teaching experience helped me realise that I love teaching, one reason being that I have enough freedom to do things the way I want to in my classes.*

Ann prefers working with groups in her classes and she stated that the idea of group teaching came along through her experiences as an active member of a socialist party. She has firm beliefs about teamwork as a means of exchanging ideas and learning effectively in a mathematics (classroom) community of practice:

Initially it happened spontaneously. We tried (in class) whatever occurred to me, in a spontaneous way. We experimented with various ideas, models and activities in class. I even had kids set and correct their own tests. The result was that a number of kids would stay back after school preparing (in teams) for next day's lessons.

Ann recalled that in the schools where she taught she was initially alone in using team work in her early years of teaching, and she also had to face strong opposition from teachers and parents who thought that her teaching approaches were inadequate for preparing their children for University entrance exams, when compared to the traditional chalk and talk approaches the other mathematics teachers were using.

Twenty two years on, and her enjoyment of learning and the desire to acquire more knowledge that can be used to become a better teacher were obvious throughout many parts of the interview. Ann admitted having pedagogical knowledge gaps as well as mathematics content knowledge gaps, due to the fact that her University classes were very theoretical and not related to mathematics teaching. Ann commented that during the first few years of her teaching career she was more comfortable teaching geometry rather than algebra and calculus, because she felt more competent in teaching geometry:

I used to think that I could comprehend geometry better than any other mathematical area. I recall that in the early years of my teaching career I used to place more emphasis on geometry in my teaching. When I felt the need to relax I would solve a geometry problem, like a crossword.

Ann commented that she enjoys teaching now more than ever and that she becomes involved in theatrical productions and environmental work at school. Ann has visited other European countries as part of Teaching Fellowship exchange programs, where she found out how other European countries' Education systems operate and since then she has adapted a number of the approaches she came across, to fit her own teaching style. In her spare time, Ann enjoys reading, gardening and walking. She has worked hard to introduce to a discourse of collaborative work to a Year 10 class, although for the majority of mathematics teachers in the secondary school where Ann works, group work in mathematics is seen as inferior to the dominant transmission view of learning.

The topic of the videotaped session under consideration was linear equations and linear programming. Ann had students engage primarily in collaborative work and her teaching was consistent with her espoused beliefs regarding the value of a socio-constructivist orientation (collaborative learning) to teaching and learning mathematics, believing that students always benefit by discussing their solutions to mathematical problems with each other, and that an effective way to teach mathematics is to provide students with interesting problems to investigate in small groups. Ann attempted to justify the consistency between her espoused and enacted beliefs during the interview by claiming that her political and ideological affiliation and involvement shaped her beliefs about collaborative learning and that it has greatly influenced her teaching practice.

In an attempt to highlight the consistency between Ann's espoused and enacted beliefs I have juxtaposed in Table 6.2.1 small but fairly representative sections of Ann's interview and video transcripts along with a sample of questionnaire items which coincide with her beliefs about the nature of mathematics, mathematics learning and mathematics teaching.

The transcript from the videotaped session shows Ann's attempts to encourage further inter-group and intra-group interactions and to emphasise the importance of justifying the mathematical statements that students make, as well as to show her students that the outcomes of collaborative work are valued by the (classroom) community of practice. The interview transcript shows Ann's satisfaction about the success of her efforts to implement a collaborative learning environment that reportedly went beyond her classroom boundaries.

Table 6.2.1
Sample of Ann's statements from video and interview transcripts along with relevant questionnaire items

	NATURE OF MATHS	MATHS LEARNING		MATHS TEACHING
QUESTIONNAIRE ITEM NUMBER	**ITEM 3**: Justifying the mathematical statements that a person makes is an extremely important part of mathematics	**ITEM 13**: Students can learn more mathematics together than by themselves	**ITEM 14**: Students always benefit by discussing their solutions to mathematical problems with each other	**ITEM 38**: An effective way to teach mathematics is to provide students with interesting problems to investigate in small groups
ANN'S VIDEOTAPED SESSION	…Lets discuss it further. … Your graph is neither a curve nor a straight line… What's your graph then?	OK, This group has done it! What about that group? Has the group done it? The group here did it as well………… Why has this group drawn points only? Why did you join them afterwards? At the beginning you had just points. Why did you then rush to join them? Why?	Let me see as well what you have done. Let's discuss it. For what reason… … Talk it over with your mates before you finish. Have you all arrived to a conclusion? Talk it over. Have you discussed it with your mates? Have you got an answer?	You have all done the same thing. The group here. Yianni, isn't that right? Good. The third group has tried it out as well but they didn't manage to draw a straight line. Let's spend some time and discuss it.
ANN'S INTERVIEW	… In my opinion, the best thing is that students can do almost anything on their own, even teach and assess their peers. They can play my part in many different ways; they can even prepare a test and assess it on their own, something my students successfully did. At the end I tried to organise their collaborative learning and even that was successful, that is, when students stayed after school, they worked in groups without my guidance, preparing their work for the next day.			

Beliefs about mathematics

Interview questions were divided in four sections, in concert with the four sections of the questionnaire survey used in the quantitative part of the study (Chapter 3, p. 62). In this part of the interview discussion focused on Ann's espoused beliefs about mathematics:

> Interviewer *(I)*: What do you think mathematics is all about?
>
> Ann (A): *Mathematics is a cultural by-product that has been acquired by the human race through the centuries. We can use mathematics to communicate with nature and to understand natural phenomena as well as the interaction between the human being and these phenomena.*

Ann held a non-traditional view about mathematics stating that mathematics is not a static collection of unrelated facts but a dynamic science, which evolved as a result of the enculturation of the human race and can be used to improve our understanding of natural phenomena.

> I: What do you think about school mathematics?
>
> A: *The mathematics we teach at school does not seem to be serving any other purpose except preparing the kids for exams. In the past, we could be more flexible in our teaching and we could improvise, but nowadays education policy makers, as well as most students and parents, think that the purpose of schooling is to prepare students for University entrance exams. I feel that I am actually doing a lot less in class nowadays than what I used to do two decades ago. The fact is that lately, I too feel that I have a responsibility to prepare them for the final exams, since it is very important for the kids and their families.*

Ann was disappointed by the way school mathematics is being taught, and by the strong emphasis being placed on the preparation of students for final exams. She holds a strong belief against mathematics being used primarily as a means to gain entry to University studies.

> I: Which factors do you consider to have a significant influence on your beliefs about mathematics?
>
> A: *When I was at the University I recall attending a Differential Geometry lecture. I had decided to be a good student so I sat on one of the front rows desks in the lecture amphitheatre and started taking notes. The Lecturer started explaining by using a wooden language full of symbols and incomprehensible jargon. I was very disappointed and I remember that I*

felt the same way very often during my University years. The greatest
disappointment was that we could pass the subjects by just memorising the
lecture material. Then one day I happened to start reading a philosophy
book written by members of the Academy of Sciences of the (then) Soviet
Union. There were a number of instances in the book were mention was
made to how Differential Geometry, Dynamics and Relativity could be
used to understand philosophy. I got the shock of my life realising that the
book offered a different – and most importantly comprehensible -
perspective of topics that I could not understand at University. From that
point onwards I started searching for answers. I wanted to find out more
about what geometry is and how is it related to dynamics, via the use of
calculus.

Ann was disappointed by the fact that mathematics university teachers
considered mathematics as an unrelated collection of facts and rules and as a
static and immutable knowledge with objective truth.

Another factor that had a significant influence on Ann's beliefs about
mathematics and its teaching was one of her mathematics teachers, a person Ann
described as a poet as well as a mathematics teacher. In her own words:

I remember J.D. who was reciting poems when teaching mathematics. I
was really shaken by his teaching methods, his attitude, and his
personality. That was definitely a time that I experienced a cognitive and a
cultural shock. I said to my self, wait a minute there is something important
about this teacher and his approach. It really touched me. These
experiences had an impact on my professional life.

Ann also mentioned that her political ideology and affiliations played a
significant role in shaping her teaching approaches:

When I found out that Marx before endeavouring in his treatise called
"The Capital" had to extensively study the applications of the derivative in
economics, I realised how important calculus and its applications were,
when used in other sciences.

Ann appeared to have experienced a cognitive shift when she started
exploring the links between philosophy and mathematics. She recalled that it was
at that particular point of time that she started wondering about what role societal
and cultural factors play in mathematics education. Ann also claimed that it was

at that time she begun to acknowledge that mathematics is a cultural as well as a scientific tool.

Beliefs about mathematics learning

In this part of the interview discussion focused on Ann's espoused beliefs about mathematics learning:

I: What can a good mathematics student do?

A: *I would like the kids to be able to work on their own and in teams, to be able to do problem solving and modelling and to be able to use mathematical proofs in their work. A good mathematics student (in Years 10-12) should be able to use abstractions and to generalise. In my classes I would like my students to be meticulous and conscientious, to work hard and persist on set tasks irrespectively of the fact of getting the answers or not. In addition, I expect a good student to perform well on tests as well as in class.*

When discussing good students Ann stated that students should be motivated, they should have a desire to learn and to be autonomous learners. Ann held a strong view about cooperative learning. Students in her classes were expected to be involved in cooperative problem solving and modelling activities, since learning is about achieving shared knowledge.

I: What accounts for the differences between a good and a poor mathematics student?

A: *A good mathematics student should be organised and to know how to study. In mathematics, the process is more important than the product. The student needs to be motivated, to have a desire to learn and to be an autonomous learner.*

According to Ann, motivating students to realise that mathematics means more than just preparing for final exams empowers them, and may result in better performance in mathematics. Ann stated that a fundamental condition for improved performance in mathematics on the part of the students is a desire to learn. Participation in meaningful activities was the key to success in mathematics according to Ann.

I: Is it possible for a teacher to help a poorly performing mathematics student become a good mathematics student?

A: *I certainly believe that a student's performance can improve and that the teacher's role is of paramount importance. If the teacher can find ways to motivate her students and to help them realise that it is worthy to make an effort to learn mathematics – and not only to pass the exams – then there is a possibility that the student's performance may improve. Each student needs to realise what interests her more and that a number of everyday applications incorporate some serious mathematical thinking. I would therefore conclude that the teacher of mathematics could help a poorly performing mathematics student become a good mathematics student, if and only if she is able to motivate her students to be systematic and organised, and instil in them the desire to learn.*

Students' learning of mathematics depends, according to Ann, primarily on the learner. Ann reiterated her strong contention that students learn mathematics through active participation in meaningful activities.

I: How do you define comprehension of a mathematical concept? topic?

A: *There is no simple answer to that question. Being able to recall the required facts and algorithms when necessary represents evidence that understanding of a concept has taken place in mathematics. When students can apply their knowledge in contexts other than the ones presented in their textbooks, is another piece of evidence that understanding has taken place. To be able to use her knowledge and skills at any time, to model any given context, and to have developed an inquiring mind, is additional evidence that mathematical understanding has taken place.*

Applying mathematics in various contexts and utilising their skills in modelling real life situations and the development of an inquiring mind are Ann's criteria that understanding has taken place in mathematics. At the same time however, Ann felt that students should both understand and master skills and algorithms. Ann espoused a socio-constructivist view to mathematics learning, one grounded on her firm belief that all students can learn mathematics and that mathematics learning is the result of students making connections and interpreting and organising the information gained from experiences.

I: Which factors do you consider to have a significant influence on your beliefs about mathematics learning?

A: *A number of factors shaped my beliefs about mathematics learning including my postgraduate studies. I firmly believe that a teacher must be a cultivated and open-minded person with rich experiences. One factor that I*

can single out as having a profound impact in shaping my beliefs about
mathematics learning was my ideological stance and my involvement in the
day-to-day business of political parties.

Being involved in ideological work in a progressive party's educational
committee for many years, had a profound impact on shaping Ann's beliefs that
collaboration among students and between the teacher and her students is the best
way to go about mathematics learning.

Beliefs about mathematics teaching

In this part of the interview discussion focused on the interviewees'
espoused beliefs about mathematics teaching:

I: Could you describe the way you teach mathematics?

A: *I would like all students in my classes to make progress and to attempt*
to maximise their potential in mathematics. I believe that even the weakest
students are able to master the basic concepts of mathematics. I try to
answer as many of their questions as possible in class. My classes are
structured around those simple principles. If I can persuade someone, who
for various reasons does not believe that she is a good mathematics
student, to be involved in the work we do in class, then I consider my
teaching successful. On many occasions, I have been taken by surprise by
students whom I considered very weak in mathematics but they performed
very well as soon as their queries were fully explained to them.

Ann promoted knowledge sharing and encouraged students to actively
participate in their learning. She clearly valued process over product and strived to
conduct her classes in a non-threatening environment.

I: What about memorisation? What is its role in mathematics teaching?

A: *During my teaching career I have gone through a number of phases*
regarding my beliefs about the role of memorisation. At first I used to think
that it was not a very important skill in mathematics learning. Having
assessed a number of students however, who did not know the tables even
in Years 10 or 11, I realised that there are aspects of mathematics that
must be memorised at various stages of mathematics learning, so that they
won't become the reason for the emergence of cognitive obstacles later.
Students need to understand the basic mechanisms in various mathematical
algorithms and they should therefore memorise some aspects of them, if

they are going to use them effectively in problem solving and modelling investigations or whenever the need arises.

Ann strived to teach topics by making connections both between concepts and topics. She also emphasised understanding over memorisation by promoting learning via problem solving and modelling activities.

I: Where did you learn to teach mathematics that way? Have you ever had graduate and/or in-service courses on how to teach mathematics?

A: *Life taught me (she laughs). By that, I mean that I had to learn many things on my own during my teaching career. I am currently participating at a regional mathematics teachers' cluster and I think that there are some positive outcomes because we discuss our daily problems and we formulate common strategies for more effective teaching. It is very important for my professional life. As far as graduate courses are concerned, I feel that I have learned a few new things in my Masters course.*

Cooperation among teachers in the region offered a platform for shared understanding and the emergence of a framework of common values, according to Ann. The impact of professional development did not seem to have had a great influence on shaping Ann' beliefs about teaching. Her daily experiences appeared to have strongly affected her beliefs about mathematics teaching.

I: Have you ever tried something different? Why?

A: *Firstly I believe that a number of traditional teaching techniques are outdated and need to be replaced by new teaching approaches. Secondly I am constantly trying to discover new approaches and educational environments that will enable the kids to fully develop as mathematics apprentices. Thirdly I believe that contemporary teaching ideas based on constructivism have given me a new purpose in teaching mathematics. I have learned a lot from my students too. If I had something in mind and tried it in class, the interaction with my students created a dialectic relationship from which a number of unexpected new ideas kept emerging.*

Ann's firm socio-constructivist stance about mathematics teaching and learning was further reinforced by her statements 'I am constantly trying to discover new approaches and educational environments that will enable the kids to fully develop as mathematics apprentices' and 'the interaction with my students created a dialectic relationship from which a number of unexpected new ideas kept emerging'. Ann valued communication and encouraged a continuous dialogue between all members of her classes.

I: What happened while attempting to introduce a new approach?

A: *I have encountered a number of problems by practising contemporary teaching methods because students are very apprehensive about their potential to enhance learning. Some students do not perceive them to be as effective as the traditional chalk and talk, and paper and pencil techniques with which they are accustomed to. Senior students who are accustomed to working individually find it very difficult to work in groups. Some students worry that their efforts will not be appreciated by their teacher, partly because they like to be protagonists in class and partly because the fear that the outcome of group's work won't be their own work alone. They also worry about how they are going to be assessed in groups and the fact that the work of their group may not be awarded top marks. Some of the students take a long time to get used to contemporary teaching techniques. The fact of the matter is however, that contemporary techniques help even the weakest students to participate in classroom work and to learn more effectively.*

Unprovoked opposition to innovative approaches was seen by Ann as an unexpected obstacle to her attempts to introduce novel teaching-learning approaches in her classes. She experienced resistance to cooperative learning from her own students who felt that they would not be rewarded for their individual efforts if they participated in group work. This is an indication of the adverse impact the system may have on students' attitudes to learning mathematics, when it is founded on traditional chalk-and-talk approaches, resulting in individual efforts and competitiveness being valued and rewarded as the approved approach to learning mathematics. Some parents expressed their opposition to cooperative learning, according to Ann (in another part of the interview), believing that their children would not be as competitively prepared for final exams as they would be with traditional methods.

I: Grouping: on what basis? Why?

A: *I started using group work in 1983. I recall that I wanted every single student to be involved in class work instead of having them passively listening to me. I (then) thought that if the class was divided in small groups then I could have a small community in each group with its*

potential to differentiate among its members and with its leaders
unknowingly acting as my assistants - without letting the class knowing
about it. All this because I will not be satisfied except when all students
participate in classroom activities.

The promotion of a community environment in Ann's classes, with its potential to encourage active participation, brainstorming, ideas exchange and to maximise each student's potential in mathematics learning, has been the driving force behind her cooperative teaching approach. The promotion of leadership qualities is also evident in her approach.

I: Probe – how do you select group membership? Do you change the groups? Why?)

A: *I allow students the freedom to decide the group they want to participate to, because I want them to be comfortable and to feel that they own the process. The less I impose the best. I intervene of course once I feel that it is necessary. I will provide an example from last year. Two of the groups the students formed, were consisting of weak students without any strong leaders or good students in them, and I felt that there were going to be problems with them. Gradually the members of those groups realised that they needed help and when I intervened and modified the group membership, things started working and a cooperative spirit emerged. I do intervene and modify group membership if in the process I realise that it is not going to work. It is a shared responsibility. I think that my approach to group work was initially experiential but it gradually became more theory laden as I started searching for theoretical evidence to support my group work approach.*

Promoting student autonomy and shared responsibility, and reducing teacher intervention to a minimum, which are fundamental ingredients in the development of a community of inquiry, was the overriding learning-teaching approach in Ann's classes.

I: What do you consider the most important characteristics of quality teaching?

A: *Getting in the students' shoes in class helps me appreciate some of the difficulties students encounter. I think that by putting students in the leading role provides adequate incentive for them to participate in class activities promotes the desire to own the process and enables them to experience that what they do is important. I consider that the development of each student's self-esteem, as well as the feeling of belonging in a group, are important elements of quality teaching. I strive to create a classroom environment, which promotes an understanding that the individual's interests and the group's interests are not always competitive. After all cooperation is more effective that competition.*

Ann's criteria of quality teaching were simple yet effective in providing incentives and in inspiring her students to be active learners: (i) placing students in the leading role provided adequate incentive for them to participate in class activities and promoted the desire to own the process and enabled them to realise that what they do is important. (ii) the development of each student's self-esteem, as well as the feeling of belonging in a group, were important elements of quality teaching. (iii) the creation of a classroom environment, which promoted an understanding that the individual's interests and the group's interests were not always in competition.

I: Which factors do you consider have had a significant influence on your ability to teach mathematics?

A: The first factor is that mathematical content knowledge is of paramount importance in being able to teach mathematics. It is necessary but not sufficient however. Teaching is not simply a job – it is a calling. It requires a combination of many skills. The classroom is a community of young people and the teacher should be knowledgeable about students' developmental stages, she should have developed strategies of how to guide them to own their learning via effective activities, and of how to develop inquiring minds in her classes. The second factor is therefore that didactical, psychological and pedagogical knowledge from the part of the teacher is of great importance.

Ann claimed that her ability to teach mathematics has been influenced by her beliefs about two teaching prerequisites (and her desire to improve on both): that the teacher should have a strong base of mathematical content knowledge, and at the same time be knowledgeable of contemporary didactical, psychological and pedagogical approaches.

I: Which factors do you consider have had a significant influence on your beliefs about mathematics teaching?

A: I believe that the education system limits the teacher's options to innovate and experiment in her classes. I sometimes feel that I have to apologise to my colleagues and to my superiors for attempting to introduce innovations in my teaching. The system - as it is today organised – forbids the teacher to use any approaches that are not 'proven'. Sometimes I feel like an outsider having to overcome - on a daily basis - time constraints, peer pressure, overt and covert opposition or disapproval from the administration, and the fact that I have to move all the desks back to their initial configuration (in rows) once I finish my classes which are based on group work. On top of that there may be opposition and disapproval from some parents and students who believe that schooling means teaching to the test and that a collaborative approach is not the best way for individual students to achieve top marks.

Ann's beliefs about mathematics teaching seem to have grown out of a desire to oppose a stagnant and inflexible system, which limits the teachers' options to innovate; to try new approaches and to strive to develop an active learning and cooperative teaching environment in her classes.

I: Which factors may explain the existence of inconsistencies between espoused beliefs and beliefs in practice?

A: *The first factor concerns the expectations of the education system that could sometimes act in ways that inhibit innovations. The second factor concerns the things you are used to do that turn out to be a lot easier than introducing innovations in your daily routine. The third factor is the fact that it is very difficult to overcome every obstacle on a daily basis in order to do what you believe is the best practice. The fourth factor is the fact that I do not have my own mathematics classroom. The fifth factor is the fact that regional mathematics consultants are more decorative than anything useful. We never get to meet them and discuss our concerns. The sixth factor concerns my family obligations, which in practice drastically limits my available time. The seventh factor concerns the lack of communication with some of my students, since they have been bred to think that schooling means teaching to the test. The eighth factor is the fact that I do not have all the required recourses at school. The ninth factor concerns the fact that the system does not provide any incentives for innovative teaching practice and the tenth factor is the fact that there is no teaching evaluation or appraisal, which could indirectly force me to be more prepared on a daily basis and to perform even better in class.*

Ann listed ten factors in her attempt to explain the existence of inconsistencies between espoused beliefs and beliefs in practice. Most of them had to do with the difficulty of introducing and sustaining innovative teaching practices in a system which had solid traditional foundations and where teaching was seen primarily as a public servant's job. The absence of a systemic teacher evaluation/appraisal system, and the lack of support for innovative teaching approaches, point to an impaired vision of education by Regional and State educational policy makers.

Beliefs about mathematics assessment

In this part of the interview discussion focused on Ann's espoused beliefs about mathematics assessment:

I: On what criteria do you select assessment methods for a topic/term/year?

A: *My assessment in mathematics is based on firm beliefs. The criteria I am using to assess my students are the following: Class involvement, keeping a journal of mathematical activities, taking notes, task involvement, degree of understanding, open-ended questions, problem solving and modelling performance, memorisation of some aspects of the course, participation in group work, student self-assessment and project work performance. It all depends on time constraints, appropriate planning and on administrative support.*

Ann assessed her students primarily via contemporary assessment methods but she felt that she also had to use traditional methods of assessment (tests, exams) in order to prepare her students for University entrance exams. She held a firm belief about problem solving and modelling as a vehicle for developing mathematical skills and she espoused a strong commitment to the development of investigative skills by all of her students.

Ann's classroom

Ann had five mathematics classes the year the study took place: A Year 10 Algebra class and a Year 10 Geometry class, a Year 11 Algebra and Calculus class, a Year 11 Geometry class, and a Year 12 Mathematical Methods class.

The lesson that is discussed in detail in this section took place in a Year 10 Algebra class. The twenty-two students who make up the class were 15-16 years of age. There were twelve girls and ten boys.

The desks in the classroom were arranged in groups of four or five and most students were at an angle or side on to the blackboard. The teacher's desk was near the front and in the middle of the classroom. There was a computer, with a couple of disks; an OH projector with transparencies that were used for the presentation of the activity; folders of teacher reference material and a small bookshelf. There was also a notice board along one wall and the classroom had many windows along two walls providing plenty of natural light.

Detailed examination of a single lesson

A single lesson of mathematics is the focus of this section. The lesson took place after a week spent observing and pretending to record in order to accustom students to the equipment. When the actual taping took place students took almost no notice of me or of the equipment. The dialogue has been transcribed as completely and accurately as the equipment would permit, by professional transcribers and double-checked by me. A professional translator, an Englishman who has lived and worked in Athens for the past thirty years, completed the transcription process. He translated all Greek transcripts to English, which were also double-checked by me.

The format of presentation is in two columns. The text of the lesson is in the left hand column, and the analysis, drawing on my criteria (indicated by symbols in brackets, e.g. (TPC 1)) for teaching practice (Appendix C4) to describe the teacher's behaviours and beliefs, is on the right hand column. The text is broken at various points to allow the teacher's voice to be heard, as she made comments while watching the taped lessons a week after her lessons were videotaped.

The aim of the lesson was an introduction to quadratic functions via a modeling activity.

ACTUAL CLASS	RESEARCHER'S COMMENTS
Teacher: We must complete a table of values, which will connect the side of a square......, and I told you to take four values each for the side and to give the corresponding values for the area.	**Provides modeling activities (TPC1 = Teaching Practice Contemporary 1)**
Teacher: What problem do we have here? We have a problem in completing the table, why? How many empty cells does it have?	**Places tasks in context**
Student 1: I don't know.	
Teacher: What don't you know? What do you mean! The Team here has done it, the Team over there? Has it done it over here? It's done it.... children; a square has sides, doesn't it? And it has a certain area, how long can the side of a square be, Annie? However long you want it to be! How long would you like the side of a square to be, how long, how many meters?	**Reinforces collaborative approach and Encourages communication (TPC5 or TPC11)** **Encourages students to take initiative**
Student 1: Two.	
Teacher: It will be two meters, OK, let's assume then that............	
Teacher: The number, how much is this?	
Student? Four?	
Teacher: Four! You're asking me, eh? Do the other children agree?	**Questioning to clarify understanding**
Class: Yes!	
Teacher: It's four. You tell me, Maria, one of the values given to the last side.	
Maria: Eh! Seven.	
Teacher: Seven, and what area did you find?	
Maria: 49.	
Teacher: 49, good. Elias, you tell me the last-but-one side.	
Elias: Yes.	
Maria: Shall I say it? Six.	

Teacher: Six, and what area did you get?

Maria: 36

Teacher: 36, very good. You, George, the first side you got.

George: 1.

Teacher: 1, and what is the area?

George: 1.

Teacher: 1! Yes! Does the whole class agree, children, with the corresponding values that we have given?

Class: Yes.

Attempts to reach consensus
(which is an essential part of a
collaborative activity, according to
Anna's interview)

While watching the tape, Ann explained her usual pedagogical strategy of providing incentives for students to attend to her instructions in class, which reflect both management strategies (keeping in touch with individuals while occupying the class) and the preference for group work, which she also expressed in the pre-instructional interview (section 6.2).

> *I have come to realise that for many activities which we (teachers) consider simple, e.g. asking students to construct a table of values and substitute the appropriate values for the area function, that type of activity requires a lot of guidance and special care by the teacher, in order to facilitate conceptual understanding of the topic under consideration. The participation of all students, especially of those who experience difficulties in understanding a particular topic, is of paramount importance in my classes. It is very important to insist that every single student fully participates and contributes to the discussions. I insist that each student attempts the set tasks individually and then discuss them with the group. I want to have students who take initiatives and do not blindly follow the work of their group. Once I realise that something has not be fully understood by all members of each group and I have to intervene and discuss it or explain it, or when I realise that something is understood but I want it to become shared knowledge, we can then move on, and we can all progress to the next stage. It is at that point that I draw the same diagram or table on the board so that we can all work together from that point onwards.*

Teacher: Good, now next to your work sheet you have a system of axes, I'll do it on the board as well and it's here on the OH transparency too, the values that I have on the board are based on the values that we took from all of you, one over here, one over there, and I want you to go and put for me on the system of axes here, putting the side here and the area here, on the basis of these values. Not your own values but the values the whole class has agreed on.

Whole class guidance on how to proceed with agreed-on outcomes

Indicates (+stresses) that collaborative results are valued products

Class: Which values?

Teacher: Those which we have on the board, where the horizontal axis is, you know what you'll do, I'm telling you, using this table of values, to draw a graph using the axis.

Practical demonstration of the teacher's belief on the importance of clarifying goals and methods

Teacher: Yes, very good, discuss it with the other children over there, discuss it a while, let me see, yes, yes, good..... Put these relationships on to the system of coordinates. OK children listen to me. On the basis of the results so far, we have the following results, first we get, children, I took the values here first of all. I am not sure about all but most of you have done this, in other words you substituted the one here, and then you substituted the next value, which is the value two, and then you substituted the value six and then you substituted seven into the function's formula. This is what I notice you have done, and here you took the values using a slightly different unit, that is, the system you used is not

Not enough wait time provided by the teacher (prefers to answer herself)

Has students clarify and Justify their ideas orally And in writing (TPC12)

Refers to prior learning (vaguely)

Offers her own interpretation of progress so far (for shared meaning)

orthonormal but orthogonal, as we said once, namely, some of you here and here (*shows on the board*) have a slightly different unit. I don't know all, with the 10, 20, 30, 40, 50 until there then, here, and I noticed that three views have been offered as to how this relationship will be represented on a graph. And the first view that has been offered by many students connects these here (*shows on the board*) correctly, the second view takes the point it goes here where the point of the next one is, which is the 6, it goes to the 36 somewhere here (*works on the board*) and the next view goes somewhere there and uses this point. So the first answer of these here, children, are these points here; the second answer which has been given is the curve which will connect, you have all done, the team here, isn't that so, Yiannis, good, and the third team tried but it didn't come out so good so as to create a line, let's discuss why and I'll start to round off..... Yours didn't come out either as a curve or a line, what did you get?

Student 2: From the beginning of the axes get a ..... And then we get a straight line.

Teacher: Let me have a look as well at what you've done. Let's discuss it a bit, children, let's discuss it a bit, and for what reason do you think,

Anthony, that the result of this relationship must be a line?

Anthony:...................

Encourages discussion but not clear if in groups or whole class

Provides snapshots of her own understanding in an attempt to break barriers and build
A community of practice climate

Uses everyday language for better communication

Poses questions that engage students (TPC10) + creates an environment that respects students' ideas (TPC6)

(The video tape demonstrated that as she goes around fairly routine corrections, she asks students from various groups, presumably to keep them all alert)

Ann frequently uses everyday language in an attempt to break the barrier between teacher and student, to communicate more effectively with her students and to create a classroom environment conducive to learning. Ann's comments reveal the importance of her own standards and beliefs in determining what occurs in her classroom.

I think that it is a conscious attempt to communicate with the kids more effectively, and it could be considered as an outcome of years of experience. I possibly do it because I want to be close to my students. Yes that's why I think I am doing it; by using friendly language familiar to them I feel that I can communicate better with them.

Ann's attempts to create an environment that respects students' ideas and efforts were in concert with her familiarity with the content and curricular goals of the activity. Ann felt that it was one of the important aspects of instilling a community of inquiry spirit to her students.

A friendly environment respects the student's ideas and secondly it is the only way to find out exactly what goes on in the student's mind at that moment. It also serves the dual purpose of helping me to form the right judgment about her current understanding and it helps the student externalise her thoughts. Sometimes the teacher does not know if the student's answer is right or wrong but in case it was wrong it enables me to assess the situation and realise how she came up with that conclusion. I then move on to the next group and ask them if they have reached a common conclusion. I keep asking them did you do this or that? How did you get this result? And so on.

Teacher: Why, Pano, do you think that it must be a line? Listen, children, to what he tells me because I am going to ask you to give me your own opinions. I didn't hear you Pano, it seems to me that we have a case of direct variation here. Do you see, yes, here, do you remember the theory from Middle School? You here, why did you use only points, I didn't hear, why did you take only points

Assumption about what the students *should* know from previous years on a line..... Don't worry, eh! Why did you join them afterwards? Why in the beginning did you have only points and then you went on to join them, why?

Team 1: Because everyone else had joined them.

Teacher: The only team which had it right, and let's see, let's discuss it, joined them because all the others tried to join them.

Class: Why shouldn't we join them?

Teacher: Let's discuss it a bit. Here we said that we have 4 values on the side of a square and the corresponding values of the area, and I asked you to draw this chart as it is, to do for me its graphic representation. This chart as it is, children, gives us these points.

Let's assume then that you all took the curve. Because Yiannis recalled the form of the functions, he also recalled that it is a parabola from his Middle School classes – what a genius! - Tell me, what is the difference; what is the difference by using only these points or the whole line, which joins them? What is the difference, what differs? And why did I rush to say that it was correct, you weren't confident enough to support it.

Vicki: Perhaps if we draw the line later and draw the vertical lines from this line we'll see that the vertical ones at 3 correspond to 13.

Teacher: But this isn't correct, why can't this be correct?

Vicki: Because it might not be valid.

Investigative questioning to clarify concepts and results (TPC10)

Teacher-groups interaction and comparison of findings

Elaborates on and attempts to guide kids to make connections (TPC12)

(Irony?)

Teacher self-reflection

(TPA5)

Ann seemed to know her students and their individual needs very well. Her discussion below, and in many parts of her interview, demonstrate knowledge of learners and her personal beliefs about how to approach students and their errors and that the teacher-student relationship should be based on a sense of familiarity. In response to the researcher's prompt regarding her expression 'what a genius' as being ironical or not, Ann claimed that it was grounded on the climate of familiarity that had emerged as a result of her attitude and her classroom approaches. It is of interest to reflect upon the extent to which the interpretation of a student's behavior (or errors) may be based upon a teacher's own set of beliefs about learning and teaching.

> *Saying to one of my students 'what a genius' was not an ironical comment. We have a special relationship with my students, since I know them for years. I want to show them that I am aware of the fact that what seems like errors from an adult point of view, could be the student's current state of understanding and that as such it is not the end of the world. At some instances, I do make intentional errors and provide false starts while solving problems, because I want my students to realise that even an expert (mathematics teacher) can err and can have false starts and that it is all part of the problem solving process.*

Teacher: Because it might not be valid, the 3 might not be connected with the 13, let's say, with the vertical line, for instance. Another opinion? Anthony, what do you say?

Clarification questioning (TPC12)

Challenges students' findings in an attempt to clarify misconceptions

Anthony: I would argue that............

Teacher: You would argue for the curve, why? Let's see now. I consider then, a point on the curve here and when I bring the corresponding vertical line this goes, if I do a good graph, here at value 3 as a side of the square. I have on this side of the table of values value 3 for the side of the square? What do you say Theo?

Observes and listens to Students to assess learning (TPC13)

Theo: We don't have a straight line, the

graph is consisting only of points.

Teacher: Yes.

Theo: Because if it's the line, the parabola takes all the other points.

Teacher: They must have the other points. I said, and perhaps you haven't understood very well, I understand your reaction because you haven't understood very well, I know that you've already done this stuff in Middle School and you've got used to it and the corresponding problem directs you to a line and you're right. But I told you and I tried to explain to you about these points only, represent only these values for me graphically. Only these points give the graph of this particular table. If we take the curve, as Theo very correctly said, then the table must also contain every other point or something else.

Student: Is this necessary?

Teacher: What?

Student: For it to contain all the other points?

Provides encouragement (TPPA6) and Focuses on specific tasks and attempts to make students aware of possible paths and strategies

Encourages student Self-reflection (TPC16)

Points out and praises correct reasoning to whole class

As mentioned earlier, it is interesting to reflect upon the extent to which interpretation of a student's behavior may be based upon a teacher's own set of beliefs about learning and teaching. Ann uses many teaching episodes to reflect on and evaluate her own performance, and to individualise the process by paying attention to the slightest detail possible. The following discussion highlights how a task, which appears to be the same for all students, may have different emphases at different times and for different students.

> *My objective is to make everyone realise that I carefully observe all my*
> *students' work. I do not want some of them to feel that I desert them and I*
> *do not care if understanding has taken place or not. I am trying to make*
> *them realise that I care about their progress and that I strive for all*

students' participation in classroom activities. Take Theo's case for example. He formed the conclusion that the graph will finally be a curve, which is correct. The fact that Theo has got the result sooner than the others does not mean that everything is fine and we can move on. I won't be comfortable to continue (just with Theo) knowing that some students may fall behind.

Teacher: I told you to draw me a curve similar to this one; I want you to reflect on this, on the table of values on the axes, to visualize this relationship for me. The relationship, which the 2 have with the 4, the 7 with the 49, the 6 with the 36, and the .... (?)

Let's take a better look at the subject, it's turned up, it didn't turn up in the other section, it turns up here and gives us an opportunity. Do you remember then, so that we can proceed - proceed a little with the next question, with what your worksheet asks you to do.

Student: The point that says "can you" or further down?

Teacher: Can you represent, we've done the graph. If x is the side of a square now, x then, what is the model (law) that relates the side x with its area? When you said that the side is 3, for example, you related the 3 with the 9. Do you know the relationship? Tell us Dana.

Dana: (?)................ x squared.

Encourages the use of Imagination (TPC22)

Visualization prompt to enable accommodation of concepts

(TPC3 - Connections)

Spontaneity of instruction as 'Emerging' in order to enable kids to make connections (goes 'off' planned track)

Provides clarifications

Ann's phrase: 'I want you to attempt to visualize', prompted discussion on the utility of visualization in enabling the processes of abstraction and generalization to take place.

I use this expression frequently as a prompt. My objective is to make my students realise that there is a relationship between algebraic abstract thinking, visualization and geometrical figures. I am trying to show them that they can graphically represent the relationship they have been working with, by using visualization as an appropriate vehicle.

Ann's ability to change plans according to the situation draws on her knowledge of content and didactics, as well as on beliefs about individual and group work, and on an awareness of what needs to be done. Ann's teaching approach could be considered as offering an alternative pattern of interaction while at the same time sharing some of the characteristics with one of the two patterns of interaction in mathematics classrooms – the funnel pattern – identified by Wood (1994). According to Wood (1994) the following two patterns of interaction appear to be dominant in mathematics classrooms:

> The *funnel pattern* can generally be described as an interaction in which the teacher creates a series of questions that act to continually narrow the student's possibilities until they arrive at the correct answer. In this situation, the teacher recognizes that the student is unable respond appropriately with the correct answer, and therefore attempts to offer guiding questions for the purpose of enabling the students to solve a problem…This form of exchange always ends with a solution of the problem at hand.

> The *focus pattern* can also be described as a situation in which the essential aspects of solving a problem are brought to fore. Furthermore, this pattern of interaction can be described as one in which the teacher's inquiries act to indicate to the child the critical features of the problem that are not yet understood. Then the teacher leaves to the child the resolution of the problem. The teacher's role is one summarizing that part which is commonly thought to be shared and then drawing the student's attention to a critical point not yet understood…In this particular interaction, students always have some aspect of the problem still to solve. (Wood, 1994, p. 160)

Ann's teaching pattern, although sharing some perspectives with the focusing pattern of interaction, is not identical to it and could be called an *emerging, spontaneous or evolving pattern of interaction.* In this particular pattern the teacher changes plans and diversifies her approach in order to accommodate all her students' needs, and to achieve her own goals for a particular segment of a mathematics lesson. Her comments demonstrate her firm beliefs on using the approach when necessary.

Sometimes I am overdoing it with this pattern of interaction. When I like an idea resulting from a spontaneous diversification of a lesson, the class may spend quite a bit of time on it. It is not always easy of course. Even when an idea is interesting and we feel that the whole class would benefit from its full exploration, there are time constraints and we usually devote a full period or even a double period to it, but it is worth doing it. In that way teaching emerges from the spontaneity of the approach and kids can rip maximum benefits from it.

Teacher: Yes, if then x is the side of the square, then the area of the square is related to its side through the law x squared. The area is equal to x squared. The area of the figure whose side is x is x squared. Let me put this problem differently for you now. If I want to represent this relationship graphically on the axes. What is it that I'm asking now that is different from before and what is it that is represented differently on the graph? Could you find a general relationship between the sides?

Natalie, what values can it take? Ah! Not how many, an infinite number, what type of values can it take?

Natalie: Eh, and negative.

Teacher: And negative the side, then, the side of a square - 2, how do you imagine them?

Natalie: Only positive.

Teacher: That is, only positive. Here I notice that the values are only integers. The side, Sophie, of one can take what else, eh? Rationals, fractions, decimals only? And irrationals. Let's have a look at such an example. Tell me a decimal, 0.3. What,

Poses a different version Of the problem

(TPC 10 - questioning)

Encourages student Self-reflection (TPC 16)

Spiro, is the area of a square which has a side of 0.3?   (TPC21)

Student: 0.3, 0.9.

Teacher: 0.9?

Student: 0.09.

Teacher: And, John, give us an example of a square with an irrational side, tell me what its side will be?

John: The root of 3.

Teacher: And what would its area be?

John: 3.

Teacher: In other words, speaking generally, to return to Natalie, the values that x takes, which values can they be then? Positive and all real numbers? In other words, all the real numbers, the entire positive. Zero, shall we put 0? Eh? What do you all say? Does a square with a side of zero exist?   (TPC3 – connections)

Class: No.

Teacher: No, in our problem here we won't put 0, a little more, eh? Good, good. So, children, when we have, when we have x side of the square, x squared is its area, the x can be all the positive real values. And now I want to ask you the following: draw me a graph of the relationship as it is now, x and x squared, what will be different from the previous question? Discuss it a little in your group before completing it. Have you all decided? Eh? Discuss it. Have you discussed it among yourselves, have you answered already? Where have you done it, children? So, Aris will give us the answer, read a little louder, Aris.

Seeks teams' responses

(TPC17)
(TPP8)

Aris: (?).................

Ann consistently encourages student self-reflection and promotes student to student and teacher to student interactions, which enable students to make connections in her classes.

Teacher: OK, yes. Yes, all the values are positive values. Do we understand now the difference between the first and the second phase, children? What do we understand of the difference now? In the previous example, x took only these 4 discrete values, for these values we had 4 values of the area and the graph was the 4 points on the Cartesian plane. Now, x can assume any real positive value, and the representation of the points, the graph of this relationship is a curve, it's not a line, Pano. The values are not directly proportional, I won't get into this discussion now, we'll discuss this some other time, but you can see that the values are not directly proportional. Good. Let's go on, children, to our next topic. Listen carefully now as to what I want you to do. If I call the area x, then x is a number, which represents the area of the square. How do we obtain the relationship between the area and the side of the square? Is there anything you want us to clarify? In the question you always read it, it says it. Ah! Yes.......... (?) by root we mean square root. I'll separate the two tables of values, if I have an area and a side here and I take different values for the area, I'll find different values for the side and

Stresses importance in attending
To teacher's explanations

it is understood that if x is the area, then the side will be the square root of x Let's look back now, children, on the basis of the relationships which we have just discussed here, let's think back to the things we did in Year 8 and Year 9. Hadn't you done it? You've done it, you've done it, and you must have done something. It's impossible that you didn't do it. You don't remember it at all. Let's think back then, if all the relationships R that I have in between 2 co-varying values, and then what does R mean? I have the side x which varies its square which varies as well and accordingly provides values for the area, are these all the same or do they vary? They vary. The area in the first relationship varies of its own accord or in accordance with the values that the side takes.

Ann and the other case study teacher (Tom) often make the assumption that the kids should know some content from previous years (see interviews)

Attempts to enable kids to make connections with prior learning

Class: ....(?)

Teacher: Ah! Yes. When, therefore, I have two values both of which vary, they are variable values, the value which varies is independent of anything else, there are no rules as to what values it takes, we can give whatever values we want to the side in our first problem. I call it an independent variable and denote it usually by an x without it always having to be denoted by an x. In Physics, for example, what is the most commonly used variable, what is it? The time t!

Encourages + promotes an interdisciplinary approach (TPC18)

Class: Ah!

Teacher: When you want to find the interval, for example, on uniformly accelerating motion without an initial speed, you say that, what do you say, Harry?

$s(t)= \frac{1}{2}at^2$. What we call the relationship between time and the interval with which a moving object covers this time, then, with a uniformly accelerating motion, it is a function. Children, there is no reason as to why only the x should be the independent variable, the values of the dependent variable we denote it usually with a y and the process which relates these two, we could also use other symbols here, for example, I denote it with an f, which is the first letter of the word 'function'. This is why I say, then, that I have the function, let's say, $f(x)=x^2$. So, what do I want now, children, I'll say a couple of things because we are a running out of time and I didn't manage to finish. The function, I'll mention the term so that we don't forget it, we'll return to it in the next lesson, is not any relation. It is a special kind of a relation between two variables; it is only the relation where for each value of the independent variable of x, let's say, I can take only one value of the dependent variable y.

At home I want you to do the following exercise: take two problems from real life, from physics, from reality, from wherever you want, which have two variables, but the relationship of one will be a function

Attempts to enable kids to make connections with prior learning

Stresses importance in attending To teacher's explanations

while the other will not be a function. And secondly, in the problem, which will be the function, the values of the independent variable will not all be real numbers but only integers. Write this exercise at home. You are to find two problems. In one of them you will find a relation between two variables, which is a function and the other will not be a function, it will be a relation. And a second problem, this will be another problem of the functional relationship of such a function, yet the values of your independent variable will be integers, the problem will be one where the values are integers, OK?

Sets real life problem for home work

End of session

Ann promoted an interdisciplinary approach in her classes and set real life problems for her students to solve believing that problem solving and modeling are the most important elements of mathematics learning.

I am deliberately trying to show my students that mathematics can be used in many other scientific disciplines, by posing examples from Economics, Physics and other sciences. My objective is to eliminate misconceptions and eliminate fixations about mathematics and its uses. Problem solving and modeling is the best way to achieve this.

6.3 The work of Tom

Introducing Tom

Tom is in his late forties and has been teaching in the Greek State school system for twenty-three years, the last ten in his current coeducational Senior High school. He has also taught at a Technical High school for one year, early in his career. He is a veteran teacher having taught at schools with students from low socio-economic backgrounds as well as in middle class suburbs. His current school is in a middle class suburb. Tom holds a four-year Bachelor of Science degree, with a major in pure mathematics, and a Postgraduate Diploma in Mathematics Education.

Tom spent his own school days at a State High school and he described himself as having been a very good student of mathematics who initially wanted to study Humanities and History of Art but in Year 11 he changed his mind and decided to become a mathematics teacher, having been influenced by one of his mathematics teachers, whose teaching approach and his charming personality made the difference to Tom's decision to take up mathematics at University. In his own words (The full interview may be found in Appendix F2):

> *When I was at high school I did not want to become a mathematics teacher. I would have preferred to study Humanities and specialize in Linguistics and the History of Art. When I was at Year 11 however, the charming personality and the teaching approaches of one of my mathematics teachers had a catalytic impact on my beliefs about mathematics and mathematics teaching, and I decided to become a mathematics teacher myself.*

Tom has taught Years 10-12 for many years and the year the study took place he was teaching Year 10, 11 and 12 classes. The video taped sessions took place in his Year 10 classes. He claimed that he loves teaching mathematics and that he was wrong about his initial feelings towards the profession:

> *I enjoy mathematics teaching and I keep reminding my students that mathematics is one of the best ways to practice and improve students' clear thinking skills.*

Tom held firm beliefs about group work as being an ineffective way of learning and teaching mathematics, which appeared to be deeply rooted. He even appeared to have a distorted view of what group work is, and the benefits kids can gain by working in groups. His views about group work are diametrically opposite to those of Ann, and they had an impact on his teaching practise. By comparing his response to the previous and the next interview questions, it can be seen that he held conflicting views about the utility of group work in his classes.

> *There is cooperation among students in my classes. Quite often when my students have a test I discuss the results in class by giving them their corrected tests back. I ask my students to exchange their test scripts and discuss them. That's O.K. but to have my students sitting in groups of four*

or five for fifteen-twenty minutes holding discussions on their own, while
our limited time is running out, that's out of the question. It doesn't serve
any purpose. I think that the kids won't benefit from this kind of approach.

Tom, along with Ann, considered that the University mathematics course that he underook was irrelevant to teaching. He felt the same way about the various professional development seminars he has participated in. That's one of the reasons that when given the opportunity, he enrolled in a Postgraduate Diploma in Mathematics Education course.

Tom firmly believed that mathematics teachers should have a wide repertoire of knowledge, not only in mathematically related areas. He also stressed that teachers should be multi-talented if they were to motivate their students. He openly expressed his love for psychoanalysis, literature and the arts.

Teachers, irrespective of their specialisation, i.e. mathematics or physics or
P.E., must be cognizant and experienced in many other fields in addition to
their own specialisation, such as History, Drama, the Arts, Literature etc.
Consider the case of Psychoanalysis. I am currently reading a book by a
French psychoanalyst, who claimed that many of the problems kids
experience at school, are the result of their upbringing and their family
environment. It is very useful for teachers to be aware of the conclusions that
a theoretical science has drawn on learning problems.

Tom has visited France as part of a Teaching Fellowship exchange program, where he found out how the French Education system operates and he claimed that he has attempted to adapt some of the approaches he came across, into his own teaching style. Tom enjoys reading and gardening in his spare time.

Beliefs about mathematics

In this part of the interview discussion focused on Tom's espoused beliefs about mathematics:

Interviewer (I): What do you think mathematics is all about?

Tom (T): Mathematics can be considered as a tool for exercising the mind.
It is the science of beauty, elegance, rigour and precision. It is a tool that is
used by most of the sciences, ranging from philosophy to medicine.

Tom expressed the view that mathematics is a beautiful, creative and useful human endeavor that is both a way of thinking and a rigorous axiomatic system base on solid foundations. His belief represents a mix of contemporary and traditional views about the nature of mathematics.

I: What do you think about school mathematics?

T: The mathematics we teach at school is consisting of fragmented and disconnected segments. I believe that by using contemporary technology we can show students the utility of each topic under consideration. There are a number of really good educational videos and CDs, which if they were made available to the teacher; they could be used to enrich mathematics teaching and learning.

Tom expressed his (espoused) belief that 'by using contemporary technology we can show students the utility of each topic under consideration', but there was no evidence of technology use in his classes (field notes of video taped sessions).

I: Which factors do you consider to have a significant influence on your beliefs about mathematics?

T: I think most of all I have been influenced by the study of the formal and rigorous axiomatic approach, which is the backbone of Euclidean Geometry. Mathematics is also a field where freedom of thought may find a fertile ground. In conclusion, I believe that mathematics is a science, which survived over the centuries due to the fact, that it is founded on solid theoretical foundations and on eternal verities.

Tom's view about mathematics coincides with the traditional view that mathematics is a static and immutable knowledge with objective truth. His preference for a rigorous axiomatic approach has influenced his views about learning and teaching, as it will be evidenced by the discussions in the next two sections.

Beliefs about mathematics learning

In this part of the interview discussion focused on Tom's espoused beliefs about mathematics learning:

I: What can a good mathematics student do?

T: Good students are the ones who can respond to the demands of academically oriented mathematics courses. Not all students can excel in mathematics nor can all of them attend Year 11 and 12 academically oriented mathematics courses. Poor students are better off attending Technical schools.

Tom's view that many students are just not able to learn mathematics echoes traditional views about mathematics being a field of study for the very few gifted individuals. It has been expressed by many educators and non-educators over the years.

I: What accounts for the differences between a good and a poor mathematics student?

T: *This is an important issue and it is related to both genetic and environmental factors. The student's socio-economic background, parents' educational level, the family environment, the school and its administration, the teachers, the resources, students' motivation to learn; all of them contribute to the development of a good or a poor student. Students have to take charge of their own learning. There is no way to acquire knowledge by being a passive observer in a classroom and expect to benefit by sitting idle on a desk all day passively copying the teachers' work. Knowledge is an active process, which is acquired via hard work and consistent effort.*

Tom's views about what accounted for the differences between a good and a poor mathematics student were in conflict with his views he expressed about good students in the previous question. Despite his expressed view that many students are just not able to learn mathematics, he claimed that knowledge is an active process and that students have to take charge of their own learning, a view that is in concert with the contemporary view that students are autonomous learners and they learn through active participation in meaningful activities.

I: Is it possible for a teacher to help a poorly performing mathematics student become a good mathematics student?

T: *By moving around in class trying to help as many students as possible, I can check their work and I can ask questions about their work. I am trying to accommodate individual differences by discussing with students who have trouble, like tutoring them one to one. I have to emphasise at this point that not all students can excel in mathematics. There are some students at Year 11 who cannot solve a linear equation.*

According to Tom, learning mathematics is the responsibility of both the teacher and the student but there is very little the teacher can do to help a poorly performing mathematics student become a good mathematics student, due to his belief that not all students can do well in mathematics.

I: How do you define comprehension of a mathematical concept? topic?

T: *I am using the tests provided by the Ministry of Education. They contain multiple choice questions, true-false questions and short answer questions. They help me a lot in forming judgements about which concepts and skills each student has (or hasn't) mastered. I am frequently using ten-minute tests, although it is hard for me to use them often since they require a lot of correction time. In that way I know when my students have mastered a particular topic and they are ready to move on to the next topic.*

Students learn mathematics when engaged in drill activities for mastery of skills, according to Tom. He espoused a sequential approach to teaching where memorisation and mastery of facts is valued more than understanding does.

I: Which factors do you consider to have a significant influence on your beliefs about mathematics learning?

T: *My beliefs about mathematics have been primarily shaped by my teaching experience. It is my deep-rooted belief that the teacher's role is not to judge students but to facilitate learning. The teacher is the student's collaborator and my objective is to help students realise that we are together in their attempts to understand, to explore, to investigate and to own their knowledge. I owe these beliefs to my colleagues and students over the years.*

Students' learning in mathematics represents their pursuit for knowledge and its attainment depends on both the teacher and the students alike, according to Tom.

Beliefs about mathematics teaching

In this part of the interview discussion focused on Tom's espoused beliefs about mathematics teaching:

I: Could you describe the way you teach mathematics?

T: *There is no typical day for my classes. One day's approach may differ dramatically from another day's approach. My teaching style varies but it is grounded on a sense of respect for my students, on my enthusiasm and on my eagerness to do the best I can, on a daily basis. As far as students' errors are concerned, I consider them part of the learning process. A mistaken answer by a student provides the spark for further discussion and elaboration on a problem or topic.*

Tom's teaching style consisted of a traditional face-to-face teaching, and the different daily approaches he referred to, were nothing more than dispensing mathematical knowledge in lecture style lessons. Tom presented mathematics in an expository style by demonstrating and explaining concepts and skills and he approached topics in isolation. He sought 'right answers' and was not concerned about students' explanations if they were not in a pre-determined 'right direction'. His espoused beliefs about the treatment of errors represent another inconsistency between his espoused and enacted beliefs. Tom espoused a contemporary view about students' errors in mathematics as being expressions of students' current understanding but in his classes he did not demonstrate any systematic effort to understand the sources of his students' errors. He instead attempted to eliminate students' misunderstandings by rewording his explanations or by follow-up instruction.

I: What about memorisation? What is its role in mathematics teaching?

T: *The human memory is a tool that should be used effectively. Mathematics learning cannot be based on the memorisation of some rules alone. There are no simple recipes. Unfortunately, many students think that memorising facts provides an easy way to pass mathematics tests. This kind of attitude constitutes a disastrous approach to mathematics learning. The role mathematics teachers play in encouraging or discouraging students to rely on memorisation alone should be examined carefully.*

Tom stated that he emphasised understanding over memorisation in his classes. He considered that the view held by some students that memorising facts provided an easy way to pass mathematics tests, constituted a disastrous approach to mathematics learning. Tom also held some mathematics teachers accountable for encouraging students to rely on memorisation alone as a vehicle for mathematics learning.

I: Where did you learn to teach mathematics that way? Have you ever had graduate and/or in-service courses on how to teach mathematics?

T: *I am learning everyday. Every single bit of knowledge in any field of human learning, has something to offer the teacher. Teaching is not a static process. It all depends on the class dynamics and the psycho-synthesis of the individual students of each class. Even when I have to teach the same concepts to two different Year 10 classes, my teaching approach is diversified to accommodate the needs of each class.*

Tom espoused an experiential approach to his own teaching approaches. He considered teaching as a dynamic process requiring a deep understanding of individual students' differences and needs.

I: Have you ever tried something different? Why? What happened?

T: *Yes I have tried to assign projects to my students but it did not work very well and soon I had to abandon it. Students did not have time to work on extended investigations, since they are being assigned a lot of homework on a daily basis.*

Tom felt that he had no time to try to facilitate his students' learning by posing challenging activities, but he acknowledged the fact that the amount of homework set by teachers on a daily basis was partly to blame (Regarding the amount of homework set, Greek students top the list of the TIMMS and PISA 2000 participating countries).

I: Grouping: On what basis? Why?

T: *I have never attempted to work with groups in my mathematics classes, I never will. With the existing school structure and the current curriculum time constraints it seems impossible. I do however, use some form of group work when I ask my students to think about a question for five minutes in groups of two. Time constraints are very prohibitive. Innovations require time and there is no time available for group work.*

Tom' approach consisted of having his students work individually all the time based on his firm belief that group work does not facilitate students' learning in mathematics. He felt that provided he had more time (once he had covered the compulsory syllabus material) he would attempt to introduce innovations, including group work.

I: What do you consider as the most important characteristics of quality teaching?

T: *I believe that quality teaching means that the students trust their teacher that there is some sort of acceptance and appreciation of what the teacher is trying to do. Quality teaching is a gift but at the same time there are some fundamental didactical principles on which teaching should be grounded. The mathematics teacher should radiate energy and knowledge and make his students feel important. I strive to use activities, which will improve my students' imagination and broaden their horizons. I do not believe that there are difficult topics to teach but poorly performing teachers instead.*

Despite the fact that he espoused using activities that would improve his students' imagination, Tom was actually using the textbook extensively. He did not use any activity other than the routine exercises presented in the textbook.

I: Which factors do you consider have had a significant influence on your ability to teach mathematics?

T: *My love for children. If the teacher loves children and can sense their eagerness to learn, that's sufficient to encourage him to be dignified, and to stand up and deliver. That is not a recipe for success however. I believe that teaching is a sociocultural process and a calling, and it should be approached as such on a daily basis.*

Tom's belief that teaching is a cultural process, had an effect on his pastoral role as a teacher but did not seem to have any effect on his (primarily) traditional teaching approach (researcher's field notes classroom observations).

I: Which factors do you consider have had a significant influence on your beliefs about mathematics teaching?

T: *My teaching practice has taught me a lot. Factors, which have had a significant impact on my beliefs, are my love for children, my devotion to my profession and the fact that I do not consider myself as a public servant but as an educationist who has a task of inspiring his students.*

Love for children, devotion to the profession and an urge to inspire his students to learn mathematics, were the characteristics, which significantly influenced Tom's beliefs about mathematics teaching.

I: Which factors may explain the existence of inconsistencies between espoused beliefs and beliefs in practice?

T: *The realisation that there are inconsistencies between espoused beliefs and beliefs in practice cause a lot of sorrow to me. It is true that many teachers use pompous words about their beliefs and when it comes to he crunch they cannot deliver. I have come across teachers who were talking about equality and a just society but in practice they deliver the minimum possible. The existence of such inconsistencies is due to the fact, that many teachers are not devoted and they are not interested in providing a good education for their students.*

The absence of adequate professional training and development is another factor that could explain the existence of inconsistencies between espoused beliefs and beliefs in practice. Most professional development seminars touch only the surface of the real issues that concern teachers by providing only theoretical support but little or no practical guidance and follow-up activities. It seems that there are a number of teachers whose espoused beliefs about mathematics teaching, learning and assessment could be classified as contemporary, but when it comes to their daily practice they resort to traditional approaches of teaching which provided a sense of security for them.

Beliefs about mathematics assessment

In this part of the interview discussion focused on Tom's espoused beliefs about mathematics assessment:

> I: On what criteria do you select assessment methods for a topic/term/year?
>
> T: *Student assessment constitutes a continuous dialogue. I am using tests with multiple choice questions, true-false questions and short answer type questions. They help me a lot in forming judgements about what each student has or has not understood. I am trying to explain to my students that the objective of testing is not grading students but finding out about individual students' (or whole class) weaknesses and misunderstandings and they enable the teacher to decide about the necessity of re-teaching the concepts that have not been mastered by students. The objective of assessment is to improve students' skills and knowledge. Grading is not the objective of assessment but since it is compulsory, I am trying to be as objective as possible when providing grades for my students.*

Tom assessed his students solely through standard quizzes and exams. His objectives were to prepare his students for university entrance type exams, to verify if students should be promoted to the next grade and to provide his students and their parents with feedback about their progress. He also felt that the development of a positive attitude towards mathematics and the utilization of a variety of mathematical skills by the students were to be included in a teacher's rationale for assessment.

Tom's classroom

Tom had five mathematics classes the year the study took place: A Year 10 Algebra class and a Year 10 Geometry class, a Year 11 Algebra and Calculus class and a Year 11 Geometry class, and a Year 12 Mathematical Methods class.

The lesson that is discussed in detail in this section took place in a Year 10 Geometry class. The twenty-eight students who make up the class were 15-16 years of age. There were fifteen girls and thirteen boys.

The desks in the classroom were arranged in rows, each desk seating two students and facing the blackboard. The teacher's desk was near the front and in the middle of the classroom. The classroom had many windows along two walls providing plenty of natural light.

Detailed examination of a single lesson

A single lesson of mathematics is the focus of this section. The teaching approaches used in this lesson represent the full spectrum of teaching approaches that have been utilized for the rest of the video taped classes.

The format of presentation is in two columns. The text of the lesson is in the left hand column, and the analysis, drawing on my criteria for teaching practice (chapter 3, section 3.8) to describe the teacher's behaviours and beliefs, is on the right hand column. The text is broken at various points to allow the teacher's voice to be heard, as she made comments while watching the taped lessons a week after her lessons were videotaped.

The discussion commenced with Tom explaining how he goes about planning for a particular lesson. His belief in the importance of clarifying purpose, goals and method, as well as explaining the relevance of activities did not appear to be very clear.

A little introduction is provided and I try to diagnose what knowledge deficiencies there are among students, so that I can introduce the topic under consideration as best as possible. Certainly I have done some preparation at home and know how to move.

There is no meaning in planning ahead. I simply know the stuff well and I have made a rough plan as to what I will teach, how I will maneuver, what sort of exercises I will assign and finally what kind of questions I am going to ask in order to make sure that my students have mastered the topic under consideration, so that we can proceed to the next topic.

Depending on the answers I get, I may re-teach a topic or proceed to the next one, without having a specific plan as to how I will present the concepts and what I will say at every single instructional step.

The instructions from the Board of Studies could have prescribed, for example, that we have to allocate eight periods for a particular topic. I might however, allocate twelve periods or seven periods, depending on students' needs. Of course, we have to follow the syllabus, but in my opinion, it is not possible to adequately cover every single aspect of it.

ACTUAL CLASS	RESEARCHER'S COMMENTS
Teacher: + y, which quadrant is this?	
Student: Which quadrant is this?	
Teacher: The first.	
Student: This is the second, this is the third, and this is the fourth.	**TP10-Questionning**
Teacher: To which quadrant does this point belong?	
Student: To the first.	
Teacher: Point B with the coordinates (-3,-2), to which quadrant does it belong?	
Student: To the third.	
Teacher: We spoke about functions, then, and I would like someone to define functions. What do we call a function?	**TPT8-Discourse-teacher**
Student: A function is a process in which we have a correspondence where point A corresponds to one and only one point of B.	
Teacher: Very good. If we assume that the whole of A is the domain of the function, it has as its elements 3, 0, and -2, and so, Con, to what is the f(3) equal to?	**Makes connection with previous topics**
Student: It's equal to 2 * 3 + 3.	
Teacher: How much is this?	
Student: 9	
Teacher: The f of 0?	

Student: 3.

Teacher: And how much is the F of -2, Theo?

Student: -4 + 3, then.

Teacher: -1. Tell me now, these ordered pairs which have been developed, which pairs are they? Tell me which pairs have been developed. When x is 3 how much is y?

Student: 9.

Teacher: When the X is 0?

Student: It's 3.

Teacher: When the X is -2?

Student: It's -1.

Teacher: I put these on to the Cartesian system, so, and we said that if I mean these then where are these three points located? I won't put them on, to save time.

Student: On to a line.

Teacher: If I assume that the domain of this function is not A, but the set of real numbers, then the graph of this function given that the domain is F will be what?

Student: A straight line.

Teacher: If the domain is these three points here (*shows the points on the board*), then what is the graph?

Student: Three points.

Teacher: Have you understood the difference? If the domain of this function is the interval $[0, +\infty)$, then the graph of this function with this interval as the domain is what, children?

Student: A semi-line.

Teacher: Which will belong to the interval $[0, +\infty)$. If the domain is the interval $[-5, 8)$, the graph of the function with this interval as domain will be what? What will it be? Tell us, Helen.

Stresses importance of
Moves and actions towards a 'goal state'

This kind of question – followed by rewording – is typical. Most things are gone through a number of times in an attempt to communicate effectively (TPTC10-questionning)

Student: A straight-line segment.

While watching the tape Tom explained his usual strategy of providing the correct answer for any question that the students could not answer and that he guided his students to a predetermined path (and answer) while attempting to solve specific questions. It is obvious from the videotape that he actually led the discussion towards a pre-determined direction with the sole objective of arriving at a pre-determined answer he had in mind, although during the interview Tom admitted that this occurred rarely and it wasn't the trend in his classes.

> *There is this aspect, certainly. When I expect a specific answer and the students cannot reach it, I might provide the full solution. But it does not always happen like this, when I want to start talking about a theoretical aspect for example, the questions might aim at a very limited answer, and I might have to provide the answer myself. However, that's not always the case.*

Tom mentioned that his approach consists of guiding the class by simultaneously making an effort not to influence the students' work.

> *I guide the discussion without influencing it. In other words, I choose who speaks I am the one who says who will speak so that we don't end up with a complete bedlam, which I can't stand at all. Students can't hold a dialogue among themselves without the guidance of the teacher. How can they decide who will speak? It should be the teacher who decides who speaks. When five hands are raised there must be one person who will co-ordinate the conversation. That's the teacher's role. Of course, I make an effort to prod and encourage my students all the time.*

Teacher: A straight-line segment, then? And so that we will be very specific, will X-5 belong to this segment?

Student: No.

Teacher: So 8 doesn't belong to this segment. Good, have you understood? Did you remember it? OK, open your books at page 73. Then I want us to do exercise 11. I think we have done 11.

TPT1 instr-text + TPT2 syll-rigid

Student: Not all of it.

Teacher: It doesn't matter, we'll do question 11 again. I would like you to do the first part of question 11: the first question, where it says that this graph corresponds to a function.

Student: No.

Teacher: No? Because it doesn't correspond to a function?

Student: ....

Teacher: So how many digits correspond to one x?

Student: Two.

Teacher: Therefore it's not?

Student: ....

Teacher: The second question.

Student: Yes, it will be.

Teacher: It will be? Why?

Student: Only one y corresponds to one x.

Teacher: Con, the third question.

Student: Me? One y corresponds to only to one x.

Teacher: What did you say? Is it or isn't it?

Student: It is.

Teacher: Do you agree, kids? And the fourth question, Con?

Student: For every x there will be two y.

Teacher: Let's go to exercise 9; which questions haven't we done?

Student: The third question.

Teacher: Good, who's coming to the board now?

Students respond according to known trend: The aim is to finish off the question. It also reflects the influence teachers' actions, methods and beliefs have on students' actions and thinking processes

Repeated emphasis on the important elements of the exercise

TPT1 instr-text +
TPT2 syll-rigid

Use of rewording while explaining a specific aspect of the activity at hand is typical in Tom's classes. Most things are gone through a number of times, in an attempt to make sure that understanding has taken place.

> Initially I'll ask some exploratory/investigative questions. Once I realise from the audience that they can answer my questions then I make a decision as to whether I will move on or not.

Tom's teaching philosophy about arriving at the answer at any cost before the end of the session became apparent when he explained the rationale of his approach.

> Students are attempting every single exercise while I provide hints and suggestions. The students never leave the classroom having doubts about whether the solutions we obtained in class were right or not. I make sure of that.

Teacher: Have you done them in your exercise books? Let me see your exercise books. So, children, let's define k so that this point says that this pair belongs to the graph. So look, children, what value does y take from here? The 8 like this and the x^1, I do a substitution, insignificant and trivial operations and we find it. Tell me, does the root of 4 here make 2 only 2 or -2? Tell us.

Student: 2 and the root is always a positive number.

Teacher: Yes, here we have a + in front.

Student: +

Teacher: What should I put here   an absolute value sign?

Student: ....

Teacher: Is what I have done here right or wrong?

Student: Right.

Teacher: But how much is the absolute value of 2?

TPT10-qustionning

Classic example of 'spoon feeding'.

The significance of the operation is diminished. (Figure of speech according to Toto – while watching the tape during a post-instructional interview)

Questions not asked in an interrogative tone but as statements to facilitate interaction and communication

Student: 2

Teacher: Tell me if I had a root of alpha squared what would it be?

Student: |a|.

Teacher: Why is it an absolute a, and not just a?

Student: ....

Teacher: Because here I don't know if it's a. I remind you that a^2 is positive since it's below the root, a however can be positive or negative, that is why I put it inside the .... OK, did we have any exercise, any query? Something that you couldn't solve from those I had told you to do? Tell me. Let's look at something else now, children. If we assume, children, that I have an axis xx', yy' and I draw a line, this line that you see forms an angle f with the axis xx', good, this angle is an acute angle as you see in the figure in contrast with this line here which forms this angle with the axis xx', this is an obtuse angle, good, did you understand that? Each line that I draw can form an angle with the axis xx' and this angle which will move when I say where it will move to; if it is parallel with the axis xx', then the angle that will be formed will be what?

Student: …

Not enough 'wait time'. Jumps from one topic to another in an attempt to finish off the topic according to the syllabus. The pressure of time constraints is evident and was acknowledged by Tom while watching the tape during a post-lesson interview)

Provides clarifications

Not enough 'wait time' provided for students to respond to his questions. Tom jumped from one topic to another in an attempt to finish off the topic with no deviation from the syllabus. The pressure of time constraints is evident and was acknowledged by Tom while watching the tape during a post-lesson interview)

On the one hand, there is the pressure of time. Often I do not tell them so as not to disappoint them. When I provide the solution to a problem, I explain to my students that they may need more time to solve some of the problems, than the time available in class. I encourage them to do the questions at home and to devote to each problem more than the three-four minutes we have available in class. The reason for not having enough time is that I must proceed to the next topic, because I ought to proceed.

Teacher: Yes 0, if it is parallel with the axis xx' then it forms with the axis xx' (0). The largest angle which can be formed by a line from the axis xx', how large is it if you consider that this line here rotates, it comes to this position, it grows and grows and comes and intersects the axis xx', then what is the maximum value this angle can take?

Student: 180 degrees.

Teacher: 180 degrees. We can assume then that each line can form with the axis xx' an angle and this angle will be ...

Student: Larger.

Teacher: Sorry, larger than 0 and smaller than 180? When it becomes 180 how much will 0 be therefore? Then each angle between 0 and 180, not 180, good. Did you understand? Children, if I consider the function F=ax+b, then the graph of this, I'm telling you now without going into details, the graph of this function is what?

Student: A straight line.

Teacher: A straight line, good, I consider the line y = ax + b here. This line is the

Self-evaluation and complementary explanations to enable students to make connections

(TPPC3-connections)

Placing tasks in context

function which has a line as its graph, I'll say that this line has the equation y = ax + b. I won't go into details; we'll do this next year, OK? Children, if I take a point on this line and draw a line down from it to the axis xx', then in Middle School you learnt the definition of the tangent of an angle on a right-angled triangle, what do you call the tangent of an acute triangle?

Assumption not always sustainable as a teaching strategy (incostistency-he does not espouse it but he does it in class)

Student: It's called................

While Tom attempted to place tasks in context he made the assumption, not always sustainable as a teaching strategy, that his students should know this topic quite well from earlier years. This led to an inconsistency between what he does in class and his espoused beliefs. Tom admitted that this is, to some extent, an inconsistency and provided the following reason for its emergence:

> *In general because here we are talking about Year 10 students and because I believe that the students are coming to the Senior High school with knowledge gaps from Junior High school mathematics classes. That's the reason I always consider that Year 10 students are like 'tabula rasa'. Sometimes however, I am forced to say that you are supposed to know this or that, since it should have been covered in Junior High school classes. This however, happens only in very few instances, very rarely.*

Teacher: Right, therefore if I take this triangle, if we put a line KLM to this right-angled triangle KLM, this is a right-angled triangle; then if I call the tangent of this angle ff and the tangent of the angle f is equal to what?

Clarification of the details of task provided but students are denied sufficient 'wait time'

Student: LM.

Teacher: With LM.

Student: Towards KM.

Teacher: Towards KM, do you agree? **Teacher explanations**

OK, children. Therefore it is demonstrated that the tangent of the triangle that this line forms with the axis xx', this equation here is not the equation of a line, this line intersects the axis xx' at some point and forms an angle, if I call the angle that is formed f, then the tangent of this corner f will be equal to the number a.

Student: ....

Teacher: This is the co-efficient of the direction of the line and is equal to this tangent φ, which is equal to what is called the gradient of my line, good? If therefore I have to give one example, I have the line y = 2x + 1, I won't draw this line so as not to waste time, this line forms an angle with the axis xx', do you get it? This angle has a tangent, what is the tangent of this angle equal to, what?

Student: To 2.

Teacher: To 2. If I assume that I have another line

u = -4x +5 and that this line forms an angle with the axis xx', if I call this angle that is formed by the line and the axis φ, then what is the tangent equal to?

Student: To -4.

Teacher: To -4. Do you understand me now? If the tangent of this angle, what did we call the tangent of this angle?

Student: The gradient.

Teacher: Good. If the gradient is a positive number, then the angle is an acute one and it isn't an angle acute like this. If the co-efficient of the direction is

Hit and run' and teacher answered questions (Questions come in a rapid-fire assault and flit from issue to issue, without allowing for connections to be made or without allowing for productive examination of any issue).

Has students clarify and justify their ideas orally

(TPC 12-justification)

negative, though?

Student: A right-angled triangle.

Teacher: A right-angled triangle. Ah! A very good question, children, look at this, a very good question; look at the tangent of an angle ω. What is it equal to?

Student: ....

Teacher: Did you get that? It makes sin/cos. Did you get that?

Student: Yes.

Teacher: When the angle is 90 degrees then what is the cos? Do you know?

Student: 0.

Teacher: 0 in this case when the cos is 0; what is the denominator?

Student: 0.

Teacher: 0, I have a fraction with the denominator 0, what happens then?

Student: It is undefined.

Teacher: It is undefined did you understand? OK, then, let's look at something else. We have the equation y = ax + b if my a is 0, then what relationship does this line have in the Cartesian system? Do you remember? If a equals 0 then the angle is 0 and the tangent is 0.

Student: .... they will be parallel with the axis of the system.

Teacher: It will be a case like that, OK, good? And since it is 0, then what equation does each line that is parallel to the axis xx' have?

Student: y = b.

Teacher: y=b, did you understand?

Focused and guided questioning becomes spoon feeding

Not enough 'wait time' provided

Student: .... if this line coincides with the axis xx', then the tangent will be 0 again.

Teacher: If my line is this one here then, tell me, what will my equation be? You heard the question, this is the axis xx', isn't it? So, and this is my line here, then what equation will this line have, let's think about it for a while.

Student: ....

Clarification of the details of task provided but students are denied sufficient 'wait-time'. It is noteworthy that the most commonly used category of unproductive questions invoked by Tom was the hit-and-run and teacher answered type questions. Tom's explanation was that quite often he had to rush through the topics in order to be in concert with the set syllabus. As a result his strategy of focused and guided questioning turns to spoon-feeding, although at certain stages of the lesson he had students clarify and justify their ideas orally.

Teacher: Your classmate says that if my line is this one on the axis, then it is the axis xx', then what will its equation be?

Student: .... $y = x$

Teacher: $y = x$, which means that when the x is 4 then the y is 4, when the x is 3, then the y is 3, hence it does not belong to the line, therefore it cannot be this one here. Let's take this point here: if I number this point here 1, 2, 3, then what coordinates does it have?

Student: (2, 0).

Teacher: This one?

Student: (1, 0).

Teacher: This one?

Student: (3, 0).

Teacher: So, the y is always what?

Attempts to involve all members of his class in the discussion. In particular the awareness of the level of involvement of a particular students suggests belief in students' involvement and current research knowledge of educational contexts (verified

Student: 0.

Teacher: Whereas the x can have what value?

Student: Whatever we want.

Teacher: The y is always 0......... What is the equation of this line?

Student: y = 0.

Teacher: y=0, do you understand that? Now, let's extend this, since we've mentioned it, to something else. I'm considering this line here, here is the 3, here is 1, 2, 3, here is the xx', and tell me, bearing in mind what we've just said, what is the equation of this line?

Student: ....

Teacher: Look at this point, what coordinates does it have, how will we work it out?

Student: ....

Teacher: Look at this point, what coordinates does it have, how will we work it out?

Student: It has (3, 0).

Teacher: Yes. What coordinates does this point have?

Student: (3, 0).

Teacher: This point?

Student: (3, 1).

Teacher: This?

Student: (3, 2).

Teacher: This?

Student: (3, 3).

Teacher: Can you tell in this way what the equation of this line will be? Is this the one it always has? What abscissa does it have?

by interview)

Provides clarifications while involving his students in the discussion

Guides his students towards a pre-determined path

Student: 3 always.

Teacher: What is its ordinate?

Student: Parallel.

Teacher: What, in your opinion, is the equation of this line?

Student: x=3?

Teacher: x=3, the x is 3; the y can be anything, understood?

Student: - when we have a constant value x it is parallel to the axis and when we have a constant value y it is perpendicular to the axis.

Tom often attempted to involve all members of his class in the discussion. In particular the awareness of the level of involvement of particular students suggests belief in students' involvement and it is an indication of awareness of current research findings regarding contemporary approaches to learning.

Teacher: Well done, did you hear? Very good. The Cartesian system has two lines on it and one is this one $y = a_1x + b_1$ and the other is, let's say this one here, which are parallel, I make them parallel, the other is $y = a_2x + b_2$ since these two lines are parallel and are intersected by a third, then? Then? Eleni, then? Then? What did we say yesterday in geometry?

Student: I can't remember.

Teacher: Anastasia? Well, my dear girl, this line is parallel with this one and intersected by a third (transversal) line, then?

Student: The corresponding angles?

Teacher: If this is φ and this is not φ.

Student: Yes, yes.

Praises student as part of a strategy to create an environment that allows students to be active learners, only occasionally however
(TPPC6-envir)

Use of friendly language and body language (gestures)

Students errors are interpreted as expressions of their current conceptual

Teacher: Eh, OK?

Student: ....

Teacher: Sorry I made a mistake, corresponding angles. Tell me, children, the tangent of φ is equal to what?

Student: ....

Teacher: Since the tangent φ is a_1 and the tangent f is a_2, then what is a equal to?

Student: To a_2.

Teacher: So, when I have two lines which are parallel, what then?

Student: The gradients are equal.

Teacher: Precisely, and the opposite, if I have two lines.......

Student: Their coordinates are also equal and thus they are parallel.

Teacher: Did you all understand?

Student: **Yes.**

understanding most of the time
(TPPC9-error)

Regularly reflects on and evaluates his own work
(TPC16 self-refl)

Productive use of non-threatening and non-interrogative questioning

Tom occasionally praises students as part of a strategy to create an environment that allows students to be active learners. Use of friendly language and gestures (my dear, my friend, my girl/boy) are common and they serve the dual purpose of breaking the barrier between the teacher and the student as well as enhancing the variability of the teaching approach.

I return to a form of conversation, a form of mutual understanding, collaboration. A 'colouring', we could say, of the teaching method. This, "my dear Anastasia", this is more how I'd talk to my own daughter.

Tom viewed students' errors as expressions of their current conceptual understanding most of the time.

Certainly I want to show to m students that we don't know everything, that we grown-ups also make mistakes.

Teacher: I'll show you another example if we have time. Look, children, I'll take two lines as that is easiest, if I take y = ax + b, if I make b zero so I take y = ax, does this line have anything characteristic about it?

Student: It passes through the origin.

Teacher: Why?

Student: Because b is 0.

Teacher: And since b is 0, it should pass through the origin, good, the b I've taken as 0 and have y = ax, what did you say was the characteristic; it passes through the origin, why should it pass through the origin?

Student: ....

Teacher: Tell us, Serg tell us quickly.

Student: In order to form a line, we join two points, one point is the beginning of the axes and the other is further in.

Teacher: For it to be this line here, it doesn't pass through the origin this one, though? I said that it must, for it to pass through, what must happen?

Student: Because when the x is 0, then the y = 0.

Teacher: When I give x the value 0, what happens to the y?

Student: 0.

Teacher: So, this point satisfies this equation, isn't that so? So, from where will its graph pass?

Student: ....

Awareness of time constraints (TPT10-quest'n)

One of the reasons offered by Tom during the post-lesson interview regarding the existence of inconsistencies between espoused beliefs and teaching practice, concerns the pressure of time constraints. This awareness seems to be a frustration factor for both the teacher and the students, irrespective of beliefs and intentions in a process where the teacher rushes to finish of a particular lesson and the students feel like they are being squeezed.

Tom's awareness of time constraints seems to be a frustration factor for both the teacher and the students, irrespective of beliefs and intentions in a process where the teacher rushes to finish of a particular lesson and the students feel like they are being pressured.

I would certainly like more time to focus on certain things that I feel I need to look at more closely. Don't forget that the time we have available for each period is not forty-five minutes. The actual instruction time is about thirty-five minutes, if we take under consideration the time kids need to settle down in class. That's why I have to rush most of the time. This is one of my basic flaws. It has some positive features, but the features are mostly negative, for me and perhaps for the children.

We need more time, I wonder too sometimes, because some children say to me that I put the squeeze on them that they feel pressurized, even squeezed. On the other hand there is very little time and we must prioritize, we must finish the work in class. I am not sure but I think that the issue of achieving a balance between content coverage, available time and mastering the concepts requires very serious consideration.

Given what I have to say and within the specific time there is pressure on me, and this pressure I unfortunately pass on to the children. Sometimes this is good, sometimes bad.

Tom argued that he was aware of the existence of such an inconsistency between his espoused and his enacted beliefs. In his own words:

No, no. Now of course, for some children this kind of work pace has positive results, for some children it doesn't. Certainly some children have another pace and if we worked at a slower pace they would have greater benefits. This is a fact. The question is to what extent we should change this pace or to what extent we should stick to it, in order to have the greatest benefit for the class in which we are working. This is a question, which I think about all the time. I haven't found a feasible solution yet.

Teacher: Did you understand, yes or no?
Student: Yes, yes.
Teacher: Look, say that I have this equation $y = a_1x$ and I draw a line which is perpendicular to this one, do you understand? I take the little triangle that I don't have and draw a vertical line, in

other words, what is this angle?

Student: 90 degrees

Teacher: I call this line here

$y = a_2x$, do you agree?

Student: Yes.

Teacher: Tell me now, if I take this point here which has the abscissa 1, that is $x = 1$, what is the value of y?

Student: ....

Teacher: Eh, you, much louder, when I substitute 1 for x, what will y become?

Student: a_1.

Teacher: x will take the value 1; the y will have what value, what coordinates will this point have?

Student: (1, 2)

Teacher: Do you all agree?

Student: Yes, yes.

Teacher: I draw a vertical line here and extend it, do you all see? What coordinates does this point have?

Student: (1, 0).

Teacher: (1, 0), and this point?

Student: $(1, -a_2)$.

Teacher: - a_2.

Student: a_2 ....

Teacher: What he said is very important. Here, Peter, what value will you give x?

Student: 1.

Teacher: If you give x the value 1, what value will the y take?

Student: a_2.

Teacher: Let him make his point.

Student: - a_2, isn't it?

Teacher: x takes the value 1; the y

Questions become more and more focused in order to accommodate time limitations (TPT10-quest'n)

Focused and directive questions from what was a TPT10 style questioning and developed into a TPPC10 style questioning during the lesson, it now falls back into a TPT10 style questioning. So the cycle of questioning due to time constraints becomes TPT10-TPPC10-TPT10

Another instance of the cycle TPT10-TPPC10-TPT10 of questioning substituted the 1, what is the y equal to?

Student: a_2.

Teacher: a_2. Because your classmate said - a_2, what made him say that?

Student: Because in the fourth quadrant the y is ....

Teacher: He got carried away and said I'll put - a_2, eh? And tell me, when I say a_2 to you, what kind of number is a_2? Positive or negative?

Student: We don't know.

Teacher: We don't put anything; the a_2 here, what number is it?

Student: Negative.

Teacher: OK, you got it? Tell me now, look at the triangle OKL, this triangle OKL, what kind of triangle is it?

Student: A right-angled triangle.

Teacher: I can't apply Pythagoras' theorem. OK, if I apply Pythagoras, what will I have? Who hasn't spoken yet? Apply Pythagoras' theorem, children. Tell us, Theo.

Student: $(KL)^2 = (OK)^2 + (OA)^2$

Teacher: Let me substitute $(KL)^2$ what is it here? I have the K and the L, the coordinates of K are $(1, a_1)$, of L, what are they?

Student: ....

Teacher: Do you remember what a rectilinear segment is the length of a rectilinear segment.................... the coordinates of its edges?

Tell us, Costas.

Student: $(1 - 1)$.

Teacher: No, $(1 - 1)$ abscissa.

Attempts to involve whole class but still TPEM8disc-equal

Knowledge of learners and beliefs about learning seem to be compatible with current research

(TPPC10-quest'n)

Spoon feeding

Student: ....

Teacher: (1 –1), sorry, I got confused.   **Individual evaluation**

Student: ....

Tom believed that this style of questioning did not constitute 'spoon feeding' but an attempt to involve all of his students in class discussions. His contention was that his teaching approach was not based on the provision of fully worked out solutions, although it happened quite often.

> *No, no, it depends on the question and on the time I have available. It also depends on what I want to focus my teaching on, but I do not provide all the answers, that is, I can't say that I always spoon feed my students by providing fully worked out solutions. No, this doesn't happen.*

Teacher: $(OK)^2$, someone else, $(OK)^2$ the coordinates of K are what?

Student: ....

Teacher: They will be .... Tell us, Costas.

Student: They will be $1 - (0)^2 + (a)^2 - (0)^2$.

Teacher: This makes 0. We take this and this away and we take this and this away and what is left here?

Student: ....

Teacher: Therefore $a_1.a_2 = -1$, what can we conclude? We've concluded what? Quickly, quickly.   **Not enough 'wait time'**

Time constraints inhibit the flow of the lesson

Student: That when two lines are perpendicular the product of the two gradients is equal to -1.

Teacher: Is that OK? Say it the other way round.   **Questions become more and more focused in order to accommodate time limitations (TPT10-quest'n)**

Student: When the product of the gradients is -1, then the lines are perpendicular.

Teacher: Children, for next time read as far as page 78. I'll return to these, do 2, 3   **Not enough time for reflection. Another sign of time/syllabus constraints and pressure**

and 4, i.e., I'll do some exercises with you,
some of the exercises, OK?

Not enough 'wait-time' provided for reflection. Time constraints had a negative impact on the smooth flow of the lesson, quite often as evidenced by Tom's way of setting the homework questions with no further explanation. In his own words:

> It depends, if there is an exercise, which is difficult for some students, I might provide suggestions, or I might ask the students to work on the exercise without me giving them suggestions and if they experience any problems then I will provide a fully worked out solution. It depends on many factors. There are cases whereby I have to explain some aspects of the course. I have to show them the right way of doing things. In some topics, we are obliged to go at a particular pace because there is a set syllabus to be covered.

An attempt was also made to tap the task specific strategies used by the teachers via a researcher-designed checklist (Appendix C3). The shaded areas in the checklist of Table 6.2.2 correspond to the observed strategies used by each teacher in his/her classes. The first seven categories in Table 3.5.1 represent traditional teaching strategies and the next thirty-eight represent contemporary teaching strategies.

6.4 Chapter summary

Tom's style was quite distinct from Ann's. There was no clear pattern of approach as there was in Ann's lessons. Frequently lessons were not complete units – a task was introduced and then deferred, due to the fact, that time was short or that because Tom's interest shifted on another aspect of the task. Ideas were not given sufficient time to percolate before the task was formally introduced.

Table 6.2.2

Task specific strategies used by participating teachers in their classes

No.	TASK SPECIFIC STRATEGIES USED IN CLASS	Tom	Ann
	TRADITIONAL		
1	Teaches solely from textbook		
2	Sole use of objective tests		
3	Uses teacher demonstration		
4	Uses drill & practice		
5	Encourages students to work independently		
6	Teaches topics in isolation		
7	Uses pencil & paper application		
	CONTEMPORARY		
8	Promotes integration of concepts by students		
9	Encourages Observing		
10	Facilitates investigations		
11	Uses physical activities		
12	Uses open ended tasks		
13	Encourages hypothesising		
14	Uses Patterning		
15	Encourages writing about maths		
16	Encourages student talk		
17	Uses video & maths		
18	Uses outdoor activities		
19	Motivates students		
20	Uses concrete materials		
21	Communicating		

22	Cooperative groups		
23	Used calculators and computers and internet		
24	Mathematical modelling		
25	Uses Journals		
26	Uses Portfolios		
27	Encourages taking risks		
28	Uses authentic and self -assessment		
29	Evaluates contexts and outcomes		
30	Uses Problem solving and posing		
31	Estimating and representing		
32	Facilitates meta-cognitive activity		
33	Facilitates use of heuristics explicitly		
34	Uses positive affirmation		
35	Encourages the use of imagination and creativity		
36	Evaluates students progress		
37	Uses non routine tasks		
38	Uses multiple modes of questioning		
39	Encourages originality and divergent thinking		
40	Provides sufficient "wait time"		
41	Extends learning beyond classroom		
42	Encourages intuitiveness		
43	Demonstrates gender sensitivity		
44	Uses debates		
45	Uses clinical interviews		

Ann on the other hand, promoted participation in meaningful activities as the key to success in mathematics. The promotion of a community environment along with the promotion of leadership qualities in Ann's classes, with their potential to encourage active participation, brainstorming, ideas exchange and to maximise each student's potential in mathematics learning, has been the driving force behind her cooperative teaching approach.

This chapter has shown Tom to be a teacher whose espoused beliefs about instruction are his students and their development as human beings. The direction of his lesson was influenced not only by the set curriculum, his own plans and his school program, but also an insistence on rote learning as a vehicle for the acquisition of mathematical knowledge. If a task suddenly appeared to be more relevant than a planned one, Tom would postpone its planned discussion until a more suitable time would be found. Tom's methods of approaching a given topic were frequently decided before the lesson was taught; the direction of a lesson was never altered in response to the reaction of the students.

Another aspect of Ann's approach, that of promoting student autonomy and shared responsibility, and reducing teacher intervention to a minimum – which were seen by her as fundamental ingredients in the development of a community of inquiry – was the overriding learning-teaching approach in Ann's classes.

Ann's and Tom's teaching styles will be discussed in more detail in chapter 7, where the characteristics that have been presented of their work are considered through a number of different lenses, and specific focus is given the research questions posed in section 3.2.

In the beginning of this chapter, it was anticipated that by attempting to interpret the nature of two veteran mathematics teachers' beliefs and the factors which influence them, it would be possible to develop a framework that would lead to the establishment of professional development programs which will inform teachers of the impact that beliefs have on everyday practice both for novice and experienced instructors of mathematics.

Ann and Tom viewed the relationship between beliefs and teaching practice as moderate and that they needed appropriate guidance in professional development seminars. They believed that mathematics teacher education and in-service training should show mathematics teachers how to teach mathematics, by demonstrating what worked and what did not work in the past and why. It should also present teachers with new approaches to mathematics teaching that can improve their instructional practice. Ann also stressed that her beliefs shaped and directly influenced her instructional practice.

I believe that one of the goals of mathematics in-service training should be to examine the development of beliefs about mathematics teaching, learning and assessment. By examining the beliefs of the two case study mathematics teachers and their classroom interactions, a lot can be learnt about the daily practices of mathematics teachers and their needs regarding professional development training programs. It seems likely that teacher pre-service and in-service training programs would have a stronger effect on practice if they focused on influencing the beliefs of practising mathematics teachers.

In the next and final chapter, conclusions will be drawn about the data in both chapters five and six and proposals for instructional practices and further research will be recommended.

CHAPTER 7

Conclusions and implications

Chapter 7 commences with the research questions and their answers, and is followed by a summary of the literature underpinning the research questions. A synthesis of the findings of the statistical analysis is then presented, followed by the findings of the qualitative analysis. The results from both parts of the main study along with the implications for learning, teaching, assessment and mathematics teachers' professional development are proposed. The closing section of the study puts forward suggestions for further research based on the study's findings.

7.1 Conclusions drawn from the quantitative part of the study

The research questions addressed in the quantitative part of the study and a summary of the results are presented below. A detailed discussion of the statistical techniques used to analyse the data was described in Chapter 5.

Summary of results

Research question 1:
What are the beliefs of Greek secondary mathematics teachers with regard to mathematics as a discipline, and learning, teaching and assessing mathematics? Specifically does there exist a typology of teachers' beliefs that correspond to that postulated in the research literature concerning Western teachers?

(i)   Beliefs about mathematics, teaching and learning of mathematics
Five factors were identified, each representing apparently differing but not mutually exclusive beliefs about mathematics, mathematics teaching and mathematics learning:

> ➤ A *socio-constructivist or contemporary orientation* to mathematics, mathematics learning and mathematics teaching.
> ➤ A *dynamic problem-driven orientation* to mathematics, mathematics learning and mathematics teaching.

> ➤ A *static - transmission orientation* to mathematics, mathematics learning and mathematics teaching.

> ➤ A *mechanistic - transmission orientation* to mathematics, mathematics learning and mathematics teaching.

> ➤ A *cooperative orientation* to mathematics learning and mathematics teaching.

From these five factors two orientations that are characteristic of secondary mathematics teachers' beliefs regarding the nature of mathematics, and the learning and teaching of mathematics were conjectured (Chapter 5, p. 91)

- A *contemporary - constructivist orientation*, consisting of the following (not mutually exclusive but complementary) views:
  - ❑ The socio-constructivist view
  - ❑ The dynamic problem driven view
  - ❑ The cooperative view

- A *traditional - transmission - information processing orientation*, consisting of the following (not mutually exclusive but complementary) views:
  - ❑ The static view
  - ❑ The mechanistic view

It was concluded that mathematics teachers' beliefs about mathematics could not be separated from their beliefs about teaching and learning mathematics.

The analysis also showed that, overall, neither the static nor the mechanistic view of mathematics, mathematics teaching and mathematics learning, were rated highly among mathematics teachers. The static view however, was stronger than the mechanistic view. It was also noticed that all dimensions of the contemporary view, that is the socio-constructivist, the problem solving and the collaborative dimensions, rated more highly among mathematics teachers than both dimensions of the traditional view, that is the static and the mechanistic dimensions.

The investigation of the existence of a typology of beliefs categories that could be used to characterise secondary mathematics teachers' beliefs relating to mathematics, and mathematics teaching and learning (Chapter 5), resulted in the following findings:

- Mathematics teachers who espouse *a socio-constructivist or contemporary orientation* and those who espouse *a dynamic problem-driven orientation* to mathematics, mathematics learning and mathematics teaching showed some leanings towards traditional teaching and learning methods. These findings could represent some uncertainty or apprehension on the part of the teachers to fully adopt contemporary mathematics education philosophies and methods. It could also be due to the number of years these teachers have been exposed to traditional mathematics education techniques.

- Mathematics teachers, who espouse *a static-transmission orientation* and those who espouse a *mechanistic - transmission orientation* to mathematics, mathematics learning and mathematics teaching, showed a drift in predictions towards a dynamic problem solving orientation.

- Mathematics teachers who espouse a collaborative view to teaching and learning mathematics hold very strong views, which are quite different from the other four groups.

(ii)   Beliefs about mathematics assessment

Three factors were identified, each representing apparently differing beliefs about mathematics assessment:

➤ A *socio-constructivist orientation* to mathematics assessment.

➤ A *problem solving orientation* to mathematics assessment.

➤ An *accountability orientation* to mathematics assessment.

It was also found that secondary mathematics teachers in the sample:

- Emphasised the use of assessment for accountability purposes.

- Used assessment for problem solving purposes.

- Used contemporary methods of assessment.

The wide range of responses to the contemporary orientation indicates that it represents a wide spectrum of approaches not coherent enough.

The investigation of the existence of a typology of beliefs categories that could be used to characterise secondary mathematics teachers' beliefs relating to mathematics assessment (Chapter 5), resulted in the following conclusions:

- Mathematics teachers who espouse *a socio-constructivist orientation to mathematics assessment* indicated a preference towards problem solving assessment methods too, which is understandable since both orientations represent contemporary assessment approaches.

- Mathematics teachers who espouse *a problem solving orientation to mathematics assessment* indicated a preference towards socio-constructivist assessment methods, which is understandable since both orientations represent contemporary assessment approaches.

- Mathematics teachers who espouse *an accountability orientation to mathematics assessment* indicated some leanings towards both problem solving assessment and socio-constructivist assessment approaches. Mathematics teachers seemed apprehensive to fully adopt a traditional orientation towards mathematics assessment.

Research question 2:

In what ways do Greek secondary mathematics teachers' characteristics, such as professional development, postgraduate studies background, years of experience background, gender and position held, influence their espoused beliefs? In other words, what differences in beliefs exist across professional development undertaken, years of experience, position held, the range of qualifications, and between female and male teachers?

(i) Teacher characteristics and their influence on their beliefs about mathematics, teaching and learning

Data were collected on five teacher characteristics, namely, gender, years of teaching experience at junior high school, years of teaching experience at Senior High school, position held and postgraduate qualifications possessed.

It was found that:

- ❏ Gender was significant for Factor 1: *A contemporary socio-constructivist orientation to mathematics, mathematics teaching and mathematics learning*. It was concluded that female teachers in this study placed more emphasis on a socio-constructivist view of mathematics, mathematics teaching and mathematics learning than did he male teachers.

- ❏ Experience at junior high school was significant for Factor 1: *A contemporary socio-constructivist orientation to mathematics, mathematics teaching and mathematics learning*. It has been argued that teachers with experience at junior high school (Years 7-9), placed more emphasis on a socio-constructivist view of mathematics, mathematics teaching and mathematics learning than did teachers with experience at other levels.

❑ The contemporary socio-constructivist orientation to mathematics, mathematics teaching and mathematics learning increases consistently between the inexperienced teachers' category (0-6 years of experience) and the experienced teachers' category (6-15 years of experience).

❑ The contemporary socio-constructivist view of mathematics, mathematics teaching and learning (factor 1) was more prevalent among experienced teachers (7-15 years experience) and veteran teachers (16+ years of experience) than among inexperienced teachers (0-6 years of experience).

❑ Teachers' beliefs about mathematics, mathematics teaching and mathematics learning were not significantly influenced by their experience at senior high school level (Years 10-12).

❑ The dynamic problem-driven orientation to mathematics, mathematics teaching and mathematics learning increases consistently across teachers' experience categories.

❑ The *dynamic problem-driven orientation to mathematics, mathematics teaching and mathematics* was more prevalent among veteran teachers (16+ years of experience) than among inexperienced teachers (0-6 years of experience) and experienced teachers (7-15 years experience).

❑ The contemporary socio-constructivist orientation to mathematics, mathematics teaching and mathematics learning decreases consistently between the principal and consultant categories.

❑ The contemporary socio-constructivist view of mathematics, mathematics teaching and learning was more prevalent among teachers and principals than among consultants, and that the static-transmission orientation to mathematics, mathematics teaching and mathematics learning was more prevalent among consultants than among teachers and principals.

❑ The mechanistic-transmission view of mathematics, mathematics teaching and mathematics learning was more prevalent among teachers with a Masters degree, and to lesser extent teachers with no postgraduate qualifications, than among teachers with a Ph.D.

(ii) Teacher characteristics and their influence on their beliefs about mathematics assessment

Data were collected on the following teacher characteristics: gender, years of teaching experience, position held, professional development background and postgraduate qualifications possessed.

It was found that:

- ❏ Gender was not a significant variable for any of the factors, suggesting that teachers' beliefs about mathematics assessment were not significantly influenced by their gender.

- ❏ Experience at Junior High school (Years 7-9) placed more emphasis on a problem solving orientation to mathematics assessment than did teachers with experience at other levels.

- ❏ The problem solving orientation to mathematics assessment increased consistently across all teachers' experience categories.

- ❏ The problem solving approach to assessment in mathematics was more prevalent among experienced teachers (7-15 years experience) and veteran teachers (16+ years of experience) than among the inexperienced teachers (0-6 years of experience).

- ❏ Teachers' beliefs about mathematics assessment were not significantly influenced by their experience at Senior High school (Years 10-12).

- ❏ The socio-constructivist orientation to mathematics assessment decreases between the teacher and principal categories, and increases between the principal and consultant categories.

- ❏ The socio-constructivist view of mathematics assessment was more prevalent among teachers than among consultants, principals and vice-principals.

- ❏ The views of teachers and principals differ significantly with regard to a socio-constructivist orientation to mathematics assessment.

- ❏ The socio-constructivist orientation to mathematics assessment increased consistently across teachers' postgraduate qualifications. Teachers with Ph.D. degrees had the lowest means for Factor 1 as compared to teachers holding a Masters degrees and a first degree in mathematics.

- ❏ The socio-constructivist view of mathematics assessment was more prevalent among teachers with Masters and first degrees in mathematics than among teachers with Ph.D. degrees. A tenable explanation for this finding is that a number of the Ph.D. degrees had been of a theoretical nature in pure mathematics, the history of mathematics or other topics, which bear no direct relevance to mathematics education.

Comparisons with previous research

(I)   Mathematics teachers' beliefs about teaching and learning

The purpose of a literature review is to establish the dimensions within which a study is placed. The determination of the context and the various models of teachers' decisions, teachers' beliefs and knowledge were of paramount importance in carrying out the literature review.

The complexity of defining *educational beliefs* was highlighted (see Chapter 2) by the fact that for research purposes the concept of beliefs has been presented in the literature as a very broad and difficult to operationalise term. Pajares (1992) cited a number of constructs which can be considered as subsets of the broadly defined 'educational beliefs' term, the most commonly used being: teacher efficacy, epistemological beliefs, attributions, anxiety, self-concept and self-esteem, self-efficacy and specific subject matter beliefs, are just in the long list.

Thompson (1992) in her review of research on mathematics teachers' beliefs reported that the findings of studies investigating the relationship between mathematics teachers' espoused (or professed) beliefs and enacted beliefs (instructional practice) have not been consistent. Some studies, according to Thompson (1992), have found a high degree of agreement between mathematics teachers' espoused beliefs and their instructional practice whereas some other studies have reported 'sharp contrasts' (Thompson, 1992, p.137). The existence of inconsistencies in the reported studies, indicate according to Thompson (1992):

> That teacher's conceptions of teaching and learning mathematics are not related in a simple cause-and-effect way to their instructional practices. Instead, they suggest a complex relationship, with many sources of influence at work; one such source is the social context in which mathematics teaching is taking place, with all the constraints it imposes and the opportunities it offers. Embedded in this context are the values, beliefs, and expectations of students, parents, fellow teachers, and

administrators; the adopted curriculum; the assessment practices; and the values and philosophical learnings of the educational system at large. (p. 138)

There is evidence from this study to partially confirm Thompson's (1992) assertion that there is a certain degree of agreement between mathematics teachers' espoused beliefs and their instructional practice.

Van Zoest, et al. (1994) used a variation of Kuhs and Ball's (1986) model for their study by collapsing two of the four components proposed by Kuhs and Ball's (1986): the classroom-focused view and the two content focused views into one they called *learner-focused with an emphasis on social interaction,* since they theorized that there was an overlap between the classroom-focused view and the two content focused views proposed by Kuhs and Ball's (1986). Van Zoest, Jones and Thornton's (1994) factor analysis of 175 pre-service primary teachers' beliefs revealed only one significant factor, which the authors labeled a *socio-constructivist orientation* to mathematics, mathematics teaching and mathematics learning. This particular orientation shares many similarities with the socio-constructivist orientation revealed by the present study, given the fact that a number of the items used in Van Zoest, et al.'s (1994) study have been also used in this study.

Perry, et al. (1999) and their colleagues (Perry et al., 1996; Howard, et al., 1997) proposed a model aimed to describe the espoused beliefs of both primary and secondary mathematics teachers, as a result of a series of studies conducted in Australia. They identified two factors, which they considered sufficient for a full description of the espoused beliefs of mathematics teachers. They defined the two beliefs factors of their model, which they called *transmission view* and *child-centredness view* as follows:

> *Transmission:* the traditional view of mathematics as a static discipline which is taught and learned through the transmission of mathematical skills and knowledge from the teacher to the learner and where "mathematics [is seen] as a rigid system of externally dictated rules governed by standards of accuracy, speed and memory".
> *Child-centredness:* students are actively involved with mathematics through "constructing their own meaning as they are confronted with learning experiences which build on and challenge existing knowledge". (Perry, Howard and Tracey, 1999, p. 40)

Perry, et al. (1999) stressed that they consider the two factors making up their model as being distinct factors and not as the two ends of a continuum of one belief factor. The researchers' (1999) factor analysis revealed two factors: the transmission factor is identical to one of the teachers' beliefs factors identified in this study - the *traditional - transmission - information processing orientation,* consisting of the following (not mutually exclusive but complementary) views:

- ❑ The static view
- ❑ The mechanistic view

Perry, Howard and Tracey's (1999) second factor, the child-centredness orientation, shares many characteristics with the *contemporary – constructivist orientation* obtained in this study consisting of the following (not mutually exclusive but complementary) views:

- ❑ The socio-constructivist view
- ❑ The dynamic problem driven view
- ❑ The cooperative view

Perry, et al. (1999) also compared the beliefs of Head mathematics teachers to those of other mathematics teachers. They found that Head mathematics teachers professed a preference to a child-centred view than to a transmission view, indicating that more experienced secondary mathematics teachers were attempting to inject a reform agenda into their practices. Although results of my study may suggest that veteran mathematics teachers' professed a preference for a socio-constructivist/child-centred view rather than a transmission view, the findings from their instructional practices indicated that there is not sufficient evidence to confirm or refute this assertion and that the reform rhetoric does not easily translate into action.

Nisbet and Warren (2000) reported that their study of primary teachers' views about mathematics and about teaching mathematics revealed four factors related to teachers' views:

- A static view of mathematics
- A mechanistic view of mathematics
- A Traditional view of teaching mathematics and
- A contemporary view of teaching mathematics

They reported however, that although their analysis led to the conclusion that two of Ernest's (1989a) three categories of views of mathematics, were reflected in their final categories of the factor solution, the one category missing from their solution was the dynamic problem-driven view of mathematics. They argued that the reason for this outcome was due to the fact that, the problem solving view was not a separate construct for the study's primary teachers cohort.

Ernest (1989a) noted that the term 'beliefs' is not an isolated construct but it consists of the mathematics teachers' beliefs system, values and ideology in much the same way as Kuhs & Ball's (1986) teachers' dispositions. The impact such conceptions have on the selection of content, styles of teaching and modes of learning, has been the subject of another model provided by Ernest (1989b). He theorised that teachers' conceptions of the nature of mathematics as a whole (Figure 2.3.2) provide the foundation for teachers' mental models regarding the teaching and learning of mathematics.

The relative positions of the elements making up his model (Chapter 2, Figure 2.3.2, p. 31), indicate Ernest's (1989b) awareness of the dominance teachers' beliefs about the nature of mathematics exert, on their espoused beliefs about teaching and learning, as well as that the social context may constraint mathematics teachers' enacted approaches concerning the teaching and learning of mathematics. In the present study, the problem solving view was identified as one of the categories of views of mathematics and mathematics teaching and learning.

There are three notable differences between this study and that of Nisbet and Warren (2000), however. The *first* concerns the fact that their study explored Australian primary teachers' views whereas this study explored Greek secondary mathematics teachers' views. The fact that pre-service secondary mathematics teachers in Greek Universities complete a four-year mathematics study cycle, consisting of many hours of solving mathematical problems, may have contributed to the existence of a distinct problem solving factor solution in my factor analysis. Cultural differences influencing the professed beliefs and instructional practices of mathematics teachers in the two countries could be a *second* factor accounting for the differences in the espoused beliefs of secondary teachers in the two countries. The *third* difference concerns Nisbet and Warren's (2000) interpretation of Ernest's (1989) categories. Their interpretation that Ernest's (1989) categories strictly refer to teachers' views about mathematics, may have contributed to a narrowness of their factor analysis results for at least two reasons:

(i)   Some of the items which loaded on the two factors describing views about mathematics (Nisbet and Warren, 2000, p. 40), i.e. the static and the mechanistic views contain items which could be considered to refer to mathematics teaching and learning as well as to mathematics. Three examples of such items are the following: *Item 26* – Students best learn by doing lots of exercises and practice, *Item 20* – The problem with low achieving students is that they don't learn the rule, *Item 11* – It is important that students use the rules learned to get answers and to solve problems.

(ii)   Ernest (1989a) stated that "teachers' conceptions of the nature of mathematics by no means have to be considered to be consciously held views; rather they may be implicitly held philosophies" (p. 20); and that "three philosophies of mathematics are distinguished *because of their observed occurrence in the teaching of mathematics*" (p.21, emphasis mine); and also that " beliefs about mathematics are reflected in teachers' models of the teaching and learning of mathematics, and hence in their practices" (p. 22). Despite Ernest's arguments and an overwhelming body of research evidence to the contrary, Nisbet and Warren (2000) have attempted to isolate teachers' views about mathematics from their views about mathematics teaching and learning, in my opinion unsuccessfully.

My interpretation of Ernest's (1989a) statements – in conjunction with the views regarding teachers' beliefs expressed by Pajares (1992); Fennema, et al. (1996); Cooney (1999); Van Zoest (1994); Askew, et al. (1997); Tanner & Jones, 1998) – is that it is not possible to separate mathematics teachers' views about mathematics from their views about mathematics teaching and learning. In this study a dynamic problem-driven component has been obtained in the questionnaire survey's factor and cluster analyses, by treating secondary mathematics teachers' views regarding mathematics, mathematics teaching and mathematics learning as an intertwined, interconnected and inseparable belief system deeply embedded into a personal philosophy or worldview.

(II)   Beliefs about assessment

As far as assessment is concerned, there has been a growing interest in mathematical assessment during the last two decades and a wealth of research reports has led to the development of authentic assessment strategies and tasks (NCTM, 1989; Webb, 1993; Clarke, 1996; Clarke & Stephens, 1996). Clarke (1996) proposed that assessment should been assigned a proactive role in the process of determining what kind of learning and instruction will be planned. He proposed that assessment should be 'constructive' in the sense that their principal aim is to inform 'a constructive consequent action' (Clarke, 1996, p. 336). A number of assessment strategies could be used to exemplify the new (constructivist) approach. Student portfolios, group work, open-ended tasks, student self-assessment, extended investigations and projects such as those used in the Victorian Certificate of Education (VCE).

Clarke and Stephens (1996) conducted a study on the instructional impact of the systemic introduction of performance assessment in mathematics. They introduced the term 'ripple effect' in an attempt to encapsulate their study that:

> The introduction of new assessment practices into existing high stakes assessment creates a climate of change, which has immediate and direct consequences for policy and instruction at the level of school and classroom. This change climate functions to stimulate and support the introduction of specific practices. The emergent hypothesis is that unless a term or practice receives the explicit sanction of inclusion in high stakes assessment it is unlikely to influence school policy or classroom practice. (Clarke and Stephens 1996, p. 70)

Clarke and Stephens (1996) used 15 items in the questionnaire part of their study and the participants were asked to indicate the degree of importance they attached to the aspect described by each item. The 15 items were designed to reflect different ways in which problem solving and investigations could be valued and used by teachers. One of the aims of the study was to compare the assessment views of teachers teaching VCE mathematics at the time, with those of teachers from Greece with no VCE (or equivalent) mathematics teaching experience.

In the present study, the 15 items used by Clarke and Stephens (1996) formed part of a larger questionnaire on secondary teachers' beliefs about assessment. Two of the items used by Clarke and Stephens have been slightly reworded for the purposes of this study. The percentage responses of Greek secondary mathematics teachers who indicated that a particular aspect of problem solving or investigation was *highly important,* on the 15 items common to both studies, is shown in Figure 7.2.1 (The numbers in brackets correspond to the items of the pilot study questionnaire (Section IV, Appendix C1).

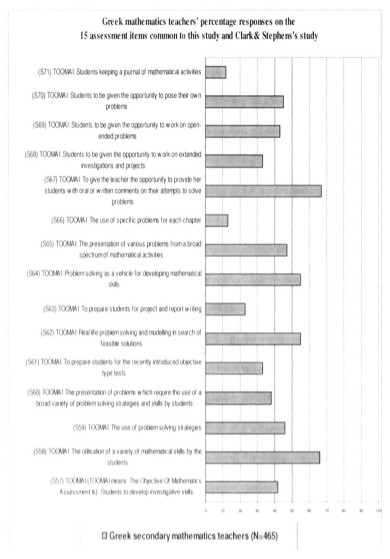

Figure 7.2.1. Greek secondary mathematics teachers' views on the 15 assessment items common to this study and Clarke& Stephen's study

Clarke & Stephens (1996, p.83) reported that 'consistently high levels of approval (50%) were given to those aspects which were strongly endorsed by VCE curriculum advice and assessment practice' (items 57 to 64 from the Victorian sample satisfy this condition). It can be seen from Figure 7.2.1 that four items from the Greek sample (58, 62, 64 and 67) satisfy the condition as well. If we reduce the (arbitrary) value of 50% to 40%, for the category of high levels of approval, then five more items from the Greek sample satisfy the condition (40% for high levels of approval or moderate approval). These items are 57, 59, 65, 69 and 70. This finding indicates Greek secondary mathematics teachers value problem solving and posing, modelling and investigations highly. In regard to Clarke and Stephens' (1996) statement that:

> The emergent hypothesis is that unless a term or practice receives the explicit sanction of inclusion in high stakes assessment it is unlikely to influence school policy or classroom practice. (p. 70)

It appears that this hypothesis can only partially be substantiated, since it is evident that Greek secondary mathematics teachers value problem solving and investigations highly, in a system where *there is no* 'explicit sanction of inclusion in high stakes assessment'.

Teachers hold beliefs towards the nature as well as the purposes and uses of assessment in mathematics. It can be conjectured that teachers' beliefs about assessment influence their teaching in many ways. There is evidence from this study that there are teachers who espouse a 'socio-constructivist' orientation to mathematics assessment, teachers who espouse a 'problem solving' orientation to mathematics assessment, and teachers who espouse an 'accountability' orientation to mathematics assessment.

The issue of whether Clarke & Stephens' (1996) emerging hypothesis can be substantiated at an international level remains open to further investigation. It would appear that the cultural climate in which assessment takes place influences teachers' beliefs about mathematics assessment and it reflects prevailing societal norms. The findings reported in this study indicate that there may be an apparent impact of the broad social and cultural climate on teachers' espoused beliefs about mathematics assessment and invites further investigation.

Nisbet & Warren (2000) extended the Clarke, Clarke & Lovitt (1990) scheme on the major uses of assessment – which focuses on three areas: teachers, students and parents – with the third area extended to become 'for accountability purposes' (Nisbet & Warren, 2000, p. 37). This extension constitutes one of the factors of the Factor Analysis in the present study. Nisbet & Warren (2000) noted that despite the fact that much has been written about the purposes of assessment 'there is a paucity of research' (p. 36) on how mathematics teachers use assessment information and on what they actually believe about assessment. The same can be said about research efforts regarding the relationship between espoused beliefs about assessment and the actual teaching practice. Assessment approaches may be considered as extensions of mathematics teachers' beliefs about mathematics, and mathematics teaching and learning.

Cooney (1999) cited a study by Senk, Beckmann and Thompson (1997), in which they found that:

> About 68% of teachers' tests focus on lower level outcomes and that only about 5% of the items require any depth of thinking. Further, they found that virtually no teachers used open-ended items on tests. (p. 167)

Cooney (1999) remarked that according to his studies: "teachers felt uncomfortable in answering and unlikely to use open-ended items with their students" (p. 167). A similar remark can be made about the present study – regarding one of the case studies teachers' (Tom) assessment classroom practices.

Regarding the introduction of contemporary assessment practices into mathematics classrooms, the role of teachers is considered pivotal. Shepard (2000) noticed that mathematics teachers' prevailing ideas about assessment could be far from what new trends on assessment aim to tackle. In that respect if mathematics educators aim to bring about change in traditional assessment practices in mathematics classrooms, then "teachers' knowledge and beliefs should be a primary site for research" (Shepard, 2000, p. 71).

7.2 Conclusions drawn from the qualitative part of the study

The case studies of the beliefs and practices of two veteran secondary mathematics teachers have provided some insights into the complex interactions involved. The existence of conflicts between what a teacher believes about teaching, learning and assessment and what can actually be achieved in the classroom has been documented in the qualitative part of this study (Chapter 6). If this is due to a lack to a coherent view of mathematics or nor, it is still to be established.

What is evident from the analysis of the case studies teachers' interviews and classroom practices is that the classroom is a complex site of political, historical, social and cultural influences (Billet, 1998).

The research question relevant to this part of the study is the following:

Research question 3:

Are there inconsistencies between Greek secondary mathematics teachers' beliefs about mathematics, mathematics teaching, mathematics learning, mathematics assessment and their teaching practice?

Teachers in this multiple-case study demonstrated that their beliefs were not always consistent with their instructional practices, as it has been documented in previous studies (Cooney, 1999; Thompson, 1992; Pajares, 1992; Ernest, 1989a; Raymond, 1997). In both cases veteran secondary mathematics teachers' beliefs about mathematics were more traditional than their beliefs about mathematics teaching and learning. An interesting finding of this study is that Greek veteran secondary mathematics teachers' beliefs about mathematics learning and teaching (including assessment) were less traditional than their actual teaching practice, much like those of the beginning primary teachers in Raymond's (1997) study. Raymond (1997) interpreted her findings as supporting an assertion that:

> Although beginning elementary school teachers often enter the teaching profession with nontraditional views beliefs about how they should teach, when faced with constraints of actual classroom teaching, they tend to implement more traditional classroom practices. (p. 573)

The fact that this finding is revealed in this study as well raises a number of issues about the relationship and interactions between teachers' espoused beliefs and their teaching practices and also about the nature and causes of inconsistencies between teachers' firmly held beliefs and their manifestations in actual mathematics teaching environments. In a number of recent studies teachers' beliefs have been found to be flexible regarding what was central to the task of teaching (Malone, 1996); to be influenced by effective practice within the boundaries of their classrooms (Buzeika, 1996), and to be influenced by a perceived pressure of known expectations of other teachers, when adopting a classroom approach (Shield, 1999).

The role that mathematics education and professional development courses should play in resolving this crisis is of paramount importance if reforms espoused by many influential documents (a *National Statement of mathematics for Australian Schools* (Australian Education Council [AEC], 1991; National Council of Teachers of Mathematics, 2000) are to be implemented successfully. The contribution of cultural influences in the formation of teachers' beliefs, and the transformation into practical approaches also needs to be addressed. It seems that prior experiences and social norms are decisive factors in the beliefs of many mathematics teachers as is the belief that if they adhere to the "tried and true" (Howard & Tracey, 1999) approaches in mathematics teaching and learning, they will not go wrong.

Overall, the analysis of the case study teachers' interviews, classroom observations and open questionnaire items (Appendix C5) indicated that both teachers in this study agreed that there is *a strong relationship between teaching practice and teachers' beliefs about mathematics, and mathematics teaching and learning.* It could also be concluded that in some cases the opposite is also true and the case studies teachers' beliefs were influenced by prior effective teaching practices. The major causes of inconsistencies suggested by the two veteran secondary mathematics teachers were the classroom situation, prior experiences and social norms. Teachers may believe for instance that group work is the best environment for exploring mathematical ideas and learning mathematics but when it comes to University entrance examinations preparation, for example, may keep them from implementing this belief into practice (Ann provided such an example). This illustrates how a single element in the classroom situation or the influence of societal and parental expectations and teaching social norms can affect teaching practice to a greater extent than the teacher's beliefs by forcing the teacher's belief system into a chaotic singularity.

Another finding of this study is that prior school experiences and personal world-views and ideologies were the main influence on the teachers' beliefs about mathematics, but their own school days experiences and their teaching experiences being the main influences on beliefs about teaching, learning and assessing mathematics. Teachers' beliefs about the nature of mathematics, the performance of their students as well as the school's ethos and established norms were named by both case study teachers as the dominant influences on the actual teaching practice. Professional development and teaching practice were viewed as having a very minimal influence on teaching practice and almost no influence on beliefs about mathematics teaching and learning.

In the case of Ann, it was clear that her beliefs about mathematics, mathematics teaching, learning and assessment were of a contemporary/socio-constructivist nature. The fact that Ann named her political ideology as a primary influence on her non-traditional teaching practice, especially on her firmly held beliefs about the power and utility of collaborative teaching and learning approaches shed light onto and enabled the interpretation of her classroom practices which were in concert with her beliefs about mathematics and mathematics learning and teaching. It was clear however, that beliefs about mathematics pedagogy and about the role of societal and cultural factors were the dominant influences in Ann's teaching practice.

According to Ann, participation in meaningful activities is the key to success in mathematics. Students' learning of mathematics depends primarily on the learner, while applying mathematics in various contexts, utilising their skills in modelling real life situations and the development of an inquiring mind were Ann's criteria regarding students' understanding. At the same time however, Ann felt that students should both understand and master skills and algorithms. Her espoused socio-constructivist view to mathematics learning was grounded on her firm belief that all students can learn mathematics and that mathematics learning is the result of students making connections, and interpreting and organising the information gained from experiences. Ann promoted knowledge sharing and encouraged students to actively participate in their learning. She clearly valued process over product and strived to conduct her classes in a non-threatening environment through making connections both between concepts and topics. She also emphasised understanding over memorisation by promoting learning via problem solving and modelling activities.

The impact of professional development did not seem to have influenced Ann' beliefs about teaching. Her daily experiences appeared to have strongly affected her beliefs about mathematics teaching. Ann's firm socio-constructivist stance about mathematics teaching and learning was further reinforced by her statements 'I am constantly trying to discover new approaches and educational environments that will enable the kids to fully develop as mathematics apprentices' and 'the interaction with my students created a dialectic relationship from which a number of unexpected new ideas kept emerging'.

Ann experienced resistance to cooperative learning from her own students, some of whom felt that they would not be rewarded for their individual efforts if they participated in group work. She also experienced opposition on the use of group work from her colleagues who expressed concerned about the value of group work in mathematics concepts and skills acquisition. Parents too, voiced their objections to the use of group work, since they felt that their children would not be as competitively prepared for final exams, as they would have been with traditional methods. All these criticisms are indications of the adverse impact the system may have on the teacher's teaching practices. When the education system is founded on traditional chalk-and-talk approaches, the result on teaching practice may be that individual efforts and competitiveness are being valued and rewarded as the approved approach to learning mathematics.

The promotion of a community environment in Ann's classes, with its potential to encourage active participation, brainstorming, ideas exchange and to maximise each student's potential in mathematics learning, has been the driving force behind her cooperative teaching approach. The promotion of leadership qualities is also evident in her approach. Promoting student autonomy and shared responsibility, and reducing teacher intervention to a minimum, which are fundamental ingredients in the development of a community of inquiry, was the overriding learning-teaching approach in Ann's classes. Ann's criteria of quality teaching were simple, yet effective in providing incentives and in inspiring her students to be active learners (Chapter 6).

Ann claimed that her ability to teach mathematics has been influenced by her two contentions (and her desire to improve on both) that the teacher should have a strong base of mathematical content knowledge, and at the same time be knowledgeable of contemporary didactical, psychological and pedagogical approaches. Ann's beliefs about mathematics teaching seem to have grown out of a desire to oppose a stagnant and inflexible system, which limits the teachers' options to innovate, to try new approaches and to strive to develop an active learning and cooperative teaching environment in her classes.

The culmination of a number of factors constituted Ann's world-view of the learning-teaching process. She listed ten factors in her attempt to explain the existence of inconsistencies between espoused beliefs and beliefs in practice. Most of them had to do with the difficulty of introducing and sustaining innovative teaching practices in a system which had solid traditional foundations and where teaching was seen primarily as a public servant's job. The absence of a systemic teacher evaluation/appraisal system and the lack of support for innovative teaching approaches point to a myopic vision by Regional and State educational policy makers. In her own words (Chapter 6, p. 142)

- *The first factor concerns the expectations of the education system that could sometimes act in ways that inhibit innovations.*
- *The second factor concerns the things you are used to do that turn out to be a lot easier than introducing innovations in your daily routine.*
- *The third factor is the fact that it is very difficult to overcome every obstacle on a daily basis in order to do what you believe is the best practice.*
- *The fourth factor is the fact that I do not have my own mathematics classroom.*
- *The fifth factor is the fact that regional mathematics consultants are more decorative than anything useful. We never get to meet them and discuss our concerns.*
- *The sixth factor concerns my family obligations, which in practice drastically limits my available time.*
- *The seventh factor concerns the lack of communication with some of my students, since they have been bred to thing that schooling means teaching to the test.*
- *The eighth factor is the fact that I do not have all the required recourses at school.*

- *The ninth factor concerns the fact that the system does not provide any incentives for innovative teaching practice, and*
- *The tenth factor is the fact that there is no teaching evaluation or appraisal, which could indirectly force me to be more prepared on a daily basis and to perform even better in class.*

Ann assessed her students primarily via contemporary assessment methods (projects, group work, self-assessment) but she felt that she also had to use traditional methods of assessment (tests, exams) in order to prepare her students for University entrance exams. She held a firm belief about problem solving and modelling as a vehicle for developing mathematical skills and she espoused a strong commitment to the development of investigative skills by all of her students. In her own words:

- *class involvement,*
- *keeping a journal of mathematical activities,*
- *taking notes,*
- *task involvement,*
- *degree of understanding,*
- *open-ended questions,*
- *problem solving and modelling performance,*
- *memorisation of some aspects of the course,*
- *participation in group work*
- *student self-assessment,*
- *project work performance,*
- *appropriate planning and administrative support.*

Ann frequently used everyday language in an attempt to break the barrier between teacher and student, to communicate more effectively with her students and to create a classroom environment conducive to learning. Her comments reveal the importance of her own standards and beliefs in determining what occurs in her classroom. Ann's attempts to create an environment that respects students' ideas and efforts were in concert with her familiarity with the content and curricular goals of the activity.

Ann's teaching pattern although sharing some perspectives with the focusing pattern of interaction is not identical to it however, and it could be called an *emerging, spontaneous or evolving pattern of interaction*. In this particular pattern the teacher changes plans and diversifies her approach in order to accommodate all her students' needs, and to achieve her own goals for a particular segment of a mathematics lesson.

Ann frequently reflected on her teaching practices. Her stated beliefs about the nature of mathematics were generally consistent with Ernest's (1989) dynamic problem-solving view. There was considerable evidence of practices that mirrored that view. She encouraged her students to take risks and attempt to find alternative solutions to problems, and they were rewarded for their efforts. Investigations were used and students' errors were capitalized on the sole purpose of facilitating learning. Ann's teaching could be described as 'learner-focused' (Appendix B1) with an emphasis on conceptual understanding. While it was apparent that most students participated in the mathematical activities and enjoyed Ann's lessons, a number of conflicts between students' expectations and classroom practices were also apparent.

Ann's classroom environment was primarily consistent with Davies' (1994) *hermeneutic listening* category (Chapter 2, page 42) of a teacher's behaviour in mathematics classrooms. This mode of teaching is concerned more with delivering a flexible response to ever-changing circumstances than of unyielding progress toward imposed goals. The rigid structure, the preset goals, the formulated explanations, the entrenched roles are being dissolved in some extent as the unanticipated, the surprising, and the intuitive find places for expression. Ann's classroom was a testimony to the kind of interaction conjectured by the model. In Ann's classroom a conflation of roles was occurring. Ann became a participant in the exploration of a shared project. The authority became collective and there was a sense of community-established standards.

Ann's hermeneutic listening reflected the participatory and negotiated nature of this manner of interaction with learners. Hermeneutic listening requires the willingness to interrogate the taken for granted and the prejudices that frame our perceptions and actions. It is a consequence of this theoretical disposition that in our joint actions we are capable of forming unities that are more complex. Ann demonstrated that what needs to be abandoned in everyday teaching activities is the belief that teaching is a matter of causing learners to acquire, master, or construct particular understandings through some pre-established instructional sequence. Ann strongly believed that learning is actually a social process, and the teacher's role is one of participating, of interpreting, of transforming, of interrogating-in short, of listening.

Ann's beliefs about mathematics teaching and learning and her consequent instructional decisions were in line with Fennema et al.' (1996) level four (Chapter 2, Table 2.3.1, pp. 45-47). Her beliefs were characterized by the acceptance of the idea that children can solve problems without direct instruction and that the mathematics curriculum should be based on children's abilities. Ann believed that her role was to find out what children knew and to use that knowledge to structure the learning environment. Ann also believed that what the children knew should be a major influence on all her instructional decisions.

Overall, Ann could be classified as a reflective connectionist mathematics teacher (Cooney's classification scheme, Appendix B1). Ann reflected on and attended to the beliefs of others as compared to her own. She attempted to resolve conflict through reflective thinking but although she did not make connections, she was able to weave them into a set of beliefs held from a relativistic and committed perspective while listening to and valuing others. Ann, as a true reflective connectionist, analysed and integrated the merits of various positions, and came to terms with what she believed in a committed way.

In the case of Tom, it was clear that his beliefs about mathematics were more traditional than his views about mathematics teaching, learning and assessment. His espoused beliefs about mathematics teaching, learning and assessment were not implemented in his teaching practice. It was clear however, that prior teaching experiences and firm beliefs on what effective practice might be were the dominant influences in Tom's teaching practice.

Tom's views about group work are diametrically opposite to those of Ann, and they had an impact on his teaching practice. He held conflicting views about the utility of group work in his classes expressing the view that it is useful but stating at the same time that he will never use this approach in his classes. Tom firmly believed that mathematics teachers should have a wide repertoire of knowledge, not only in mathematically related areas.

Tom's view about mathematics coincides with the non-constructivist view that mathematics is a static and immutable knowledge with objective truth. His preference for a rigorous axiomatic approach had a dominant influence his views about learning and teaching. Despite his expressed view that many students are just not able to learn mathematics, he claimed that knowledge is an active process and that students have to take charge of their own learning, a view that is in concert with the contemporary view that students are autonomous learners and they learn through active participation in meaningful activities. Students learn mathematics when engaged in drill activities for mastery of skills, according to Tom. He espoused a sequential approach to teaching where memorisation and mastery of facts is valued more than understanding. According to Tom students' learning in mathematics is an individual pursuit for knowledge and it depends on both the teacher and the student alike. In his own words (Chapter 6, p. 165):

My beliefs about mathematics have been primarily shaped by my teaching experience. It is my deep-rooted belief that the teacher's role is not to judge students but to facilitate learning. The teacher is the student's collaborator and my objective is to help students realise that we are together in their attempts to understand, to explore, to investigate and to own their knowledge. I owe these beliefs to my colleagues and students over the years.

Tom's teaching style consisted of a traditional face-to-face teaching, and the different daily approaches he referred to were nothing more than dispensing mathematical knowledge in lecture style lessons. He presented mathematics in an expository style by demonstrating and explaining concepts and skills and he approached topics in isolation. He sought 'right answers' and was not concerned about students' explanations if they were not in a pre-determined 'right direction'.

His espoused beliefs about the treatment of errors represent another inconsistency between his espoused and enacted beliefs. Tom espoused a contemporary view about students' errors in mathematics as being expressions of students' current understanding but in his classes, he did not demonstrate any systematic effort to understand the sources of his students' errors. He instead attempted to eliminate students' misunderstandings by rewording his explanations or by follow-up instruction.

Tom adopted an experiential approach to his own teaching approaches. He considered teaching as a dynamic process requiring a deep understanding of individual students' differences and needs. He felt that, provided he had more time, he would attempt to introduce innovations. He expressed the view that quality teaching is a gift (Chapter 6, pp. 167-168):

I believe that quality teaching means that the students trust their teacher that there is some short of acceptance and appreciation of what the teacher is trying to do. Quality teaching is a gift but at the same time there are some fundamental didactical principles on which teaching should be grounded. The mathematics teacher should radiate energy and knowledge and make his students feel important. I strive to use activities, which will improve my students' imagination and broaden their horizons. I do not believe that there are difficult topics to teach but poorly performing teachers instead.

Tom, despite the fact that he espoused using activities that would improve his students' imagination and broaden their horizons, was actually using the textbook like a Bible. He did not use any activity other than the routine exercises presented by the textbook. Tom's belief that teaching is a socio-cultural process had an effect on his pastoral role as a teacher but did not seem to have any effect on his (primarily) traditional teaching approach.

Tom assessed his students solely through standard quizzes and exams, his objectives being to prepare his students for university entrance type exams, to verify if students should be promoted to the next grade and to provide his students and their parents with feedback about their progress.

Tom provided the correct answers for any question that the students could not answer and that he guided his students to a predetermined path (and answer) while attempting to solve specific questions. He primarily led most classroom discussion towards a pre-determined direction with the sole objective of arriving at a pre-determined answer he had in mind.

One of the reasons regarding the existence of inconsistencies between his espoused beliefs and teaching practice offered by Tom during the post-lesson interview, concern the pressure of time constraints. This awareness seems to be a frustration factor for both the teacher and the students, irrespective of beliefs and intentions in a process where the teacher rushes to finish of a particular lesson and the students feel like they are being squeezed. Tom argued that he was aware of the existence of such an inconsistency between his espoused and his enacted beliefs. In his own words (Appendix F2).

> *For some children this kind of work pace has positive results, for some children it doesn't. Certainly some children have another pace and if we worked at a slower pace they would have greater benefits. This is a fact. The question is to what extent we should change this pace or to what extent we should stick to it, in order to have the greatest benefit for the class in which we are working. This is a question, which I think about all the time. I haven't found a feasible solution yet.*

Tom's stated beliefs about the nature of mathematics were a combination of Ernest's (1989) dynamic – problem solving and Platonist views. He believed that mathematics is a continually expanding field of inquiry and its results are open to revision. It is also a field of creativity and invention and a cultural product (problem-solving view). He also believed that mathematics is a set of immutable structures and truths, and a unified body of expert knowledge (Platonist view).

There was considerable evidence of practices that mirrored the Platonist view, also. Tom did not use investigations, and students' errors were not capitalized during the course of teacher-student interactions. Tom tended to direct his students toward a pre-determined solution. His teaching could be described as 'content-focused' with an emphasis on procedural understanding. It was apparent that a number of students participated in the mathematical activities but did not enjoy Tom's lessons, and a number of conflicts between students' expectations and classroom practices were also apparent.

Tom's classroom environment was consistent with Davies' (1994) *evaluative listening* category (Chapter 2, page 42) of a teacher's behaviour in mathematics classrooms. The primary reason for listening in such mathematics classrooms tends to be limiting and limited. Tom was not interested in what his students were saying and the communication was constrained by the fact that he was listening *for* something in particular (his own pre-determined answer) rather than listening *to* the student. Tom's actions – including his questions – were generally pre-determined and allowed little room for deviation. As a result, students frequently felt that their contributions were not valued. In his classes, listening occurred at a trivial level. Tom had a correct answer in mind and he would strive for unambiguous explanations and well-structured lessons. It was apparent that in his interactions with his students, potentially powerful learning opportunities were not being picked up and the opportunity to capitalise on them was lost.

Tom's beliefs about mathematics teaching and learning and his consequent instructional decisions were in line with Fennema et al.' (1996) level three (Appendix B1). His beliefs were characterized by the acceptance of the idea that children would learn mathematics as they solved many problems and discussed their solutions. Just providing (what he thought were) rich experiences (just helping, or providing different kinds of problems-harder and easier, or providing a larger amount of problems) appeared to be sufficient for him.

Overall, Tom could be classified as a naïve connectionist mathematics teacher (Cooney's classification, Appendix B1). Tom reflected on and attended to the beliefs of others as compared to his own. He failed however, to resolve conflict or differences in beliefs. There is not sufficient evidence however, to determine whether this lack of resolution emerged as a result of a lack of his commitment to teaching or from his inability to resolve contradictions.

7.3 Limitations of the study

The study aimed to examine teachers' beliefs regarding mathematics, and mathematics learning and teaching. It is recognized that case study teachers who felt inhibited or embarrassed in expressing their views were free to respond in any way they preferred. In a number of cases teachers were drawing upon memories of learning and teaching mathematics, the accuracy of recollections could be called into question. The method adopted in this study was to analyse the recollections of the events without consideration of the way they were recalled by each case study participant, thus limiting the depth of the analysis.

The case studies were limited by the number of teachers who were prepared to participate in this aspect of the research. While a number of teachers who were invited to be involved took advantage of the opportunity, various factors forced two of them to decline to be involved in the case studies or in specific parts of the case studies. The reasons cited were personal commitments, lack of time and a fear of being formally evaluated while participating in the study. It would have been desirable to have more than two teachers participating in the case studies, since that would have enabled me to investigate the resulting factors in more detail.

Videotape provided a rich set of data. The findings of the data analysis, despite the fact that it was time-consuming and tedious, illustrated the limitation of inferences drawn from self-report measures. Although many classes of each teacher were observed and video taped, a decision was made that only a single lesson of mathematics would be used as the focus for full analysis and interpretation. Alternatively I could have chosen to discuss more briefly a greater number of lessons taught by Ann and Tom, but to do so it would have necessitated the fragmentation of the process of teaching and it would not have allowed me to focus on an exploration of the many aspects of classroom life. It could also have led me to forego my intention of acknowledging the complexity of mathematics teachers' work.

Six hundred survey forms were mailed to a random selection of grade 7-12 mathematics teachers. Of these 465 mathematics teachers responded. The size of this sample was considered to be appropriate for the principal component and factor analysis. Tabachnick & Fidell (1996) suggest that a sample size of at least 300 cases is appropriate.

A limitation of this study is that all results must be considered in the context that responses to the questionnaire items depend on the interpretations assigned to them by each respondent.

7.4 Future directions for research and teacher training

Teachers' beliefs influence their classroom practices, the beliefs are formed early and beliefs about teaching are well established by the time a prospective teacher starts attending University classes. It is therefore important to mathematics educators, researchers and curriculum designers, to understand the impact teachers' beliefs have on their cognitions and classroom practices. In this study we have explored the complex terrain of mathematics teachers' beliefs regarding the teaching and learning of mathematics.

Ann and Tom considered the relationship between teacher preparation and teaching practice to be minimal and viewed the relationship between beliefs and teacher preparation as strong. Helping pre-service teachers become aware of their beliefs before they commence teaching could help them in the first years of teaching. Having an understanding of teachers' world-views of teaching at the beginning could help teachers evaluate their instructional practice with honesty.

Ann's teaching approach could be considered as offering an alternative pattern of interaction while at the same time sharing some of the characteristics with one of the two patterns of interaction in mathematics classrooms – the funnel pattern – identified by Wood (1994). According to Wood (1994), the funnel and focus patterns of interaction appear to be dominant in mathematics classrooms. Ann's teaching pattern, although sharing some perspectives with the focusing pattern of interaction is not identical to it, and it could be called an *emerging, spontaneous or evolving pattern of interaction.* In this particular pattern the teacher changes plans and diversifies her approach in order to accommodate all her students' needs and to achieve her own goals for a particular segment of a mathematics lesson. Ann's comments demonstrate her firm beliefs on using the approach when necessary: "Sometimes I am overdoing it with this pattern of interaction … In that way teaching emerges from the spontaneity of the approach and kids can reap maximum benefits from it" (Chapter 6, p. 157).

The absence of adequate professional training and development is another factor that could explain the existence of inconsistencies between espoused beliefs and beliefs in practice. Most professional development seminars touch only the surface of the real issues that concern teachers by providing only theoretical support but little or no practical guidance and follow-up activities. It seems that there are a number of teachers whose espoused beliefs about mathematics teaching, learning and assessment could be classified as contemporary, but when it comes to their daily practice, they resort to traditional approaches of teaching, which provided a sense of security for them.

The awareness of one's beliefs systems could stipulate the examination and development of beliefs about mathematics, and mathematics teaching and learning because teacher preparation and in-service programs are likely to exert more influence on beliefs than on instructional practice. Initial teacher education may not have the power to influence teaching practices significantly, but in-service programs could prove more effective in this endeavour. It could be conjectured that both pre-service and in-service teacher education programs may indirectly affect teachers' instructional practice if their objective concerned influencing the belief systems of teachers via training programs. Hiebert, Gallimore & Stigler (2002) argued that effective professional development programs yields the best results when they are:

> Long-term, school based, collaborative, focused on students' learning, and linked to curricula. In such programs, teachers examine student work, develop performance assessments and standards-based report cards, and jointly plan, teach, and revise lessons. Teachers, who traditionally have worked in isolation, report favourably on programs that bring them in close contact with colleagues in active work on improving practice. (p. 3)

Since a growing number of professional development programs draw from the available research evidence in their effort to altering teachers' beliefs about their instructional practices, Hiebert, Gallimore & Stigler (2002), reminded us that "teachers rarely draw from a shared knowledge base to improve their practice" (p. 3) and that "there is a persistent concern that educational research has too little influence on improving classroom teaching and learning" (p. 3). It could be claimed that professional development programs such as those espoused by Hiebert, Gallimore & Stigler (2002), might lead to a "professional community mind-set" among mathematics teachers by providing them with the opportunity to rely on the dynamics and the collective wisdom of the team. In that way teachers may develop an increased predilection for reflection and critical analysis of their own teaching and of their own beliefs about teaching and learning. The results of this study support the idea that mathematics teachers need to be provided with systematic guidance in developing the skills for critical reflection and self-appraisal.

Data such as that gathered from the lessons of Ann and Tom could be used in pre-service and in-service professional development courses in several ways. Excerpts could be used as the basis of discussion on mathematics teaching and learning matters, of those factors that influence teachers in their daily practices, of the pressures they are faced with, how they respond to them, and of the inconsistencies identified between espoused beliefs and beliefs in practice. Such excerpts could be used in an open ended way for participants to consider what they might have done in the same situation and why. Valuable knowledge could be acquired by teachers by exploring the daily routines they use and by examining the inconsistencies identified. Observed inconsistencies may also point to deficiencies in the planning and the implementation of professional development courses.

It is hoped that the findings of the study will be of value to potential or practising mathematics teacher evaluators or appraisers and principals. It is deemed necessary to understand what mathematics teachers do before the commencement of an appraisal session or before attempting to evaluate their performance. The outcomes of the study could also be used by teacher educators in encouraging the development of reflective practice by prospective teachers or teacher practitioners.

The findings of this study invite research into several issues which are discussed in this section. Through an examination of the Principal Component Analysis factors an analysis of particular dimensions of the deep structure of mathematics teachers' beliefs have been elaborated and a new model has been proposed. Two major orientations have been identified (Chapter 5, p. 90) that are characteristic of secondary mathematics teachers' beliefs with regard to the nature of mathematics and the learning and teaching of mathematics: A *contemporary – constructivist orientation*, and a *traditional – transmission – information processing orientation*. Replication of particular findings would substantiate some of the conclusions drawn.

The study also attempted to explore the influence beliefs exert on mathematics teachers' instructional practice. More work is needed in observing behaviours in the classroom setting to infer beliefs.

Consideration might be given to the development of a scale which measures the extent to which mathematics teachers consider mathematics as a static-mechanistic or a dynamic body of knowledge, and the extent to which mathematics teaching and learning is viewed as a constructivist-oriented or as a transmission-oriented endeavour.

The findings of this study suggest that the broad social and cultural climate of the classroom may impact on teachers' espoused and enacted beliefs about mathematics, and mathematics learning, teaching and assessment. This possibility invites further investigation.

7.5   *Final words*

While teachers' beliefs are difficult to change, making teachers aware of the influence of those beliefs is a first step in assisting them to transform any counter-productive beliefs into a positive force to enhance mathematics teaching and learning.

It is my contention that in attempting to transform current transmission-oriented teaching practices, understanding the complexity of the region where teachers' espoused and enacted sets of beliefs intersect, is of paramount importance. Taking into consideration the recent interest expressed by the mathematics education community in the importance of values in teaching, and on their interrelationship to belief systems, I believe that such an understanding will constitute the motivation for future reform in, and the delivery of both in-service and pre-service programs for mathematics teachers.

My journey into the complex topology of mathematics teachers' beliefs has come to an end. But what a journey has it been! The richness of the experiences of such a journey have been captured by the words of the Greek poet Kavafis in his poem '*Ithaca*', in which he described the saga of Odysseus, the King of Ithaca, in his twenty year return home journey:

Have Ithaca always in your mind
Arriving there is what you are destined for
But do not in the least hurry the Journey
Better it last for years
So that when you reach the island you are old
Rich with all that you have gained in the way
Not expecting Ithaca to give you wealth
Ithaca gave you your splendid Journey
Without her you would not have set out
She hasn't anything else to give you

And if you find her poor, Ithaca hasn't deceived you
So wise have you become, of such experience
That already you have realized
What Ithacas mean

REFERENCES

Abelson, R. (1979). Differences between belief systems and knoeledge systems. *Cognitive Science, 3,* 355-366.

Aiken, L. R. (1974). Two scales of attitude toward mathematics. *Journal for Research in Mathematics Education, 5,* 67-71.

Aiken, L. R. (1976). Update on attitudes and other affective variables in learning mathematics, *Review of Educational Research, 46* (2), 293-311.

Alexander, P. A., & Dochy, F. J. R. C. (1995). Conceptions of knowledge and beliefs: A comparison across varying cultural and educational communities. *American Educational Research Journal, 32* (2), 413 - 442.

Assessment of Performance Unit. (1982). *A review of monitoring in mathematics 1978-1982.* London, Department of Education and Science.

Askew, M, Brown, M., Rhodes, V., Johnson, D. & Wiliam, D. (Feb. 1997). *Effective teachers of numeracy, Final report.* Report of a study carried out for the Teacher Training Agency 1995-96 by the School of Education, King's College London.

Atweh, B., Forgasz, J. H. & Nebres, B. (2001). *Sociocultural research on mathematics education. An international perspective.* NJ: Lawrence Erlbaum Associates.

Australian Education Council and Curriculum Corporation. (1991). *A National Statement on Mathematics for Australian Schools.* Carlton, Victoria: Curriculum Corporation.

Baird, J. R. (2001). Learning and teaching: From ignorance to understanding. Chapter 11 in D. Clarke (Ed.), *Perspectives on practice and meaning in mathematics and science classrooms.* (pp. 255-289). Dordrecht: Kluwer Academic Publishers.

Barkatsas, A. & Hunting, R. P. (1996). A review of recent research on cognitive, metacognitive and affective aspects of mathematical problem solving. *Nordic Studies in Mathematics Education, 4* (4), 7-30.

Barkatsas, A. N. Forgasz, H. J. & Leder, G. C. (In press). The stereotyping of mathematics: Gender and cultural factors. *THEMES in Education.*

Barkatsas, A. N. & Malone, J. (2002). Secondary mathematics teachers' beliefs about teaching and learning: Some significant factors. In B. Barton, K. C. Irwin, M. Pfannkuch & O.J. Thomas (Eds.), *Mathematics Education in the South Pacific.Mathematics Education in the South Pacific.*(Proceedings of the 25th Annual Conference of the Mathematics Education Group of Australasia, Vol. 1, pp. 115-122). Auckland: MERGA.

Barkatsas, A. N. (2001). Secondary mathematics teachers' beliefs about mathematics assessment: A European perspective. In C. Vale, J Horwood & J. Roumeliotis (Eds.), *2001: A mathematical odyssey* (pp. 369-378). Brunswick Melbourne: M.A.V.

Bauersfeld, H. (1998). Interactions, construction, and Knowledge: Alternative perspectives for mathematics education. In D.A. Grouws, T.J. Cooney and D. Jones (Eds.), *Perspectives on research on effective mathematics teaching.* Reston , VA: Lawrence Erlbaum and Associates.

Beaton, A. E., Mullis, I. V. S., Martin, Gonzalez, E. J., Kelly, D. L., & Smith, T. A. (1996). *Mathematics achievement in the middle school years.* Boston: International Association for the Evaluation of Educational Achievement.

Berger, P. (1999). The hidden dimensions in maths teaching and learning processes. Exploring entrenched beliefs, tacit knowledge, and ritual behaviour via metaphors. In G. Philippou (Ed.). *Research on Mathematical Beliefs.* MAVI-8 Proceedings. Eight European Workshop. University of Cyprus, Nicosia, Cyprus.

Berger, P. (2000). Multiple Realities and the Making of Worlds. A Multi-perspective Approach to Mathematical Belief Systems. In S. Gotz & G Torner (Eds.), *Research on Mathematical Beliefs.* Proceedings of MAVI-9 European Workshop. University of Vienna, Austria.

Billet, S. (1998). Transfer and social practice. *Australian & New Zealand Jouranl of Vocational Education Research, 6*(1), 1-25.

Bishop, A. J. (1988). *Mathematical Enculturation,* Dordrecht: Kluwer.

Borg, W. A. & Gall, M, D. (1983). *Educational research. An introduction.* (4th edition). Longman, NY.

Bowling, J.M. (1976). *Three scales of attitude toward mathematics.* Unpublished Doctoral Dissertation, Ohio State University.

Bromme, R. (1994). Beyond subject matter: A psychological topolofy of teachers' professional knowledge. In R. Biehler, R. W. Scholtz, R Straver & R Winkelmann (Eds.), *Didactics of Mathematics as a scientific Discipline,* 73-88. Kluwer Academic Publishers: The Netherlands.

Buzeika, A. (1996). Teachers' beliefs and practice: The chicken or the egg? In P.C. Crarkson (Ed.), *Technology in mathematics education* (Proceedings of the 19th annual Conference of the Mathematics Education Group of Australasia, pp. 93-100). Melbourne: MERGA.

Clark, C. M., & Peterson, P. L. (1986). Teachers' thought processes. In M. Wittrock (Ed.), *Handbook of research on teaching* (3rd ed., pp. 255-296). New York: Macmillan.

Clarke, D. J. (2001). Complementary accounts methodology. In D. Clarke (Ed.), *Perspectives on practice and meaning in mathematics and science classrooms.* (pp. 13-32). Dordrecht: Kluwer Academic Publishers.

Clarke, D. J. & Stephens, W. M. (1996). The Ripple effect: The instructional impact of the systemic introduction of performance assessment in mathematics. In M. Birenbaum & F. Dochy (Eds.), *Alternatives in Assessment of Achievements, Learning Processes and Prior Knowledge,* Kluwer, Dortrecht, 63-92.

Clarke, D. J., Clarke, D. M., & Lovitt, C. J. (1990). Changes in mathematics teaching call for assessment alternatives. In T. Cooney & C. Hirsch (Eds.), *Teaching and learning mathematics in the 1990s.* Reston, Va: NCTM.

Clarke, D. J. (1996). Assessment in mathematics. In A. J. Bishop (Ed.), *International Handbook of Mathematics education.* Kluwer, Dortrecht, 327-370.

Coakes S. J. & Steed L. G. (1999). *SPSS: Analysis without anguish.* John Wiley and Sons, Australia, Ltd.

Cockcroft, W.H. (1982). *Mathematics counts,* Report of the Committee of Inquiry in-to the Teaching of Mathematics in Schools, HMSO, London.

Confrey, J. (1990). What constructivism implies for teaching. In R.B. Davis, C.A. Maher, and N. Noddings (Eds.), *Constructivism views on the teaching and learning of mathematics.* Monograph Number 4 of the *Journal for Research in Mathematics Education.* Reston, VA: NCTM, pp. 107-122.

Cooney, T. J. (1999). Conceptualizing teachers' ways of knowing. *Educational Studies in Mathematics. 38,* 163-187.

Cooney, T. J., Shealy, B. E. & Arvold, B. (1998). Conceptualising belief structures of preservice secondary mathematics teachers. *Journal for Research In Mathematics Education, 29* (3), 306-333.

Cronbach, L. J. & Suppes, P. (Eds.). (1957). *Research for tomorrow's schools: Disciplined inquiry for education.* New York: MacMillan.

Davis, P.J. & Hearsch, R. (1981). *The mathematical experience.* Boston: Houghton Mifflin.

Davis, B. (1998). Listening for differences: An evolving conception of mathematics teaching. *Journal for Research in Mathematics Education, 28*(3), 355-376.

Dengate, B. & Lerman, S. (1995). Learning theory im mathematics education: Using the wide angle lens and not just the microscope. *Mathematics Education Research Journal, 7,* (1), 26-36.

Department of Employment, Education and Training. (1989). *Discipline review of teacher education in mathematics and science.* Canberra, Australian Government Publishing Service.

Department of Education and Science and Welsh Office. (1989). *Mathematics in the National curriculum.* London, HMSO.

Dreyfus, T., & Eisenberg, T. (1986). On the aesthetics of mathematical thought. *For the Learning of Mathematics, 6,* 2-10.

Driver, R. & Oldham, V. (1986). A constructivist approach to curriculum development in science. *Studies in Science Education, 13,* 105-122.

Ellerton, N. and Clements, M.A. (1992). Some Pluses and Minuses of Radical Constructivism in Mathematics Education. Paper presented at The Fifteenth Annual Meeting of the Mathematics Education Research Group of Australia held at the University of Western Sydney, July, 1992.

Ellerton, N.F., & Clements, M.A. (1991). *Mathematics in language: Language factors in mathematics learning*. Geelong: Deakin University.

Ernest, P. (1994). The philosophy of mathematics and the didactics of mathematics. In R. Biehler, R. W. Scholtz, R Straver & R Winkelmann (Eds.), *Didactics of Mathematics as a scientific Discipline*, 335-349. Kluwer Academic Publishers: The Netherlands.

Ernest, P. (1989a). The knowledge, beliefs and attitudes of the mathematics teacher: A model. *Journal of Education for Teaching. 15*, 13-34.

Ernest, P. (1989b). The impact of beliefs on the teaching of mathematics. In P. Ernest (Ed.), *Mathematics teaching: The state of the art*. New York, NY:Falmer.

Fennema, E., Carpenter, t. P., Franke, M. L., Jacobs, V. R. & Empson, S. B. (1996). A longitudinal study of learning to use children's thinking in mathematics education. *Journal for Research in Mathematics Education, 27* (4), 403-434.

Fennema, E., & Sherman, J. (1976). Fennema-Sherman Mathematics Attitudes Scales. Instruments Designed to Measure Attitudes Toward the Learning of Mathematics by Females and Males. *Abstracted in the JSAS Catalog of Selected Documents in Psychology, 6* (1), 31. (Ms No. 1225)

Fennema, E., P. Wolleat and J. D. Pedro. (1979). Mathematics Attribution Scale. JSAS: *Catalog of selected Documents in psychology, 95* (6), 26. (Ms. No. 1837)

Fennema, E., & Leder, G. C. (Eds.) (1993). *Mathematics and gender*. St. Lucia, Queensland: Queensland University Press.

Fennema, E., & Sherman, J. A. (1976). Fennema-Sherman Mathematics Attitude Scales. *Catalog of selected documents in psychology, 6*, 31 (Ms. No. 1225).

Fenstermacher, G. D. (1994). The knower and the known: The nature of knowledge in research on teaching. In L. Darling-Hammond (Ed.), *Review of Research in Education*, (Vol. 20, pp. 1-56).Washington, DC: American Educational Research Association.

Firestone, W. A. (1987). Meaning in method: The rhetoric of quantitative and qualitative research. *Educational Researcher, 16*(7), 16-21.

Forgasz, J. H. (1995). *Learning mathematics: Affect, gender, and classroom factors.* Unpublished doctoral thesis. Monash University, Clayton, Australia.

Ginsburg, H. and Opper, S. (1979). *Piaget's Theory of Intellectual Development.* (2nd Ed.) N.I.: Prentice-Hall.

Green, T. (1971). *The activities of teaching.* New York: McGraw-Hill.

Guba, G.E. and Lincoln, S.L. (1989). *Fourth Generation Evaluation. California:* SAGE Publications Inc.

Hiebert, J., Gallimore, R. & Stigler, W. (2002). A knowledge base for the teaching profession: What would it look like and how can we get one? *Educational Researcher, 31*(5), 3-15.

Hofer, B. K. & Pintrich, P. R. (1997). The Development of Epistemological Theories: Beliefs about the Knowledge and Knowing and Their Relation to Learning. *Review of Educational Research, 67* (1), 88-140.

Holden, C. (1987). Female maths anxiety on the wane. *Science, 234,* 660-661.

Hollingworth, S. (1989). Prior beliefs and cognitive change in learning to teach. *American Educational Research Journal, 26,* 160-189.

Hox, J.J. (1994). Hierarchical regression models for intervewer and respondent effects. *Sociological Methods & Research, 22* (3), 300-318.

Howard, P., Perry, B. & Lindsay, M. (1997). Secondary mathematics teachers beliefs about the learning and teaching of mathematics. In F. Biddulph & K. Carr (Eds.), *People in mathematics Education.(pp. 231-238).* Rotorua, NZ.

Hunting, R.P. (1983). Emerging methodologies for understanding internal processes governing children's mathematical behaviour. *The Australian Journal of Education, 27* (1), 45 - 61.

Hunting, R.P. (1987). Issues shaping school Mathematics Curriculum development in Australia. *Curriculum Perspectives, 7* (1), 29 37.

Karageorgos, D. (2000). *Το Πρόβλημα και η Επίλυση του. Μια Διδακτική Προσέγγιση.* [The mathematical problem and its solution. A teaching approach]. Athens, Greece: Savvalas.

Katsikas, C. (2000, *18 Nov.*). Το «φύλο» ... των θετικών επιστημών! Μύθος και Πραγματικότητα για τη διαφορά επίδοσης μεταξύ αγοριών και κοριτσιών στα Φυσικομαθηματικά [The 'gender' of Physical Sciences: Myth and reality regarding performance differences between boys and girls in the Physical Sciences]. *Financial Post, 48*(2428), 83-85.

Kilpatrick, J. (2000). Research in mathematics education across the centuries. In M. A. (Ken) Clements, H. H. Tairab & W. K. Yoong (Eds.), *Science, Mathematics and Technical education in the 20th and the 21st centuries.* University of Brunei Darussalam.

Kulm, G. (1980). Research on mathematics attitude. In R.J. Shumway (ed.), *Research in Mathematics education.* Reston V.A: National Council of Teachers of Mathematics, pp.356-387.

Kuhs,T. & Ball, D. (1986). *Approaches to teaching mathematics: Mapping the domains of knowledge, skills and dispositions* (Research Memo). Lansing, MI: Centre on Teacher Education, Michigan State University.

Kvale, S. (1996). *InterViews: An introductionto qualitative research interviewing.* Thousand Oaks, CA: SAGE Publications.

Leder, G. C., Pehkonen, E and Torner, G. (2002). *Beliefs: A hidden variable in mathematics education?* Dordrecht: Kluwer.

Leder, G. C. (1993). Reconciling affective and cognitive aspects of mathematical learning: Reality or a pious hope? In I. Hirabayashi, N. Nohda, K. Shigemathu & F-L, Lin. (Eds.), *Proceedings of the 17th PME Conference* (pp. 46-65). Tsukuba, Ibaraki: University of Tsukuba, Japan.

Leder, G. C. (1992). Measuring attitudes to mathematics. *Fifteenth Annual Conference of the Mathematics Association of Australasia,* Conference Proceedings, Richmond, N.S.W.

Leder, G. C. (1993). Reconciling affective and cognitive aspects of mathematical lear-ning: Reality or a pius hope? In I. Hirabayashi, N. Nohda, K. Shigemathu & F-L, Lin. (Eds.), *Proceedings of the Seventeenth PME Conference* (pp. 46-65). Tsukuba, Ibaraki: University of Tsukuba, Japan.

Lerman, S. (1994). *Cultural perspectives on the mathematics classroom.* Dordrecht: Kluwer Academic Publishers.

Lester, F. K. & Garofalo, J. (1987). *The influence of affects, beliefs and metacognition on problem solving behaviour: some tentative speculations.* ERIC Document Reproduction Service No. ED 281758.

Lincoln, Y. S. & Guba, E. E. (Feb. 1985). *Research, Evaluation, and Policy Analysis: Heuristics for disciplined inquiry.* Unpublished research monograph.

Linn, R. L. (1992). Uantitaive methods in research on teaching. In M. C. Wittrock (Ed.), *Handbook for Research on Teaching.* (3rd ed.) (pp. 92-118). New York: Macmillan.

Malone, J. A. (1995). Determining preservice teachers' beliefs about their role in teaching mathematics. In A. Richards (Ed.), *FLAIR: Forging Links and Integrating Resourses* (Proceedings of the 15th biennial conference of the Australian Association of Mathematics Teachers, pp. 264-269). Darwin: AAMT.

Malone, J. A. (1996). Preservice secondary teachers' beliefs: Two case studies of emerging and evolving perceptions. In l. Puig & A. Guteriez (Eds.), *Proceedings of the 20th Conference of the International Group for the Psychology of Mathematics Education* (Vol. 3, pp. 313-320). Valencia, Spain: PME.

Malone, J. A., Thornton, C. A., Langrall, C. W., & Jones, G. A. (1997). Modyfying Preservice teachers' beliefs about their role in teaching mathematics. In D.Fisher & T. Rickards (Eds.), *Science, Technology and Mathematics Education Development.* (pp. 355-363). Vietnam.

Mandler, G. (1989). Affect and learning: Causes and consequences of emotional interactions', In D. B.McLeod & V. M. Adams (Eds.). *Affect and mathematical problem solving: A new perspective* (pp. 3-19). New York: Springer-Verlag.

Maturana, H. (1978). Biology of language: The epistemology of reality. In G. A. Miller & E. Lenneberg (Eds.), *Psychology and biology of language and thought* (pp. 27-64). New York: Academic Press.

McLeod, D. B. (1989). The role of affect in mathematical problem solving. In D. B. McLeod & V.M. Adams (eds.), *Affect and mathematical problem solving: A new perspective* (pp. 20-36). New York: Springer-Verlag.

McLeod, D. B. (1992). Research on affect in mathematics education: A reconceptualisation. In D. A. Grouws (ed.), *Handbook of Research on Mathematics Teaching and Learning* (pp. 575-596). New (pp. 575-596). New York: MacMillan.

Miles, M. B. & Huberman, A. M. (1994). *An expanded sourcebook: Qualitative Data Analysis.* Thousand Oaks, CA: SAGE Publications.

Munby, H. (1982). The place of teachers' beliefs in research on teacher thinking and decision making, and an alternative methodology. *Instructional Science, 11,* 201-225.

National Council of teachers of Mathematics (2000). *Principles and Standards for School Mathematics,* Reston, VA: NCTM.

National Council of Teachers of Mathematics (1989). *Curriculum and evaluation standards for school mathematics.* Reston, VA: Author.

National Council of Teachers of Mathematics (1980). *An agenda for action.* Reston, Virginia: Author.

Nespor, J. (1987). The role of beliefs in the practice of teaching. *Journal of Curriculum Studies, 19,* 317-328.

Nisbet, S., & Warren, E. (2000). Primary school teachers' beliefs relating to mathematics, teaching and assessing mathematics and factors that influence these beliefs. *Mathematics Teacher Education and Development. 2*(2), 34-47.

OECD (1996, March). *Educational Policy Review: Greece. Examiners' Report.* Athens: Ministry of National Education and Religious Affairs.

Pajares, M. F. (1992). Teachers' beliefs and educational research: cleaning up a messy construct. *Review of Educational Research, 62* (3), 307-322.

Pekhonen & Safuanov (1996). Pupil's views of mathematics teaching in Finland and Tatarstan. *Nordic Studies in Mathematics Education, 4* (4), 31-59.

Perry, W. G. (1970). *Forms of intellectual and ethical development in the college years.* New York: Holt, Rinehart & Winston.

Perry, B., Vistro-Yu, C., Howard, P., Wong, N. & Keong, F. (2002). Beliefs of primary teachers about mathematics and its teaching and learning: Views from Singapore, Philippines, Mainland China, Hong Kong, Taiwan and Australia. In B. Barton, K. C. Irwin, M. Pfannkuch & O.J. Thomas (Eds.), *Mathematics Education in the South Pacific.* (Proceedings of the 25th Annual Conference of the Mathematics Education Group of Australasia, Vol. 1, pp. 551-558). Auckland: MERGA

Perry, B., Howard, P., & Tracey, D. (1999). Head mathematics teachers' beliefs about the learning and teaching of mathematics. *Mathematics Education Research Journal. 11*(1), 39-57.

Perry, B. Howard, P., & Conroy, J. (1996). K-6 teachers' beliefs about the learning and teaching of mathematics. In P.C. Crarkson (Ed.), *Technology in mathematics education.* (Proceedings of the 19th Annual Conference of the Mathematics Education Group of Australasia, Vol. 1, pp. 453-460). Melbourne: MERGA.

Piaget, J. (1971). *Biology and Knowledge.* Chicago: The University of Chicago Press.

Pirie, S. (1998). Where do we go from here? Chapter 7 in A. Teppo (Ed.) *Qualitative research methods in mathematics education.* Monograph Number 9 of the *Journal for Research in Mathematics Education.* Reston, VA: NCTM, pp. 156-163.

Poincare, H. (1946). *The foundations of science.* (G. B. Halstead, Trans.), Lancaster, PA: Science Press (Original work published 1913).

Raymond, A. M. (1997). Inconsistency between a beginning elementary school teacher's mathematics beliefs and teaching practice. *Journal for Research in Mathematics Education, 28* (5), 550-576.

Rokeach, M. (1960). *The open and closed mind.* New York: Basic Books.

Rokeach, M. (1968). *Beliefs, attitudes, and values: A theory of organization and change.* San Francisco: Jossey-Boss.

Richardson, V., Anders, P., Tidwell, D., & Lloyd, C. (1991). The relationship between teachers' beliefs and practices in reading comprehension instruction. *American Educational Research Journal*, 28 (3), 559 - 586.

Schaller, J. S. & Tobin, K. (1998). Quality criteria for the genres of interpretive research. In J. A. Malone, B. Atweh and J. R. Northfield (Eds.), *Research and supervision in mathematics Education.* (pp. 39-60). Mahwah, NJ; Laurence Erlbaum Associates.

Schoenfeld, A. H. (2000). *Purposes and methods of research in Mathematics Education.* To appear in the *Notices* of the American Mathematical Society.

Schoenfeld, A. H. (1987). What's all the fuss about metacognition? In A. H. Schoenfeld (Ed.), *Cognitive science and mathematics education* (pp. 189-215). Hillsdale, NJ: Lawrence Erlbaum.

Schoenfeld, A.H. (1989). Explorations of students' mathematical beliefs and behavior. *Journal for Research in Mathematics Education, 20*, 338-355.

Schoenfeld, A. H. (1985a). *Mathematical problem solving.* Orlando, FL: Academic Press.

Schoenfeld, A. H. (1985b). Understanding and teaching the nature of mathematical thinking. In I. Wirszup & R. Streit (Eds.), *Developments in School Mathematics Education Around the World* , Reston, VA: National Council of Teachers of Mathematics, pp.362-368.

Schoenfeld, A. H. (1992). Learning to think mathematically: Problem solving, metacognition, and sense making in mathematics. In D. A. Grouws (Ed.), *Handbook of research on mathematics teaching and learning*, New York: Macmillan, 334-370.

Shephard, L. (2000). The Role of Classroom Assessment in Teaching and Learning. *CSE Technical Report 517. CRESST.*

Shield, M. (1999). The conflict between teachers' beliefs and classroom practices: Ethnicity and the stereotyping of mathematics. In J. M. Truran & K. M. Truran (Eds.), *Making the difference.* Proceedings of the 22nd Annual Conference of the Mathematics Education Group of Australasia, pp. 439-445). Adelaide: MERGA.

Shulman, L. S. (1988). Disciplines of inquiry in Education: An overview. In R. M. Jaeger (Ed.), *Complementary methods for research in Education.* American Educational Research Association. Washington, DC.

Shulman, L. S. (1987). Knowledge and Teaching: Foundations of the new reform. *Harverd Education Review. 57*(1), 1-22.

Shulman, L. S. (1986). Those who understand: Knowledge growth in teaching. *Educational Researcher, 15,* 4-14.

Silver, E. A. (1994). On mathematical problem posing. *For the Learning of Mathematics,* 14 (1), 19-28.

Stanbridge, B. (1990). A constructivist model of learning used in the teaching of Junior Science. *Australian Teachers Journal,* 36 (4), 20-28.

Steffe, L.P. (Ed.) (1991). *Epistemological foundations of mathematical experience.* New Yourk: Springer-Verlag.

Steffe, L.P. (Ed.) (1990). Mathematics curriculum design: A constructivist's perspective. In L.P. Steffe & T. Wood (Eds.), *Transforming children's mathematics education: international perspectives* (pp. 389-398). Hillsdale, NJ: Lawrence Erlbaum.

Steffe, L. P. (1985). *Children's mathematics: A new perspective for mathematics education.* Paper presented at the 63rd Annual Meeting of the National Council of Teachers of Mathematics, San Antonio, Tx.

Tabachnick, B. G. & Fidell, L.S. (1996). *Using Multivariate statistics* (3rd ed.). New York: Harper Collins.

Tanner, H. & Jones, S. (1998). Dynamic scaffolding and reflective discourse: Successful teaching styles observed within a project to teach mathematical thinking skills. In C. Kanes, M. Goos & E. Warren (Eds.), *Teaching Mathematics in New Times.* (Proceedings of the 21st annual Conference of the Mathematics Education Group of Australasia, Vol. 2, pp. 596-604). Brisbane: MERGA.

Thompson, A. G. (1992) Teachers' beliefs and conceptions: A synthesis of the research. In D. A. Grouws (Ed.), *Handbook of Research on Mathematics Teaching* (pp. 127-146). New York and Ontario: Macmillan. von Glasersfeld,

E. (Ed.) (1991). *Radical constructivism in mathematics education.* Dortrecht: Kluwer.

Van Zoest, L, R., Jones, G. A. & Thornton, C. A. (1994). Beliefs about mathematics teaching held by pre-service teachers. *Mathematics Education Research Journal, 6* (1), 37-55.

von Glasersfeld, E. (1990). Environment and communication. In L. Steffe & T. Wood (Eds), Transforming children's mathematics education: International Perspectives (pp. 30-38). Hillsddale NJ: Lawrence Erlbaum.

von Glaserfeld, E. (1984, June). Reconstructing the concept of knowledge. Seminar on constructivism. Archives Team Piaget, Geneva.

von Glaserfeld, E. (Ed.). (1991a). *Radical constructivism in mathematics education.* Dortrecht: Kluwer.

von Glasersfeld, E. (1991b). Abstraction, representation, and reflection: An interpretation of experience and Piaget's approach. In L. P. Steffe (Ed.), Epistemological Functions of mathematical experience (pp. 45 - 67). New York: Springer-Verlag.

von Glasersfeld, E. (1990). Environment and communication. In L. P. Steffe & T. Wood (Eds.), Transforming children's mathematics education: International Perspectives (pp. 30 - 38). Hillsdale NJ: Lawrence Erlbaum.

Wertsch, J. V. (1985). *Vygotsky and the social formation of mind.* Harvard University Press. Cambridge, Massachusetts.

White, A. L. (2002). Research into teacher beliefs: Can the past stop endless repetitions? In B. Barton, K. C. Irwin, M. Pfannkuch & O.J. Thomas (Eds.), *Mathematics Education in the South Pacific.* (Proceedings of the 25th annual Conference of the Mathematics Education Group of Australasia, Vol. 2, pp. 690-697). Auckland: MERGA.

Wiersma, W. (1986). *Research methods in education: An introduction.* (4th ed.). Boston: Allyn and Bacon.

Wood, T. (1994). Patterns of interaction and the culture of mathematics classrooms. In S. Lerman (Ed.), *Cultural perspectives on the mathematics classroom* (pp. 149-168). Dordrecht: Kluwer Academic Publishers.

APPENDICES

Appendix B1

Mathematics teachers' beliefs models: A comparative overview (Part I)

FENNEMA et.al. (1996)	COONEY (1999)	TANNER & JONES (1998)
LEVEL 1	**ISOLATIONIST:**	**TASKERS:**
Teachers in this category believe *that students learn best by being told how to do mathematics.* They also believe that children either could not invent problem solutions for themselves or that it was a waste of time to ask them to solve problems before demonstrations were provided *consistently.*	Tends to have belief structures in such a way that beliefs remain separated or clustered away from others. Accommodation is not a theme that characterizes an isolationist. The isolationist tends to reject the beliefs of others at least as they pertain to his/her own situation. More importantly, the rejection is rooted in a circular array of beliefs impervious to empirical evidence. It is a person who 'knows' the right way to teach and believes that any in-service program, hasn't anything to offer to him/her.	Taskers focus on the demands of the task rather than the targeted skills (cognitive or metacognitive)
LEVEL 2:	**NAÏVE IDEALIST:**	**RIGID SCAFFOLDERS:**
Are beginning *to question the idea that children needed to be shown how to do mathematics, but they have conflicting beliefs.* Sometimes they believe that children could solve problems without instruction, but at other times they believe that *when dealing with certain ideas, children need to be led to do things correctly.* Sometimes *they hold different beliefs about groups of children who they perceived differed in ability.*	Tends to be a received knower in that, unlike the isolationist, he/she absorbs what others believe to be the case but often without analysis of what he/she believes. He/she could be relying on others to provide the evidence and substance of what they know. He/she did not reject ideas, as does the isolationist. Rather he/she uncritically accepts them.	Focus on planning, but rather than helping students to develop their own plans, aimed to share their own plans with the class. The support and questioning provided, constrains students' thinking leading them down a pre-determined path.

LEVEL 3:	NAÏVE CONNECTIONIST:	DYNAMIC SCAFFOLDERS:
Teachers thought *that children would learn mathematics as they solved many problems and discussed their solutions*. They did not indicate however, that specific knowledge about their students should inform their selection of mathematical experiences. Just providing (what they thought were) rich experiences (just helping, or providing different kinds of problems-harder and easier, or providing a larger amount of problems) appeared to be sufficient.	This position emphasises reflection and attention to the beliefs of others as compared to one's own. He/she fails however, to resolve conflict or differences in beliefs. It is not clear whether this lack of resolution emerges as a result of a lack of commitment to teaching or from inability to resolve contradictions.	They grant significant autonomy to students, particularly at the early ages of planning. The scaffolding in this case is dynamic in character, and it is based on participation in a discourse in which differences are valued and encouraged. *Validates conjectures and uses focusing questions to control the direction of discourse, ensuring that an acceptable whole class plan (or a result) is generated*. This framework is equivalent to 'legitimate peripheral participation' within an apprenticeship model of learning. Articulation and objectification of explanation is encouraged making the explanation itself the object of the discourse.

LEVELS 4A AND 4B:	REFLECTIVE CONNECTIONIST:	REFLECTIVE SCAFFOLDERS:
These beliefs were characterized by the acceptance of the idea that children can solve problems without direct instruction and that the mathematics curriculum should be based on children's abilities. They also believed that their role was to find out what children knew and to use that knowledge to structure the learning environment. They in fact believed that what the children knew should be a major influence on all instructional decisions. Belief differences between the two levels 4A and 4B centered on the degree to which *the teacher believed that children's thinking should be used to make instructional decisions.* Level B teachers, *more than* level A teachers, reported that they *should use their knowledge of children's thinking consistently.*	This position emphasises reflection and attention to the beliefs of others as compared to one's own. He/she however, resolves conflict through reflective thinking. He/she does not make connections but he/she is able to weave them into a set of beliefs held from a relativistic and, perhaps, committed perspective while listening to and valuing others. It follows that the reflective connectionist integrates voices, analyses the merits of various positions, and comes to terms with what he or she believes in a committed way. It sets the stage for becoming a reflective practitioner.	The characteristic feature of this category of teachers is their focus on evaluation and reflection. Peer and self-assessment is encouraged to make through group presentations of draft reports before redrafting for assessment. Reflective discourse is thus deliberately generated. Collective discourse does not of course equal reflective abstraction but it is conjectured that during collective reflection opportunities arise for students to reflect on and to objectify their previous actions as they engage in reflective discourse.

Appendix B2

Mathematics teachers' beliefs models: A comparative overview (Part II)

ASKEW et.al. (1997)	Van ZOEST et.al. (1994)
TRANSMISSION:	**CONTENT PERFORMANCE** (Teachers' actions during:)
Beliefs about what it is to be a numerate pupil • Primarily the ability to perform standard procedures or routines • A heavy reliance on paper and pencil methods • Selecting a method of calculation primarily on the basis of the operation involved • Confidence in separate aspects of the mathematics curriculum • Able to 'decode' context problems to identify the particular routine or technique required	*(1) Problem statement & clarification* Directs towards a predetermined solution *(2) Solution exploration* Checks on progress and discourages deviation
Beliefs about pupils an d how they learn to become numerate • Pupils become numerate through individual activity based on following instructions • Pupils learn through being introduced to one mathematical routine at a time and remembering it • Pupils vary in their ability to become numerate • Pupils' strategies for calculating are of little importance – they need to be taught standard strategies • Pupil misunderstandings are the result of failure to 'grasp' what was being taught and need to be remedied by further reinforcement of the correct method	*(3) Impasse relief* Intercedes immediately by directing to the predetermined solution method *(4) Solution presentation and interpretation* Evaluates student answers as either right or wrong. If wrong reviews predetermined solution method. Ignores student methods
Beliefs about how best to teach pupils to become numerate • Teaching is seen as separate and having priority over learning • Mathematics teaching is based on *verbal explanations* so that pupils understand teachers' methods. • Learning about mathematical concepts precedes the ability to apply the concepts • Mathematical ideas need to be introduced in discrete packages • Application is best approached through 'word' problems: contexts for calculating routines	

DISCOVERY:	CONTENT UNDERSTANDING: (Teachers' actions during:)
Beliefs about what it is to be a numerate pupil Being numerate involves: o Finding the answer to a calculation by any method o A heavy reliance on practical methods o Selecting a method of calculation primarily based on the operation involved o Confidence in separate aspects of the mathematics curriculum o Being able to use and apply mathematics using practical apparatus *Beliefs about pupils and how they* *learn to become numerate* o Pupils become numerate through individual activity based on actions on objects o Pupils need to be ready before they can learn certain mathematical ideas o Pupils vary in the rate at which their numeracy develops o Pupils own strategies are most important o Pupils misunderstandings are the result of pupils not being 'ready' to learn the ideas *Beliefs about how best to teach pupils to become numerate* o Learning is seen as separate from and having priority over teaching o Mathematics teaching is based on practical activities so that pupils can discover methods for themselves o Learning about mathematical concepts precedes the ability to apply these concepts o Mathematical ideas need to be introduced in discrete packages o Application is best approached through use of practical equipment	*(1) Problem statement & clarification* Models the initial stages of one or more solution methods *(2) Solution exploration* Allows students to work individually on their chosen method then asks them to compare solutions *(3) Impasse relief* Intercedes fairly quickly with suggestions for the kids to try *(4) Solution presentation and interpretation* Accepts right and wrong answers in a non-evaluative way while refraining from discussing unsuccessful solution methods

CONNECTIONIST:	LEARNER INTERACTION: (Teachers' actions during:)
Beliefs about what it is to be a numerate pupil Being numerate involves: • The use of methods of calculation which are both effective and efficient • Confidence and ability in mental methods • Selecting a method of calculation on the basis of both the operation and the number involved • Awareness of the links between different aspects of the mathematics curriculum • Reasoning, justifying and eventually, proving results about number *Beliefs about pupils an dhow they learn to become numerate* • Pupils become numerate through purposeful interpersonal activity based on interactions with others • Pupils learn through being challenged and struggling to overcome difficulties • Most pupils are able to become numerate • Pupils have strategies for calculating but the teacher has responsibility for helping them refine their methods • Pupils misunderstandings need to be recognized, made explicit and worked on *Beliefs about how best to teach pupils to become numerate* • Teaching and learning are seen as complementary • Numeracy teaching is based on *dialogue* between teacher and pupils to explore understandings • Learning about mathematical concepts and the ability to apply these concepts are learned alongside each other • The connections between mathematical ideas need to be acknowledged in teaching • Application is best approached through challenges that need to be reasoned about	*(1) Problem statement & clarification* Provides just enough information to establish the intent of the activity *(2) Solution exploration* Encourages mathematical dialogue and consensus with students sharing their strategies and solution methods *(3) Impasse relief* Facilitates continuation of the dialogue without providing substantive mathematical suggestions. Encourages the kids to persist to figure out the problem for themselves. *(4) Solution presentation and interpretation* Accepts right and wrong answers in an non-evaluative way and probes solution methods regardless of their success. Assists in verbalising all solution attempts

Appendix C1

Initial questionnaire for the Pilot study

(Section I)   Nature of mathematics

(1) Although there are some connections between different areas, mathematics is mostly made up of unrelated topics

(2) In mathematics problems can be solved without using rules

(3) Justifying the mathematical statements that a person makes is an extremely important part of mathematics

(4) Mathematics is a static and immutable knowledge with objective truth

(5) Mathematics is computation

(6) Mathematics problems given to students should be quickly solvable in a few steps

(7) Mathematics is the dynamic searching for models and problems and their results are open to review

(8) Mathematics is no more sequential than any other subject

(9) Mathematics is a beautiful, creative and useful human endeavor that is both a way of knowing and a way of thinking

(10) Right answers in mathematics are much more important than the ways in which you get them

(Section II)   Mathematics learning

(11) The most effective way to learn mathematics is by listening carefully to the teacher explaining a mathematics lesson

(12) Mathematics is best learned individually

(13) Students can learn more mathematics together than by themselves

(14) Students always benefit by discussing their solutions to mathematical problems with each other

(15) Mathematics knowledge is the result of the learner interpreting and organising the information gained from experiences

(16) Students are rational decision-makers capable of determining for themselves what is right and what is wrong

(17) Mathematics learning is being able to get the right answer quickly

(18) Periods of uncertainty, conflict, confusion, surprise are a significant part of the mathematics learning process

(19) Students are capable of much higher levels of mathematical thought than has been suggested traditionally

(20) The memorisation of mathematical facts is important in mathematics learning

(21) Mathematics learning is enhanced by activities which build upon and respect students' experiences

(22) Mathematics learning is enhanced by challenging activities within a supportive environment

(Section III)　Mathematics teaching

(23) A key responsibility of a teacher is to encourage students to explore their own mathematical ideas

(24) Ignoring the mathematical ideas generated by the students can seriously limit their learning

(25) Encouraging multiple ways of mathematical thinking is insufficient and may confuse children

(26) A vital task for the teacher is motivating students to resolve their own mathematical problems

(27) Teachers should encourage their students to strive for elegant solutions when they solve problems

(28) Teachers should create a non-threatening environment for learning mathematics for all students

(29) I would feel uncomfortable if a student suggested a solution to a mathematical problem that I hadn't thought of previously

(30) Mathematics teachers should be fascinated with how students think and intrigued by alternative ideas

(31) The main function of a teacher is to provide her students with solutions to their mathematical problems

(32) Teachers should be able to present mathematical ideas in a variety of ways

(33) Persistent questioning by the teacher has a significant effect on students' mathematical learning

(34) Teachers always need to hear students' mathematical explanations before correcting their errors

(35) Effective mathematics teachers enjoy learning and 'doing' mathematics themselves

(36) If a student's explanation of a mathematical problem does not make sense to the teacher it is best to ignore it

(37) It is important to cover all the topics in the mathematics curriculum in the textbook sequence

(38) An effective way to teach mathematics is to provide students with interesting problems to investigate in small groups

(39) It is not necessary for teachers to understand the source of students' errors; follow-up instruction will eliminate their difficulties

(40) Telling students the answer is an efficient way of facilitating their mathematics learning

(41) It is the teacher' responsibility to provide students with clear and concise solution methods for mathematical problems

(42) It is important for students to be provided with opportunities to reflect on and evaluate their own mathematical understanding

(43) There must be a set syllabus to be followed by the teacher

(44) Mathematics material is best presented in an expository style: demonstrating, explaining, and describing concepts and skills

(45) My mathematics teachers would often show me different ways to solve a problem

(46) It is important that mathematics content be presented to students in the correct logical sequence

(47) Teachers or the textbook-not the student-are the authorities for what is right or wrong

(48) The role of the mathematics teacher is to transmit mathematical knowledge and to verify that learners have received that knowledge

(49) Teachers should negotiate social norms with the students in order to develop a cooperative learning environment in which students can construct their knowledge

(50) Teachers should recognise that what seems like errors from an adult point of view are students' expressions of their current understanding

(51) The comprehension of mathematical concepts by students should correspond to their cognitive development and it should be a decisive factor in the content sequence to be taught

(52) Students can solve non-routine problems in mathematics even when they haven't been taught some relevant procedures

(53) Students should be given the opportunity to feel confident and to attempt to maximise their potential in mathematics

(54) The education system should be preparing critically thinking citizens who are able to utilise their mathematical skills

(55) All students are able to be creative and do original work in mathematics

(56) Teachers should respect the mathematical knowledge of their students which is consisting of a nexus of experiences, beliefs, attitudes, representations, concepts, strategies, connections, values, judgements and emotions

(Section IV)   Mathematics assessment

(S57) TOOMAI (TOOMAI means: The Objective Of Mathematics Assessment
Is): Students to develop investigative skills

(58) TOOMAI: The utilisation of a variety of mathematical skills by the students

(59) TOOMAI: The use of problem solving strategies

(60) TOOMAI: The presentation of problems which require the use of a broad variety of problem solving strategies and skills by students

(61) TOOMAI: To prepare students for the recently introduced objective type tests

(62) TOOMAI: Real life problem solving and modelling in search of feasible solutions

(63) TOOMAI: To prepare students for project and report writing

(64) TOOMAI: Problem solving as a vehicle for developing mathematical skills

(65) TOOMAI: The presentation of various problems from a broad spectrum of mathematical activities

(66) TOOMAI: The use of specific problems for each chapter

(67) TOOMAI: To give the teacher the opportunity to provide her students with oral or written comments on their attempts to solve problems

(68) TOOMAI: Students to be given the opportunity to work on extended investigations and projects

(69) TOOMAI: Students to be given the opportunity to work on open-ended problems

(70) TOOMAI: Students to be given the opportunity to pose their own problems

(71) TOOMAI: Students keeping a journal of mathematical activities

(72) TOOMAI: The development of a positive attitude towards mathematics

(73) TOOMAI: The encouragement of student participation via properly designed activities

(74) TOOMAI: To promote students' communication skills by means of the mathematical language both orally and in writing

(75) TOOMAI: To mark student' work and to verify if the student should be promoted to the next grade

(76) TOOMAI: The use of authentic methods involving a broad spectrum of methods and approaches and reflecting and documenting the complexity of mathematical learning

(77) TOOMAI: The evaluation of both the efficiency and the effectiveness of teaching as well as further planning

(78) TOOMAI: Students to be provided with the opportunity for self-assessment and collaborative assessment

(79) TOOMAI: To provide students and parents with feedback

(80) TOOMAI: To succeed in University entrance exams

Appendix C2

Final questionnaire for the main study

(The symbols in the brackets signify the items that have been selected for the main study for comparison purposes: M=Main study item and P=Pilot study item)

(Section I) Nature of mathematics

(Main1+Pilot3) Justifying the mathematical statements that a person makes is an extremely important part of mathematics

(M2+P4) Mathematics is a static and immutable knowledge with objective truth

(M3+P5) Mathematics is computation

(M4+P7) Mathematics is the dynamic searching for models and problems and their results are open to review

(M5+P8) Mathematics is no more sequential than any other subject

(M6+P9) Mathematics is a beautiful, creative and useful human endeavor that is both a way of knowing and a way of thinking

(Section II) Mathematics learning

(M7+P11) The most effective way to learn mathematics is by listening carefully to the teacher explaining a mathematics lesson

(M8+P13) Students can learn more mathematics together than by themselves

(M9+P14) Students always benefit by discussing their solutions to mathematical problems with each other

(M10+P15) Mathematics knowledge is the result of the learner interpreting and organising the information gained from experiences

(M11+P16) Students are rational decision-makers capable of determining for themselves what is right and what is wrong

(M12+P20) The memorisation of mathematical facts is important in mathematics learning

(M13+P22) Mathematics learning is enhanced by challenging activities within a supportive environment

(Section III) Mathematics teaching

(M14+P24) Ignoring the mathematical ideas generated by the students can seriously limit their learning

(M15+P26) A vital task for the teacher is motivating students to resolve their own mathematical problems

(M16+P27) Teachers should encourage their students to strive for elegant solutions when they solve problems

(M17+P30) Mathematics teachers should be fascinated with how students think and intrigued by alternative ideas

(M18+P32) Teachers should be able to present mathematical ideas in a variety of ways

(M19+P34) Teachers always need to hear students' mathematical explanations before correcting their errors

(M20+P38) An effective way to teach mathematics is to provide students with interesting problems to investigate in small groups

(M21+39) It is not necessary for teachers to understand the source of students' errors; follow-up instruction will eliminate their difficulties

(M22+P40) Telling students the answer is an efficient way of facilitating their mathematics learning

(M23+P41) It is the teacher' responsibility to provide students with clear and concise solution methods for mathematical problems

(M24+P42) It is important for students to be provided with opportunities to reflect on and evaluate their own mathematical understanding

(M25+P43) There must be a set syllabus to be followed by the teacher

(M26+P46) It is important that mathematics content be presented to students in the correct logical sequence

(M27+P47) Teachers or the textbook-not the student-are the authorities for what is right or wrong

(M28+P48) The role of the mathematics teacher is to transmit mathematical knowledge and to verify that learners have received that knowledge

(M29+P50) Teachers should recognise that what seems like errors from an adult point of view are students' expressions of their current understanding

(M30+P51) The comprehension of mathematical concepts by students should correspond to their cognitive development and it should be a decisive factor in the content sequence to be taught

(M31+P53) Students should be given the opportunity to feel confident and to attempt to maximise their potential in mathematics

(M32+P54) The education system should be preparing critically thinking citizens who are able to utilise their mathematical skills

(M33+P55) All students are able to be creative and do original work in mathematics

(M34+P56) Teachers should respect the mathematical knowledge of their students which is consisting of a nexus of experiences, beliefs, attitudes, representations, concepts, strategies, connections, values, judgements and emotions

(Section IV)   Mathematics assessment

(M35+P57) TOOMAI (*TOOMAI means: The Objective Of Mathematics Assessment Is*): Students to develop investigative skills

(M36+P58) TOOMAI: The utilisation of a variety of mathematical skills by the students

(M37+P59) TOOMAI: The use of problem solving strategies

(M38+P60) TOOMAI: The presentation of problems which require the use of a broad variety of problem solving strategies and skills by students

(M39+P62) TOOMAI: Real life problem solving and modelling in search of feasible solutions

(M40+P63) TOOMAI: To prepare students for project and report writing

(M41+P65) TOOMAI: The presentation of various problems from a broad spectrum of mathematical activities

(M42+P66) TOOMAI: The use of specific problems for each chapter

(M43+P67) TOOMAI: To give the teacher the opportunity to provide her students with oral or written comments on their attempts to solve problems

(M44+P68) TOOMAI: Students to be given the opportunity to work on extended investigations and projects

(M45+P69) TOOMAI: Students to be given the opportunity to work on open-ended problems

(M46+P70) TOOMAI: Students to be given the opportunity to pose their own problems

(M47+P71) TOOMAI: Students keeping a journal of mathematical activities

(M48+P72) TOOMAI: The development of a positive attitude towards mathematics

(M49+P73) TOOMAI: The encouragement of student participation via properly designed activities

(M50+P74) TOOMAI: To promote students' communication skills by means of the mathematical language both orally and in writing

(M51+P75) TOOMAI: To mark student' work and to verify if the student should be promoted to the next grade

(M52+P79) TOOMAI: To provide students and parents with feedback

(M53+P80) TOOMAI: To succeed in University entrance exams

Appendix C3

Criteria for the categorisation of interviewees' responses

(i)   Teachers' beliefs about the nature of mathematics

TRADITIONAL	PRIMARILY TRADITIONAL	EVEN MIX OF TRADITIONAL AND CONTEMPORARY	PRIMARILY CONTEMPORARY	CONTEMPORARY
MT1 Mathematics is an unrelated collection of facts, rules and skills	MPT1 Although there are some connections between different areas, mathematics is mostly made up of unrelated topics			MC1 Mathematics is dynamic, problem driven and continually expanding
MT2 Mathematics is a static and immutable knowledge with objective truth	MPT2 Mathematics is primarily fixed, predictable, absolute, certain and applicable		MPC2 Mathematics involves problem solving	MC2 Mathematics is the dynamic searching for models and problems and their results are open to review
MT3 Mathematics is computation				MC3 Mathematics is the study of patterns
MT4 Mathematics problems given to students should be quickly solvable in a few steps				MC4 Mathematics can be surprising, relative, doubtful and aesthetic
MT5 Right answers in mathematics are much more important than the ways in which we find them				MC5 Mathematics is a beautiful, creative and useful human endeavor that is both a way of knowing and a way of thinking

(ii)   Teachers' beliefs about mathematics learning

TRADITIONAL	PRIMARILY TRADITIONAL	EVEN MIX OF TRADITIONAL AND CONTEMPORARY	PRIMARILY CONTEMPORARY	CONTEMPORARY
LT1 Students passively receive/consume knowledge that is transmitted from the teacher	**LPT1** Students learn mathematics better by working individually most of the time	**LM1** Students learn mathematics through both problem solving and textbook work	**LPC1** Students primarily learn mathematics via problem solving tasks	**LC1** Students learn mathematics through problem solving and inquiry activities
LT2 Students learn mathematics better by working individually	**LPT2** Students primarily engage in drill activities (repeated practice) for mastery of skills	**LM2** Students should do equal amounts of individual and group work	**LPC2** Students primarily learn mathematics from working with other students	**LC2** Students can learn more mathematics by working cooperatively than by themselves
LT3 The most effective way to learn mathematics is by listening carefully to the teacher explaining a mathematics lesson	**LPT3** The teacher is more responsible for learning than the student	**LM3** Learning mathematics is equally the responsibility of students and teacher	**LPC3** Students are more responsible for their learning than the teacher	**LC3** The student is an autonomous learner
LT4 Students learn mathematics solely from the textbook and worksheets	**LPT4** Students learn mathematics primarily from the textbook and worksheets	**LM4** Students learn mathematics equally from the textbook and worksheets, and through active participation in meaningful activities	**LPC4** Students learn mathematics primarily through active participation in meaningful activities	**LC4** Students learn mathematics solely through active participation in meaningful activities
LT5 Memorisation and mastery of algorithms signify learning	**LPT5** Memorisation and mastery of algorithms provide primary evidence of learning	**LM5** Students should both understand and master skills and algorithms	**LPC5** Students should show evidence of understanding their work	**LC5** Learning is evidenced more by the student's capacity to explain understanding than through memorization and performance on algorithms
LT6 Many students are just not able to learn mathematics	**LPT6** Some students are just not able to learn mathematics	**LM6** Some students can learn mathematics and some can't	**LPC6** Most students can learn mathematics	**LC6** All students can learn mathematics

LT7	LPT7	LM7	LPC7	LC7
Students' learning of mathematics depends solely on the teacher	Students' learning of mathematics depends primarily on the teacher	Students' learning of mathematics depends equally on the teacher and the learner	Students' learning of mathematics depends primarily on the learner	Each student learns mathematics in his or her own way
LT8 Mathematics learning is being able to get the right answer quickly				**LC8** Mathematics learning is the result of the learner making connections, and interpreting and organising the information gained from experiences
LT9 Students learn when engaged in drill activities for mastery of skills				**LC9** Students learn when engaged in investigative activities with periods of uncertainty, conflict and confusion
LT10 Mathematics learning is an individual pursuit for knowledge				**LC10** Mathematics learning is about achieving shared knowledge

(iii)   Teachers' beliefs about mathematics teaching

TRADITIONAL	PRIMARILY TRADITIONAL	EVEN MIX	PRIMARILY CONTEMPORARY	CONTEMPORARY
TT1 The teacher lectures and dispenses mathematical knowledge	**TPT1** The teacher primarily lectures	The teacher equally lectures and facilitates learning by posing challenging questions	**TPC1** The teacher primarily facilitates and guides with little lecturing	**TC1** The teacher facilitates learning by posing challenging questions
TT2 The teacher presents mathematics in an expository style by demonstrating and explaining concepts and skills				**TC2** The teacher promotes knowledge sharing and allows students to actively participate in their learning
TT3 The teacher seeks 'right answers' and is not concerned with explanations	**TPT3** The teacher primarily values right answers over process	**TM3** The teacher equally values product and process	**TPC3** The teacher values process somewhat more than product	**TC3** The teacher clearly values process over product

TT4				TC4
The teacher approaches mathematics topics in isolation				The teacher strives to approach topics by making connections
TT5		**TM5**		**TC5**
The teacher emphasizes mastery and memorization of skills and facts over understanding		The teacher equally emphasizes memorization and understanding		The teacher emphasises understanding over memorisation
TT6	**TPT6**	**TM6**	**TPC6**	**TC6**
The teacher instructs solely from the textbook	The teacher primarily (but not exclusively) teaches from the textbook	The teacher uses textbook and other resources equally	The teacher primarily uses resources other than the textbook when teaching	The teacher uses resources other than the textbook when teaching
TT7	**TPT7**	**TM7**	**TPC7**	**TC7**
Lessons are planned and implemented without deviation	Lessons are planned and implemented without deviation most of the time	Lesson plans are followed explicitly at times and flexibly at others	Lesson plans are followed flexibly most of the time	The teacher does not follow explicit, inflexible lessons
TT8	**TPT8**	**TM8**	**TPC8**	**TC8**
The teacher assesses students solely through standard quizzes and exams	The teacher assesses students solely through standard quizzes and exams most of the time	The teacher assesses students equally through exams and contemporary assessment methods	The teacher assesses students mostly via contemporary assessment methods	The teacher assesses students solely via contemporary assessment methods (projects, folios, clinical interviews, etc.)

TT9	TPT9		TPC9	TC9
Lessons and activities follow the same pattern daily	The teacher includes a limited number of opportunities for problem solving		The teacher teaches makes problem solving an integral part of the class	The teacher teaches only via problem solving and modeling activities
TT10	**TPT10**	**TM10**	**TPC10**	**TC10**
The teacher has students work individually all the time	The teacher has students work individually most of the time	The teacher has students work in groups and individually in equal amounts	The teacher has students work in cooperative groups most of the time	The teacher has students work in cooperative groups all the time
TT11	**TPT11**	**TMT11**	**TPC11**	**TC11**
The teacher provides the correct answers all the time	The teacher provides the answers most of the time	The teacher provides the answers and promotes students' autonomy equally	The teacher promotes students' autonomy most of the time	The teacher promotes students' autonomy
TT12	**TPT12**		**TPC12**	**TC12**
The teacher does not demonstrate any gender sensitivity in his/her interaction with his/her students	The teacher demonstrates gender sensitivity in some aspects of his/her interaction with his/her students		The teacher demonstrates gender sensitivity in most aspects of his/her interaction with his/her students	The teacher demonstrates gender sensitivity in all aspects of his/her interaction with his/her students
TT13				**TC13**
The teacher doesn't have to understand the source of students' errors; follow-up instruction will eliminate their difficulties				The teacher recognises that what seems like errors from an adult point of view are students' expressions of their current understanding
TT14				**TC14**
The teacher conducts her classes in a autocratic way				The teacher strives to conduct her classes in a non-threatening environment

(iv)   Teachers' beliefs about mathematics assessment

TRADITIONAL

The objective of mathematics assessment is:

AT1	AT2	AT3	AT4	AT5
To prepare students for the recently introduced objective type tests	To mark student' work and to verify if the student should be promoted to the next grade	To succeed at University entrance exams	The evaluation of both the efficiency and the effectiveness of teaching as well as further planning	To provide students and parents with feedback

CONTEMPORARY

The objective of mathematics assessment is:

AC1	AC9
The presentation of various problems from a broad spectrum of mathematical activities	Students keeping a journal of mathematical activities
AC2	**AC10**
To give the teacher the opportunity to provide her students with oral or written comments on their attempts to solve problems	Students to be given the opportunity to pose their own problems
AC3	**AC11**
Real life problem solving and modelling in search of feasible solutions	To promote students' communication skills by means of the mathematical language both orally and in writing
AC4	**AC12**
To prepare students for project and report writing	The use of authentic methods involving a broad spectrum of methods and approaches and reflecting and documenting the complexity of mathematical learning
AC5	**AC13**
Students to be given the opportunity to work on open-ended problems	Students to develop investigative skills
AC6	**AC14**
Students to be given the opportunity to work on extended problem solving and modeling projects	The utilisation of a variety of mathematical skills by the students
AC7	**AC15**
Students to be provided with the opportunity for self-assessment and collaborative assessment	Students to be given the opportunity to work on extended investigations and projects
AC8	**AC16**
The development of a positive attitude towards mathematics	Problem solving as a vehicle for developing mathematical skills

Appendix C4

Criteria for the analysis of video- taped sessions

TRADITI-ONAL	PRIMARILY TRADITIO-NAL	EVEN MIX OF TRADITIONAL AND CONTEMPO-RARY	PRIMARILY CONTEMP0-RARY	CONTEMPORA-RY
The teacher: (TPT1instr-text) Instructs solely from the textbook	*The teacher:* (TPPT1 instr-text) Instructs mainly from the textbook	*The teacher:* (TPEM1 instr-equal) Teaches equally from textbook and problem-solving/modeling activities	*The teacher:* (TPPC1instr-p.s.) Primarily engages students in problem-solving/mode ling tasks	*The teacher:* (TPC1 instr-p.s.) Solely provides problem-solving/modeling tasks
(TPT2 syll-rigid) Follows the prescribed syllabus rigidly	(TPPT2 syll-divers) Follows the prescribed syllabus with occasional diversions			(TPC2 patt-outd) Extends learning beyond the classroom
(TPT3 topic-isol) Approaches mathematics topics in isolation	(TPPT3 topic-isol) Approaches mathematics topics in isolation most of the time		(TPPC3 syll-conn) Primarily selects tasks that stimulate students to make connections	(TPC3 syll-conn) Selects tasks that stimulate students to make connections
(TPT4 patt-same) Approaches mathematics instruction in the same pattern daily	(TPPT4 patt-same) Approaches mathematics instruction in the same pattern most of the time		(TPTC4 topic-chall.) Primarily selects challenging tasks based on students' interests and experiences	(TPC4 topic-chall.) Selects challenging tasks based on students' interests and experiences
(TPT5 eng-p+p) Has students engage only in individual paper-and-pencil tasks	(TPPT5 eng-p+p) Has students engage primarily in individual paper-and-pencil tasks with occasional assignment of group work		(TPPC5 eng-coll) Has students engage primarily in collaborative work	(TPC5 eng-coll) Facilitates cooperative student work, encouraging communication

(TPT6 env)	(TPPT6 env)	(TPEM6 env)	(TPPC6 env)	(TPC6 env)
Creates an environment in which students are passive learners	Creates an environment in which students are passive learners, occasionally calling on them to play a more active role	Creates an environment that at times allows students to be passive learners and at times active learners	Creates an environment that at times allows students to be active learners occasionally having them play a more passive role	Creates an environment that reflects respect for students' ideas and structures the time necessary to grapple with ideas and problems
(TPT7 eval) Evaluates students solely via exams seeking 'right answers'	(TPPT7 eval) Evaluates students primarily via standard quizzes and exams, only occasionally using alternative methods	(TPEM7 eval) Evaluates students' learning equally via standard quizzes and exams and alternative assessment methods	(TPPC7 eval) Evaluates students' learning using primarily alternative assessment methods	(TPC7 eval) Evaluates students' learning using alternative assessment methods (projects, investigations, portfolios, etc.)
(TPT8 disc-teach) Primarily encourages teacher-directed discourse	(TPPT8 disc-teach) Primarily encourages teacher-directed discourse, only occasionally allowing for student-directed interactions	(TPEM8 disc-equal) Encourages equally teacher-directed discourse and student-directed discourse	(TPPC8 disc-stud) Encourages mostly student-directed discourse	(TPC8 disc-stud) Encourages student-directed discourse
(TPT9 error) Students' errors are considered as cognitive deficiency or weakness or inability to grasp concepts	(TPPT9 error) Students' errors are considered as cognitive deficiency or weakness or inability to grasp concepts most of the time	(TPEM9 error) Students' errors are sometimes interpreted as expressions of their current conceptual understanding and sometimes as cognitive deficiency or weakness or inability to grasp concepts	(TPPC9 error) Students' errors are interpreted as expressions of their current conceptual understanding most of the time	(TPC9 error) Students' errors are interpreted as expressions of their current conceptual understanding

(TPT10 quest'n) Poses questions in search of specific pre-determined responses using unproductive questions (e.g. too complex, tricky, trivial, abstract, ambiguous)	(TPPT10 quest'n) Poses questions in search of specific pre-determined responses using unproductive questions most of the time (e.g. too complex, tricky, trivial, abstract, ambiguous)	(TPEM10 quest'n) Poses questions using a mix of unproductive and productive questioning	(TPPC10 quest'n) Poses questions that engage multiple modes of questioning (e.g. justifying, inferring, generalizing, categorizing, establishing criteria, testing hypotheses, extrapolating, etc.) most of the time	(TPC10 quest'n) Poses questions that engage multiple modes of questioning (e.g. justifying, inferring, generalizing, categorizing, establishing criteria, testing hypotheses, extrapolating, etc.)
CONTEMPORARY CATEGORIES				
(TPC11 comm'n) Selects tasks that promote communication about mathematics	(TPC12 jystif'n) Has students clarify and justify their ideas orally and in writing	(TPC13 observ'n) Observes and listens to students to eveluate learning	(TPC14 risk) Encourages students to take risks while solving problems	(TPC15 tech'n) Facilitates an effective/efficient/creative use of technology
(TPC16 self-refl) Regularly reflects on and evaluates his/her own work	(TPC17 comm-inq) Aims for a community of inquiry in his/her classes	(TPC18 Interdisc) Uses an interdisciplinary approach	(TPC19 journ) Encourages and facilitates the use of student journals	(TPC20 self-refl) Encourages student self-reflection
(TPC21 meta-cog) Facilitates and encourages meta-cognitive activities	(TPC22 creat) Encourages and facilitates the use of creativity and imagination			

Appendix C5

Aims and objectives of interviews and classroom observations, and interview schedule

The aims and objectives of the interview and classroom observations were to obtain information about and to explore teachers':

- pedagogical knowledge
- students' knowledge and beliefs
- understanding of teaching mathematics
- exploration of beliefs and teaching methods/strategies
- mathematical interconnection of ideas
- exploration of <u>critical incidents</u> related to the above
- their own perception of what made them successful teachers of maths including reasons and factors identified
- specific details related to teaching arising from observations - significant incidents identified both by the researcher and by the teacher
- aims and planning
- differences between teacher's self perception and observations
- self confidence
- self concept
- classroom management
- further details on training and development

The prompt questions used in the interview were divided into the eight categories listed below:

1. *Background:*
   - Number of years teaching?
   - Grade levels?
   - Types of students being taught?
   - Why did you become a mathematics teacher?
   - Your development so far in terms of P.D., Post Grad. studies, and career?
   - Any innovative instruction in your class?

- Hobbies?

2. *Mathematics:*
    - What do you think mathematics is all about?
    - Which factors do you consider to have a significant influence on your beliefs about mathematics?

3. *Mathematics learning:*
    - When a student enters into grade ___, what should the student be able to do in terms of mathematics?
    - What can a good mathematics student do?
    - When a student leaves grade __, what can she do?
    - What accounts for the differences between a good and a poor mathematics student?
    - Is it possible for a teacher to help a poorly performing mathematics student become a good mathematics student?
    - How do you define comprehension of a mathematical concept? topic?
    - How do you know a student understood a particular lesson?
    - Which factors do you consider to have a significant influence on your beliefs about mathematics learning?
    - Can you describe the learning environment in your class?

4. *Mathematics teaching:*
    - Could you describe the way you teach mathematics?
    - Questioning students—why? what do you consider a good response? what is a poor response? what is a creative response?
    - Where did you learn to teach mathematics that way?
    - Have you ever had graduate/in-service courses on how to teach it? (**Probe--** duration? when was the last one undertaken)?
    - Have you ever tried something different? Why? What happened?
    - Have you ever wanted to do something different?
    - Grouping: on what basis? why?
    - Do you do different things in different groups? why?
    - What indicates to you that a lesson is going poorly?
    - Do you ever feel that you are getting behind in mathematics?

- What are the most important characteristics of quality teaching?
- Which is the most effective way to teach mathematics?
- Which factors do you consider to have a significant influence on your ability to teach mathematics?
- Which factors do you consider to have a significant influence on your beliefs about mathematics teaching?
- Which factors may explain the existence of inconsistencies between espoused beliefs and beliefs in practice
- What could the constituents of an effective mathematics teaching model be?

5. *Assessment:*
   - Based on what criteria do you select the appropriate assessment method for a topic/term/year?

6. *The students:*
   - Describe the students in your class
   - Do they have a pretty good chance of making it through school?
   - Describe a student who is having great difficulty in mathematics
   - Describe a student who is just behind—not terrific, but not a real problem
   - Describe a student who is really doing well
   - Describe a gifted and talented student in your class

7. *The school:*
   - Do you feel there is a characteristic way of teaching mathematic in this school?
   - Do you know what the other mathematics teachers are doing? I mean sort of?
   - How do you know?
   - Do you ever observe in other classrooms?
   - Do you exchange materials, ideas, methods with other maths (or any other discipline) teachers?
   - Communication with other teachers? Consultants? Other specialists (Researchers, Lecturers, Board of Studies personnel)?

8.   *Personal Reading:*

- What types of things do you read now? (When you have a chance)

Participants were also given the opportunity to respond to take-home open response items, which are listed below along with their headings:

Throughout this survey we would like you imagine a mathematics lesson, at any year level, where students are learning, for example, to estimate the volume of various objects, or to add/subtract fractions, or to evaluate integrals, or to solve differential equations, or to analyse/interpret information from a given graph.

(a) Could you please write down the most important characteristics which a *quality* mathematics lesson on any of these concepts/skills would usually have.

(b) Could you please write down what could the reason(s) for the existence of *inconsistencies* between espoused beliefs and actual classroom practice be, on topics such as beliefs about mathematics, mathematics teaching, mathematics learning and mathematics assessment?

(c) Could you please prioritise (using nos 1-10 in order of preference, i.e. 1=top priority, 10=lowest priority) the factors and establish their connections by using the given arrows, on the following diagram, which you deem to be the most significant for the inconsistencies identified in (b) above?

Box	Past school experiences
Box	Teacher education program
Box	Social teaching norms
Box	Teacher's life outside school
Oval	Mathematics beliefs
Box	Immediate classroom situation
Oval	Mathematical teaching practices
Box	Early family experiences
Box	Students' lives outside school
Box	Personality characteristics of the teacher

Indicates strong influence

Indicates moderate influence

Indicates slight influence

Appendix C6

Traditional and contemporary task specific strategies

	No.	TASK SPECIFIC STRATEGIES USED	Tom	Ann
T R A D I T I O N A L	1	Teaches solely from textbook		
	2	Uses objective tests solely		
	3	Uses teacher demonstration solely		
	4	Uses drill & practice solely		
	5	Uses independent work solely		
	6	Teaches topics in isolation		
	7	Uses pencil & paper applications solely		
C o n t e m p o r a r y	8	Encourages integration of concepts		
	9	Observes students for evaluation purposes		
	10	Incorporates investigations		
	11	Uses physical activities		
	12	Uses open ended tasks		
	13	Uses hypothesising		
	14	Uses patterning		
	15	Uses writing about maths activities		
	16	Encourages student talk		
	17	Utilises the video		
	18	Uses outdoor activities		
	19	Motivates students		
	20	Uses concrete materials		
	21	Uses communicating		
	22	Uses cooperative groups		
	23	Uses calculators and computers and internet		
	24	Uses mathematical modelling		
	25	Uses Journals		
	26	Uses Portfolios		
	27	Encourages taking risks		
	28	Authentic and self -assessment		

Contemporary

29	Evaluates contexts and outcomes		
30	Problem solving and posing		
31	Estimating and representing		
32	Facilitates meta-cognitive activity		
33	Facilitates use of heuristics explicitly		
34	Uses positive affirmation		
35	Encourages the use of imagination and creativity		
36	Evaluates students progress		
37	Uses non routine tasks		
38	Uses multiple modes of questioning		
39	Encourages originality and divergent thinking		
40	Provides sufficient "wait time"		
41	Extends learning beyond classroom		
42	Encourages intuitiveness		
43	Demonstrates gender sensitivity		
44	Uses debates		
45	Uses clinical interviews		

Appendix D1

Criteria used to eliminate items from the Pilot study's questionnaire

Using SPSS$_{WIN}$

(1) For 80 items, **descriptives** with mean, standard deviation, skewness, kurtosis

(2) **Reliability analysis** (Alpha analysis) for each factor

(3) **Exploratory factor analysis** (for 80 items): forced to 3+3 factors; replace missing data with means (insufficient number of cases due to large loss through listwise deletion); varimax rotation; loading only above .3 accepted

(4) Printouts for 2-3 above analysed

From (1) above items deleted if:

- 1 sd above/below mean is outside score range for item (1-5+1-4 respectively)
- both normality criteria also examined
  ie. contravened if skewness & kurtosis: ratio of skewness/kurtosis:SE >2

From (2) above, items deleted if:

- r_{it} <.3 (ie. item to rest of scale correlations <.3)
- alpha would increase if item removed

These deletions were checked against (5) below

From (3) above, items deleted if, from varimax:

- items did not load on factor interpretable
- items loaded >.3 on more than one factor

(5) Reliability and factor analysis re-run as many times as required- remove items as described for (2) and (3) above

Appendix D2

Reasons for elimination of items from the questionnaire of the Pilot study

Qn	Item	Reason
Q 23	A key responsibility of a teacher is to encourage students to explore their own mathematical ideas	FA: First factor analysis double loading, factor 1 with factor 3
Q 44	Mathematics material is best presented in an expository style: demonstrating, explaining, and describing concepts and skills	FA: First factor analysis double loading, factor 1 with factor 2
Q 17	Mathematics learning is being able to get the right answer quickly	FA: First factor analysis double loading, factor 2 with factor 3
Q 49	Teachers should negotiate social norms with the students in order to develop a cooperative learning environment in which students can construct their knowledge	FA: Did not load at all
Q 19	Students are capable of much higher levels of mathematical thought than has been suggested traditionally	FA: Did not load at all
Q 21	Mathematics learning is enhanced by activities which build upon and respect students' experiences	FA: Did not load at all
Q 1	Although there are some connections between different areas, mathematics is mostly made up of unrelated topics	FA: Did not load at all
Q 28	Teachers should create a non-threatening environment for learning mathematics for all students	FA: Did not load at all
Q 35	Effective mathematics teachers enjoy learning and 'doing' mathematics themselves	FA: Did not load at all
Q 27	Teachers should encourage their students to strive for elegant solutions when they solve problems	FA: Did not load at all
Q 12	Mathematics is best learned individually	FA: Did not load at all
Q 33	Persistent questioning by the teacher has a significant effect on students' mathematical learning	FA: Did not load at all
Q 55	All students are able to be creative and do original work in mathematics	FA: Did not load at all
Q 3	Justifying the mathematical statements that a person makes is an extremely important part of mathematics	FA: Did not load at all
Q 6	Mathematics problems given to students should be quickly solvable in a few steps	FA: Did not load at all
Q 50	Teachers should recognise that what seems like errors from an adult point of view are students' expressions of their current understanding	FA: Did not load at all
Q 7	Mathematics is the dynamic searching for models and problems and their results are open to review	FA: Did not load at all

Qn	Item	Reason
Q 2	In mathematics problems can be solved without using rules	FA: Did not load at all
Q 45	My mathematics teachers would often show me different ways to solve a problem	FA: Did not load at all
Q 37	It is important to cover all the topics in the mathematics curriculum in the textbook sequence	FA: Did not load at all
Q 31	The main function of a teacher is to provide her students with solutions to their mathematical problems	Alpha reliability improved if deleted
Q 29	I would feel uncomfortable if a student suggested a solution to a mathematical problem that I hadn't thought of previously	Alpha reliability improved if deleted
Q 10	Right answers in mathematics are much more important than the ways in which you get them	Alpha reliability improved if deleted
Q 36	If a student's explanation of a mathematical problem does not make sense to the teacher it is best to ignore it	Alpha reliability improved if deleted
Q 25	Encouraging multiple ways of mathematical thinking is insufficient and may confuse children	Alpha reliability improved if deleted
Q 52	Students can solve non-routine problems in mathematics even when they haven't been taught some relevant procedures	Alpha reliability improved if deleted
Q 18	Periods of uncertainty, conflict, confusion, surprise are a significant part of the mathematics learning process	Alpha reliability improved if deleted
Q 9	Mathematics is a beautiful, creative and useful human endeavor that is both a way of knowing and a way of thinking	Alpha reliability improved if deleted
Q 34	Teachers always need to hear students' mathematical explanations before correcting their errors	Alpha reliability improved if deleted
Q 19	Students are capable of much higher levels of mathematical thought than has been suggested traditionally	Alpha reliability improved if deleted
Q 49	Teachers should negotiate social norms with the students in order to develop a cooperative learning environment in which students can construct their knowledge	Alpha reliability improved if deleted
Q 72	TOOMAI (TOOMAI means: The Objective Of Mathematics Assessment Is): The development of a positive attitude towards mathematics	FA: First factor analysis double loading, factor 1 with factor 2
Q 61	TOOMAI: To prepare students for the recently introduced objective type tests	FA: First factor analysis double loading, factor 2 with factor 3
Q 77	TOOMAI: The evaluation of both the efficiency and the effectiveness of teaching as well as further planning	FA: First factor analysis double loading, factor 1 with factor 3
Q 78	TOOMAI: Students to be provided with the opportunity for self-assessment and collaborative assessment	FA: First factor analysis double loading, factor 1 with factor 3
Q 67	TOOMAI: To give the teacher the opportunity to provide her students with oral or written comments on their attempts to solve problems	FA: First factor analysis double loading, factor 1 with factor 3
Q 64	TOOMAI: Problem solving as a vehicle for	FA: Second factor analysis double loading,

Qn	Item	Reason
	developing mathematical skills	factor 1 with factor 2
Q 66	TOOMAI: The use of specific problems for each chapter	FA: Third factor analysis double loading, factor 1 with factor 3
Q 76	TOOMAI: The use of authentic methods involving a broad spectrum of methods and approaches and reflecting and documenting the complexity of mathematical learning	FA: Fourth factor analysis double loading, factor 1 with factor 2
Q 74	TOOMAI: To promote students' communication skills by means of the mathematical language both orally and in writing	FA: Fifth factor analysis double loading, factor 1 with factor 3

Appendix F1

Ann's interview

Ann's beliefs about mathematics

In this part of the interview discussion focused on the interviewees' espoused beliefs about mathematics:

Interviewer *(I)*: What do you think mathematics is all about?

Ann (A): *Mathematics is a cultural by-product that has been acquired by the human race through the centuries. We can use mathematics to communicate with nature and to understand natural phenomena as well as the interaction between the human being and these phenomena.*

I: What do you think about school mathematics?

A: *The mathematics we teach at school do not seem to be serving any other purpose except preparing the kids for exams. In the past, we could be more flexible in our teaching and we could improvise, but nowadays education policy makers, as well as most students and parents, think that the purpose of schooling is to prepare students for University entrance exams. I feel that I am actually doing a lot less in class nowadays than what I used to do two decades ago. The fact is that lately, I too feel that I have a responsibility to prepare them for the final exams, since it is very important for the kids and their families.*

I: Which factors do you consider to have a significant influence on your beliefs about mathematics?

A: *When I was at the University I recall attending a Differential Geometry lecture. I had decided to be a good student so I sat on one of the front rows desks in the lecture amphitheatre and started taking notes. The Lecturer started explaining by using a wooden language full of symbols and incomprehensible jargon. I was very disappointed and I remember that I felt the same way very often during my University years. The greatest disappointment was that we could pass the subjects by just memorising the lecture material. Then one day I happened to start reading a philosophy book written by members of the Academy of Sciences of the (then) Soviet Union. There were a number of instances in the book were mention was made to how Differential Geometry, Dynamics and Relativity could be used to understand philosophy. I got the shock of my life realising that the book offered a different – and most importantly comprehensible - perspective of topics that I could not understand at University. From that point onwards I started searching for answers. I wanted to find out more about what geometry is and how is it related to dynamics, via the use of calculus.*

I remember J.D. who was reciting poems when teaching mathematics. I was really shaken by his teaching methods, his attitude, and his personality. That was definitely a time that I experienced a cognitive and a cultural shock. I said to my self, wait a minute there is something important about this teacher and his approach. It really touched me. These experiences had an impact on my professional life.

When I found out that Marx before endeavouring in his treatise called "The Capital" had to extensively study the applications of the derivative in economics, I realised how important calculus and its applications were, when used in other sciences.

Ann's beliefs about mathematics learning

In this part of the interview discussion focused on the interviewees' espoused beliefs about mathematics learning:

I: What can a very good mathematics student do (is the difference between a very good and a poor mathematics student qualitative or quantitative)?

A: *I would like the kids to be able to work on their own and in teams, to be able to do problem solving and modelling and to be able to use mathematical proofs in their work. A good mathematics student (in Years 10-12) should be able to use abstractions and to generalise. In my classes I would like my students to be meticulous and conscientious, to work hard and persist on set tasks irrespectively of the fact of getting the answers or not. In addition, I expect a good student to perform well on tests as well as in class.*

I: What accounts for the differences between a good and a poor mathematics student? (Probe – parents? genetic? good teaching? learning style?)

A: *A good mathematics student should be organised and to know how to study. In mathematics, the process is more important than the product. The student needs to be motivated, to have a desire to learn and to be an autonomous learner.*

I: Is it possible for a teacher to help a poorly performing mathematics student become a good mathematics student?

A: *I certainly believe that a student's performance can improve and that the teacher's role is of paramount importance. If the teacher can find ways to motivate her students and to help them realise that it is worthy to make an effort to learn mathematics – and not only to pass the exams – then there is a possibility that the student's performance may improve. Each student needs to realise what interests her more and that a number of everyday applications incorporate some serious mathematical thinking. I would therefore conclude that the teacher of mathematics could help a poorly performing mathematics student become a good mathematics student, if and only if she is able to motivate her students to be systematic and organised, and instil in them the desire to learn.*

I: How do you define comprehension of a mathematical concept? topic?

A: *There is no simple answer to that question. Being able to recall the required facts and algorithms when necessary represents evidence that understanding of a concept has taken place in mathematics. When students can apply their knowledge in contexts other than the ones presented in their textbooks, is another piece of evidence that understanding has taken place. To be able to use her knowledge and skills at any time, to model any given context, and to have developed an inquiring mind, is additional evidence that mathematical understanding has taken place.*

I: Which factors do you consider to have a significant influence on your beliefs about mathematics learning?

A: *A number of factors shaped my beliefs about mathematics learning including my postgraduate studies. I firmly believe that a teacher must be a cultivated and open-minded person with rich experiences. One factor that I can single out as having a profound impact in shaping my beliefs about mathematics learning was my ideological stance and my involvement in the day-to-day business of political parties.*

Ann's beliefs about mathematics teaching

In this part of the interview discussion focused on the interviewees' espoused beliefs about mathematics teaching:

I: Could you describe the way you teach mathematics? (Probe – typical day? remembering ideas? memorizing facts?)

A: *I would like all students in my classes to make progress and to attempt to maximise their potential in mathematics. I believe that even the weakest students are able to master the basic concepts of mathematics. I try to answer as many of their questions as possible in class. My classes are structured around those simple principles. If I can persuade someone, who for various reasons does not believe that she is a good mathematics student, to be involved in the work we do in class, then I consider my teaching successful. On many occasions, I have been taken by surprise by students whom I considered very weak in mathematics but they performed very well as soon as their queries were fully explained to them.*

I: What about memorisation? What is its role in mathematics teaching?

A: *During my teaching career I have gone through a number of phases regarding my beliefs about the role of memorisation. At first I used to think that it was not a very important skill in mathematics learning. Having assessed a number of students however, who did not know the tables even in Years 10 or 11, I realised that there are aspects of mathematics that must be memorised at various stages of mathematics learning, so that they won't become the reason for the emergence of cognitive obstacles later. Students need to understand the basic mechanisms in various mathematical algorithms and they should therefore memorise some aspects of them, if they are going to use them effectively in problem solving and modelling investigations or whenever the need arises.*

I: Where did you learn to teach mathematics that way? Have you ever had graduate and/or in-service courses on how to teach mathematics?

A: *Life taught me (she laughs). By that, I mean that I had to learn many things on my own during my teaching career. I am currently participating at a regional mathematics teachers' cluster and I think that there are some positive outcomes because we discuss our daily problems and we formulate common strategies for more effective teaching. It is very important for my professional life. As far as graduate courses are concerned, I feel that I have learned a few new things in my Masters course.*

I: Have you ever tried something different? Why?

A: *Firstly I believe that a number of traditional teaching techniques are outdated and need to be replaced by new teaching approaches. Secondly I am constantly trying to discover new approaches and educational environments that will enable the kids to fully develop as mathematics apprentices. Thirdly I believe that contemporary teaching ideas based on constructivism have given me a new purpose in teaching mathematics. I have learned a lot from my students too. If I had something in mind and tried it in class, the interaction with my students created a dialectic relationship from which a number of unexpected new ideas kept emerging.*

I: What happened while attempting to introduce a new approach?

A: *I have encountered a number of problems by practising contemporary teaching methods because students are very apprehensive about their potential to enhance learning. Some students do not perceive them to be as effective as the traditional chalk and talk, and paper and pencil techniques with which they are accustomed to. Senior students who are accustomed to working individually find it very difficult to work in groups. Some students worry that their efforts will not be appreciated by their teacher, partly because they like to be protagonists in class and partly because the fear that the outcome of group's work won't be their own work alone. They also worry about how are they going to be assessed in groups and the fact that the work of their group may not be awarded top marks. Some of the students take a long time to get used to contemporary teaching techniques. The fact of the matter is however, that contemporary techniques help even the weakest students to participate in classroom work and to learn more effectively.*

I: Grouping: on what basis? Why?

A: *I started using group work in 1983. I recall that I wanted every single student to be involved in class work instead of having them passively listening to me. I (then) thought that if the class was divided in small groups then I could have a small community in each group with its potential to differentiate among its members and with its leaders unknowingly acting as my assistants - without letting the class knowing about it. All this because I will not be satisfied except when all students participate in classroom activities.*

I: Probe – how do you select group membership? Do you change the groups? Why?)

A: *I allow students the freedom to decide the group they want to participate to, because I want them to be comfortable and to feel that they own the process. The less I impose the best. I intervene of course once I feel that it is necessary. I will provide an example from last year. Two of the groups the students formed, were consisting of weak students without any strong leaders or good students in them, and I felt that there were going to be problems with them. Gradually the members of those groups realised that they needed help and when I intervened and modified the group membership, things started working and a cooperative spirit emerged. I do intervene and modify group membership if in the process I realise that it is not going to work. It is a shared responsibility. I think that my approach to group work was initially experiential but it gradually became more theory laden as I started searching for theoretical evidence to support my group work approach.*

I: What do you consider the most important characteristics of quality teaching?

A: *Getting in the students' shoes in class helps me appreciate some of the difficulties students encounter. I think that by putting students in the leading role provides adequate incentive for them to participate in class activities promotes the desire to own the process and enables them to experience that what they do is important. I consider that the development of each student's self-esteem, as well as the feeling of belonging in a group, are important elements of quality teaching. I strive to create a classroom environment, which promotes an understanding that the individual's interests and the group's interests are not always competitive. After all cooperation is more effective that competition.*

I: Which factors do you consider to have a significant influence on your ability to teach mathematics?

A: *The first factor is that mathematical content knowledge is of paramount importance in being able to teach mathematics. It is necessary but not sufficient however. Teaching is not simply a job it is a calling. It requires a combination of many skills. The classroom is a community of young people and the teacher should be knowledgeable about students' developmental stages, she should have developed strategies of how to guide them to own their learning via effective activities, and of how to develop inquiring minds in her classes. The second factor is therefore that didactical, psychological and pedagogical knowledge from the part of the teacher is of great importance.*

I: Which factors do you consider to have a significant influence on your beliefs about mathematics teaching?

A: *I believe that the education system limits the teacher's options to innovate and experiment in her classes. I sometimes feel that I have to apologise to my colleagues and to my superiors for attempting to introduce innovations in my teaching. The system - as it is today organised – forbids the teacher to use any approaches that are not 'proven'. Sometimes I feel like an outsider having to overcome - on a daily basis - time constraints, peer pressure, overt and covert opposition or disapproval from the administration, and the fact that I have to move all the desks back to their initial configuration (in rows) once I finish my classes which are based on group work. On top of that there may be opposition and disapproval from some parents and students who believe that schooling means teaching to the test and that a collaborative approach is not the best way for individual students to achieve top marks.*

I: Which factors may explain the existence of inconsistencies between espoused beliefs and beliefs in practice?

A: *The first factor concerns the expectations of the education system that could sometimes act in ways that inhibit innovations. The second factor concerns the things you are used to do (the teacher's habitus) that turn out to be a lot easier than introducing innovations in your daily routine. The third factor is the fact that it is very difficult to overcome every obstacle on a daily basis in order to do what you believe is the best practice. The fourth factor is the fact that I do not have my own mathematics classroom. The fifth factor is the fact that regional mathematics consultants are more decorative than anything useful. We never get to meet them and discuss our concerns. The sixth factor concerns my family obligations, which in practice drastically limits my available time. The seventh factor concerns the lack of communication with some of my students, since they have been bred to thing that schooling means teaching to the test. The eighth factor is the fact that I do not have all the required recourses at school. The ninth factor concerns the fact that the system does not provide any incentives for innovative teaching practice and the tenth factor is the fact that there is no teaching evaluation or appraisal, which could indirectly force me to be more prepared on a daily basis and to perform even better in class.*

Ann's beliefs about mathematics assessment

In this part of the interview discussion focused on the interviewees' espoused beliefs about mathematics assessment:

I: Based on what criteria do you select the appropriate assessment method for a topic/term/year?

A: *My assessment in mathematics is based on firm beliefs. The criteria I am using to assess my students are the following: Class involvement, keeping a journal of mathematical activities, taking notes, task involvement, degree of understanding, open-ended questions, problem solving and modelling performance, memorisation of some aspects of the course, participation in group work, student self-assessment and project work performance. It all depends on time constraints, appropriate planning and on administrative support.*

Appendix F2

Tom's interview

Tom's beliefs about mathematics

In this part of the interview discussion focused on the interviewees' espoused beliefs about mathematics:

Interviewer (I): What do you think mathematics is all about?

Tom (T): Mathematics can be considered as a tool for exercising the mind. It is the science of beauty, elegance, rigour and precision. It is a tool that is used by most of the sciences, ranging from philosophy to medicine.

I: What do you think about school mathematics?

T: The mathematics we teach at school is consisting of fragmented and disconnected segments. I believe that by using contemporary technology we can show students the utility of each topic under consideration. There are a number of really good educational videos and CDs, which if they were made available to the teacher; they could be used to enrich mathematics teaching and learning.

I: Which factors do you consider to have a significant influence on your beliefs about mathematics?

T: I think most of all I have been influenced by the study of the formal and rigorous axiomatic approach, which is the backbone of Euclidean Geometry. Mathematics is also a field where freedom of thought may find a fertile ground. In conclusion, I believe that mathematics is a science, which survived over the centuries due to the fact, that it is founded on solid theoretical foundations and on eternal verities.

Tom's beliefs about mathematics learning

In this part of the interview discussion focused on the interviewees' espoused beliefs about mathematics learning:

I: What can a very good mathematics student do (is the difference between a very good and a poor mathematics student qualitative or quantitative)?

T: *Good students are the ones who can respond to the demands of academically oriented mathematics courses. Not all students can excel in mathematics nor can all of them attend Year 11 and 12 academically oriented mathematics courses. Poor students are better off attending Technical schools.*

I: What accounts for the differences between a good and a poor mathematics student? (Probe – parents? genetic? good teaching? learning style?)

T: *This is an important issue and it is related to both genetic and environmental factors. The student's socio-economic background, parents' educational level, the family environment, the school and its administration, the teachers and the resources used, students' motivation to learn; all of them contribute to the development of a good or a poor student. Students have to take charge of their own learning. There is no way to acquire knowledge by being a passive observer in a classroom and expect to benefit by sitting idle on a desk all day passively copying the teachers' work. Knowledge is an active process, which is acquired via hard work and consistent effort.*

I: Is it possible for a teacher to help a poorly performing mathematics student become a good mathematics student?

T: *By moving around in class trying to help as many students as possible, I can check their work and I can ask them questions about their work. I am trying to accommodate individual differences by discussing with students who have trouble, like tutoring them one to one. I have to emphasise at this point that not all students can excel in mathematics. There are some students at Year 11 who cannot solve a linear equation.*

I: How do you define comprehension of a mathematical concept? topic?

T: *I am using the tests provided by the Ministry of Education. They contain multiple choice questions, true-false questions and short answer questions. They help me a lot in forming judgements about which concepts and skills each student has (or hasn't) mastered. I am frequently using ten-minutes tests, although it is hard for me to use them often since they require a lot of correction time. In that way I know when my students have mastered a particular topic and are ready to move on to the next topic.*

I: Which factors do you consider to have a significant influence on your beliefs about mathematics learning?

T: *My beliefs about mathematics have been primarily shaped by my teaching experience. It is my deep-rooted belief that the teacher's role is not to judge students but to facilitate learning. The teacher is the student's collaborator and my objective is to help students realise that we are together in their attempts to understand, to explore, to investigate and to own their knowledge. I owe these beliefs to my colleagues and students over the years.*

Tom's beliefs about mathematics teaching

In this part of the interview discussion focused on the interviewees' espoused beliefs about mathematics teaching:

I: Could you describe the way you teach mathematics? (Probe – typical day? Role of students' errors?)

T: *There is no typical day for my classes. One day's approach may differ dramatically from another day's approach. My teaching style varies but it is grounded on a sense of respect for my students, on my enthusiasm and on my eagerness to do the best I can, on a daily basis. As far as students' errors are concerned, I consider them part of the learning process. A mistaken answer by a student provides the spark for further discussion and elaboration on a problem or topic.*

I: What about memorisation? What is its role in mathematics teaching?

T: *The human memory is a tool that should be used effectively. Mathematics learning cannot be based on the memorisation of some rules alone. There are no simple recipes. Unfortunately, many students think that memorising facts provides an easy way to pass mathematics tests. This kind of attitude constitutes a disastrous approach to mathematics learning. The role mathematics teachers play in encouraging or discouraging students to rely on memorisation alone should be examined carefully.*

I: Where did you learn to teach mathematics that way? Have you ever had graduate and/or in-service courses on how to teach mathematics?

T: *I am learning everyday. Every single bit of knowledge in any field of human learning, has something to offer the teacher. Teaching is not a static process. It all depends on the class dynamics and the psycho-synthesis of the individual students of each class. Even when I have to teach the same concepts to two different Year 10 classes, my teaching approach is diversified to accommodate the needs of each class.*

I: Have you ever tried something different? Why? What happened?

T: *Yes I have tried to assign projects to my students but it did not work very well and soon I had to abandon it. Students did not have time to work on extended investigations, since they are being assigned a lot of homework on a daily basis.*

I: Grouping: On what basis? Why?

T: *I have never attempted to work with groups in my mathematics classes, I never will. With the existing school structure and the current curriculum time constraints it seems impossible. I do however, use some form of group work when I ask my students to think about a question for five minutes in groups of two. Time constraints are very prohibitive. Innovations require time and there is no time available for group work.*

I: What do you consider as the most important characteristics of quality teaching?

T: *I believe that quality teaching means that the students trust their teacher that there is some short of acceptance and appreciation of what the teacher is trying to do. Quality teaching is a gift but at the same time there are some fundamental didactical principles on which teaching should be grounded. The mathematics teacher should radiate energy and knowledge and make his students feel important. I strive to use activities, which will improve my students' imagination and broaden their horizons. I do not believe that there are difficult topics to teach but poorly performing teachers instead.*

I: Which factors do you consider to have a significant influence on your ability to teach mathematics?

T: *My love for children. If the teacher loves children and can sense their eagerness to learn, that's sufficient to encourage him to be dignified, and to stand up and deliver. That is not a recipe for success however. I believe that teaching is a sociocultural process and a calling, and it should be approached as such on a daily basis.*

I: Which factors do you consider to have a significant influence on your beliefs about mathematics teaching?

T: *My teaching practice has taught me a lot. Factors, which have had a significant impact on my beliefs, are my love for children, my devotion to my profession and the fact that I do not consider myself as a public servant but as an educationist who has a task of inspiring his students.*

I: Which factors may explain the existence of inconsistencies between espoused beliefs and beliefs in practice?

T: *The realisation that there are inconsistencies between espoused beliefs and beliefs in practice, causes a lot of sorrow to me. It is true that many teachers use pompous words about their beliefs and when it comes to he crunch they cannot deliver. I have come across teachers who were talking about equality and a just society but in practice they deliver the minimum possible. The existence of such inconsistencies is due to the fact, that many teachers are not devoted and they are not interested in providing a good education for their students.*

Tom's beliefs about mathematics assessment

In this part of the interview discussion focused on the interviewees' espoused beliefs about mathematics assessment:

I: Based on what criteria do you select the appropriate assessment method for a topic/term/year?

T: *Student assessment constitutes a continuous dialogue. I am using tests with multiple choice questions, true-false questions and short answer type questions. They help me a lot in forming judgements about what each student has or has not understood. I am trying to explain to my students that the objective of testing is not grading students but finding out about individual students' (or whole class) weaknesses and misunderstandings and they enable the teacher to decide about the necessity of re-teaching the concepts that have not been mastered by students. The objective of assessment is to improve students' skills and knowledge. Grading is not the objective of assessment but since it is compulsory, I am trying to be as objective as possible when providing grades for my students.*

Wissenschaftlicher Buchverlag bietet

kostenfreie

Publikation

von

wissenschaftlichen Arbeiten

Diplomarbeiten, Magisterarbeiten, Master und Bachelor Theses
sowie Dissertationen, Habilitationen und wissenschaftliche Monographien

Sie verfügen über eine wissenschaftliche Abschlußarbeit zu aktuellen oder zeitlosen
Fragestellungen, die hohen inhaltlichen und formalen Ansprüchen genügt,
und haben **Interesse an einer honorarvergüteten Publikation**?

Dann senden Sie bitte erste Informationen über Ihre Arbeit per Email
an info@vdm-verlag.de. Unser Außenlektorat meldet sich umgehend bei Ihnen.

VDM Verlag Dr. Müller Aktiengesellschaft & Co. KG
Dudweiler Landstraße 125a
D - 66123 Saarbrücken

www.vdm-verlag.de

Printed in the United Kingdom
by Lightning Source UK Ltd.
134140UK00001B/333/P